THE COMPLETE
ENCYCLOPEDIA OF

ANTIQUE CARS

Sport & Passenger Cars 1886 - 1940

THE COMPLETE ENCYCLOPEDIA OF

ANTIQUE CARS

Sport & Passenger Cars 1886 - 1940

Informative text with over 800 color photographs

ROB DE LA RIVE BOX

CHARTWELL
BOOKS, INC.

© 1998 Rebo International b.v., The Netherlands

Text and photographs: Rob de la Rive Box
Edited by Pieter Smit
Editing, production, and coordination: TextCase, Groningen
Design and layout: Signia, Winschoten
Cover design: Minkowsky Graphics, Enkhuizen

ISBN 0-7858-1872-3

This edition published in 2003 by
CHARTWELL BOOKS, INC.
A division of BOOK SALES, INC.
114 Northfield Avenue
Edision, New Jersey 08837

Contents

Foreword

More than a hundred years ago Mr. Daimler and Mr. Benz built their first 'automobiles'. The vehicles that were built in the early years looked more like carriages than cars. These first prototypes nevertheless formed the basis for all present-day models fitted with modern electronics. The first cars were built by professional producers, but also by enthusiastic tinkerers, who put all of their money into their car, but often saw their life's work end in financial ruin. But what was actually the first 'automobile' ever built?

According to the French, Edouard Delamare-Deboutteville's vehicle from 1884 was the first one, which gave the French cause to celebrate the 100th anniversary of the car in 1984. The Austrians claim that Siegfried Marcus made the first trial run in a car in 1870.

And then there was Nicolas-Joseph Cugnot's three-wheeler, which terrorised the streets of Paris in 1769. The car ended up against a brick wall, but was in fact more like a steam engine than a car. This model therefore does not count. The land yacht with which the Frenchman Hayquet wanted to become the talk of the town in 1834 also belongs on this list. No, everyone (except for the French) agrees that the Germans Daimler and Benz, simultaneously and independently of each other, built the first motorised carriages in 1886. Before the war, there were slightly more than 3,000 car manufactureres in America alone! As far as Europe was concerned, we see that there were many thousand more.

This means that it is impossible to include all of the models made in the period between 1886 and 1945 in this

This vehicle, which was built by the Russian Ivan Kutibin in 1752, can now be found in a museum in Moscow.
The Russians call it an automobile.

In particular in the nineteenth century, numerous steam vehicles were built. This most ancient American vehicle dates from 1892. But is it in fact a 'car'?

encyclopedia, so we have restricted ourselves to the most important and outstanding ones.

I hope that you will very much enjoy reading this extensive reference book, which covers more than 200 famous and less well known models from before the war.

Rob de la Rive Box

In 1769 Nicolas-Joseph Cugnot drove through the streets of Paris with this monster. Because the vehicle could hardly be controlled, its first trial run ended in an accident.

The Frenchman Hayquet designed this land yacht in 1834.

Adler

An Adler advertisement from 1920.

America had had a head start on Europe in the technical field for quite some time. When the German businessman Heinrich Kleyer made a business trip through the 'land of endless opportunities' in 1880, he noticed that almost everyone was using a bicycle, which was still a relatively unknown form of transport in Europe. Even at that time it was already possible to refer to it as a mass-produced product! Kleyer decided to start importing bicycles from the US. This proved to be a good decision. The demand was so great that he soon decided to set up a production linc himself. As early as in 1898, the 100,000th bicycle left the factory under the name of Adler. In addition to bicycles, typewriters were also taken into production that same year, followed by the first automobile in 1900. The vehicle was powered by a one-cylinder De Dion engine placed in the front and was fitted with a three speed gearbox with a column gearshift. In 1904 Edmund Rumpler – who would later become famous with his own streamlined cars –

The Adler Favorit, this picture shows a car from 1928, was especially popular as a taxi. The model was in production from 1928 to 1933.

The dashboard of the Trumpf from 1935. Note the steering column gearshift and the round knob above it with which the windscreen could be opened slightly.

In 1938 Hans Otto Lhoer and Paul von Guilleaume's Adler won its class at Le Mans. The car's streamlined body was designed by Paul Jaray.

designed Adler engines with two and four cylinders. The factory in Frankfurt produced small, inexpensive cars, but also large and more expensive models with engines with a capacity of up to 7.5 litres, which only delivered 50 bhp! Kaiser Wilhelm II was a regular customer of Adler's, something that generated a great deal of free publicity.

One of the four Adlers that appeared at the start in Le Mans in 1937. The car was driven by Mrs. Anne Rose and Baron Fritz Huschke von Hanstein.

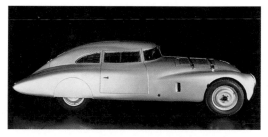

Yet another Ambi-Budd product: a two-door Trumpf Junior, which was in production between 1936 and 1939.

The Trumpf Junior Sport, as built between 1935 and 1937. With its 28 bhp four-cylinder 995 cc engine it was able to reach a top speed of 69 mph (110 kph).

In 1938 the Adler Trumpf also became available with a 2.0 litre engine. The model could be recognised by the special rims that were fitted with holes.

In those days the dashboard of the 2.0 litre Trumpf was very comprehensive. Incidentally, the bodies of this model were made by Karmann in Osnabrück..

In 1913, Adler had eight different models in its range. But World War I threw a spanner in the works. As a result of tremendous post war inflation the company almost went bankrupt. Fortunately the Deutsche Bank took things over, so that the Adler car make could be saved. It was, however, not until 1925 that Adler was able to start selling two new models. Both models were powered by a six-cylinder engine with a cylinder capacity of 2.5 or 4.7 litres, but the cars were not a great success because of their high price. Fortunately the factory had better luck with the Favorit, an inexpensive car with a 2.0 litre four-cylinder engine. In 1932 Gustav Röhr became Adler's chief engineer. Between 1928 and 1930, Röhr had been building cars under his own name, but had stopped doing so due to lack of success. He was more successful working for Adler.

Rohr, for example, designed the Adler Trumpf, which was highly advanced in those days. Among other features, the car had front wheel drive, four independently sprung wheels and hydraulic shock absorbers that could be adjusted with the aid of a knob on the dashboard. The bonnet was very long, because the gearbox was positioned in front of the engine, but behind the front axle. The first Trumpfs were powered by four-cylinder engines with a capacity of 1.5 litres, but in 1933 they were bored out to 1.7 litres, making 38 bhp available. In that same year, the sports version of the Trumpf was introduced. For this model the 1.7 litre engine had been tuned up to 47 bhp. This was followed in 1934 by the Trumpf Junior with a 1.0 litre engine. Just like its big brother, this model was regularly used in rallies, races and record-breaking attempts.

The streamlined bodies had in most cases been specially designed for this purpose by Paul Jaray. The Adlers were particularly successful in the 24 hour Le Mans race. The Adler Trumpf became a resounding success. Between 1932 and 1941 no fewer than 102,840 of them were built in Frankfurt. The model was furthermore produced under licence by Imperia (Belgium) and Rosengart (France) In 1934, the factory made another attempt at making big cars with 3.0 and 2.5 litre six-cylinder engines. But this so-called Adler Diplomat also failed to sell anywhere near as well as the small Trumpf. Adler stopped with the production of cars after the war. The company limited its activities to the production of typewriters and motorbikes.

Aero

The Aero company, established in a Prague suburb, built sports planes and (from 1928 onwards) small sports cars. The Aero 10 was powered by a one-cylinder two-stroke 499 cc engine delivering 10 bhp at 2700 rpm. It was a front-wheel drive vehicle. In 1931, the small two-seater was succeeded by the Aero 18. The engine now had two cylinders, with a cylinder capacity of 622 cc, delivering 18 bhp. No fewer than 2,575 of these highly successful cars were made up until 1934. The model was succeeded by the Aero 20, the Aero 30 and finally the Aero 50 with a four-cylinder engine that consisted of two cylinder blocks. The Aero 30 was the most successful model. The car was available in different body designs, namely as a convertible, as a roadster and as a limousine. In all cases, the Aero offered room for four people. With its cut-out doors it looked very sporty, in particular, the roadster version. The chassis of the Aero 30 was made up of square pipes. The bottom of the car was completely smooth and axle half shafts were placed at the front

An Aero 18 built in the year 1931. A total of 2,575 cars of this model, which was in production between 1931 and 1934, were sold.

and rear. The cast iron motor block had an aluminium cylinder head, which improved the cooling. An interesting detail was the use of the connecting rod bearings with pins, a principle that was only ever used in super sports cars. In 1936, Aero introduced a sports car, the Aero 50. This model was powered by a heavier four-cylinder engine with a bore/stroke ratio of 85 x 88 mm and a capacity of 1997 cc. The two-stroke engine delivered 45 bhp and ensured a top speed of 81 mph (130 kph). The bodies of the open-top Aeros were made by the Czech firm Sodomka.

During the war, two more prototypes were built at Aero, the Pony and the Record. The models were never taken

This Aero 50 was powered by a four-cylinder two stroke engine. The 50 was built from 1936 to 1941. The factory produced a total of 1,205 of these cars.

The two-cylinder engine of the Aero 18 delivered 18 bhp, enough for a top speed of 47 mph (75 kph).

An Aero 30 as four-seater roadster. The linen hood was fully removable.

into production, however. By order of the new government, Aero had to restrict itself to building aeroplanes. The Aero-Minor, which was sold in the Netherlands in large numbers immediately after the war, was no longer produced by Aero.

Despite its top speed of barely 60 mph (100 kph) this Aero 30 was also used in races.
The car even was a right-hand drive one, like all true sports cars in those days.

The Aero 30 was just as sporty-looking as, for example, an MG or a Morgan. The model was built between 1934 and 1940.

The dashboard of the Aero. Note the gear lever, which is pushed in or pulled out.

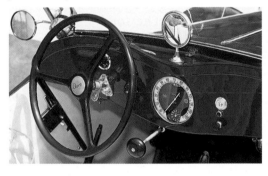

The small engine was lost underneath the long bonnet. The two-cylinder engine delivered 28 bhp at 3200 rpm.

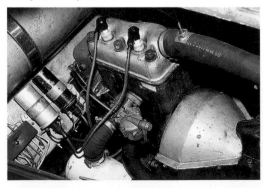

Alfa Romeo

In 1906, the French manufacturer Alexandre Darracq opened a branch in Italy at which he wanted to start building his cars under licence. It turned out to be a big flop and in 1909 Darracq was forced to sell his factory to a group of Italian businessmen. The new company went by the name of A.L.F.A. (Società Anonima Lombarda Fabbrica Automobili). Alfa was already building its own cars of the type 24 HP in 1910. They left the factory in the Milanese district of Portello as saloon or sports cars. The four-cylinder side valve engine had a capacity of 4084 cc and delivered between 42 and 45 bhp. Because the open body weighed between 870 and 1000 kg, (1914–2200 lb) the top speed of 69 mph (110 kph)

Two Zenith carburettors saw to the correct petrol-air mixture in the RL. The engine had a capacity of 3.0 litres and delivered between 56 and 83 bhp.

was nothing special. In 1914, the first Grand Prix car was introduced. It was powered by a 4492 cc four-cylinder engine with two overhead camshafts and four, yes four, valves per cylinder, a double ignition with two spark plugs per cylinder and dry-sump lubrication. In December 1915, Alfa got into financial difficulties. The company was taken over by Nicola Romeo and from then on became known as Alfa Romeo. Alfa and Alfa Romeo did not exclusively build sports and racing cars, but the racing cars were the most important product. Racing drivers like Enzo Ferrari, Alberto Ascari Senior and Guiseppe Campari made an important contribution to the make's fame.

In 1921, Alfa built its touring car of the type 20-30E. This model was available between 1914 and 1922, but only 504 were sold.

This Tipo RM-Sport from 1924 can be admired in the 'Museo Storico Alfa Romeo' in Arese close to Milan. 500 of these cars were built between 1923 and 1927.

The top of the range: a 6C1750 with Zagato body and a double camshaft engine with compressor. The 6C1750 was the most widely sold Alfa. A total of 2,579 were sold between 1929 and 1933.

With its 84 bhp compressor engine the 6C15000 achieved a top speed of 90 mph (145 kph). 1.074 of these cars were built between 1927 and 1929.

In 1920, Giuseppe Merosi developed the Tipo RL, which could be used as a saloon as well as a racing car. The fact that they were fast was proven for example in 1923, when two Alfas were in the first two places in the Targa Florio. Another famous constructor was Vittorio Jano who built, among others, the P-2 Grand Prix car with an eight-cylinder compressor engine. In the 1924 Grand Prix in Monza, the P-2s occupied the first four places in the finals. The design of the 6C15000 sports and saloon car also came from Jano's drawing board. This model was the 6C1750's predecessor, which was probably the most famous pre-war Alfa.

This 6C1750 was powered by an engine with one overhead camshaft. This six-cylinder engine delivered 46 bhp at 4000 rpm.

Most of the 188 8C23000s were sold as rolling chassis. The roadster with Zagato body became famous. This car dates from 1933.

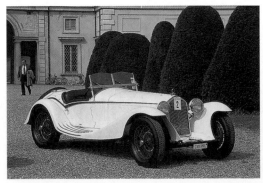

The 1750 was also available with different bodies. But the one that became really famous was the model with the two-seater body by Zagato. The sports cars of the type 8C2900 were very special. With their eight-cylinder in-line engines with two compressors these were really full-blooded Grand Prix cars with a sports car body.

In 1937, Jano moved to Lancia. He was succeeded by Gioaccino Colombo. Colombo also designed racing cars and engines that were to go on and win a great many championships even after the war. Alfa not only won a great deal of money in the GP-races, they also did extremely well in long-distance races, for example in the Mille Miglia, the

The dashboard of the 8C2300 was fully comprehensive and left nothing to be desired.

The 8C2900 was an extremely expensive car. As a result, only 30 of these cars were sold.

The car in the picture was fitted with a body by Stabilimenti Farina in 1938.

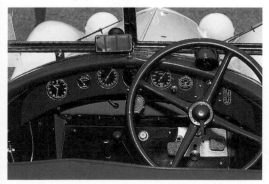

*The Swiss bodywork builder Hermann Graber
constructed the body of this 6C2500.
A total of 1,759 of these cars were built in 1952.*

such as a GP-car with a 3.0 litre V16 engine and the Biturbo, which had engines at the front and at the back. In 1939, Alfa Romeo built the first 6C2500, which was to remain in production as a saloon until 1952.

Alldays

1000 mile (1600 km) road race right across Italy. With the exception of 1931 and 1940 (won by respectively Mercedes and BMW) the race was won continuously by an Alfa up to and including 1947. The racing department of Alfa was headed by Enzo Ferrari for a long time. Under his supervision a number of very special cars were built,

The cars of the 'Alldays & Onions Pneumatic Engineering Company' were sold under the name of Alldays. The first cars left the factory in Birmingham in 1898. In contrast to many other makes of the time, the cars had an proper round steering wheel. The car was powered by a one-cylinder De Dion-engine from France. In 1905, this model was followed by a car with a two-cylinder engine and a year later the Alldays also became available with a

The headlights of this Alldays work on carbide but the parking lights and the back lights work on petroleum.

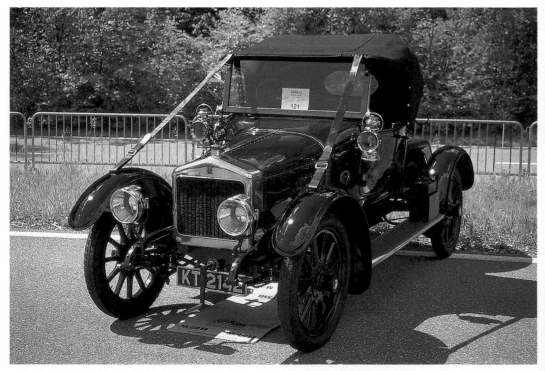

four-cylinder side valve engine. The cars were highly suitable for everyday use but also did very well in the hill climbs and trials that were very popular in England. In 1911, the 30/35 bhp model, with a big six-cylinder engine was introduced. The car in the picture is an Alldays Victoria Coupe built in 1914.

The four-cylinder in-line engine has a capacity of 2025 cc and delivers 14 bhp. The foot brake only allows you to brake with the back wheels. The hand brake works on the cardan shaft. The car is 390 cm long and 119 cm wide. The top speed is 40 mph (65 kph), but the current owner has never been able to reach this speed. After the First World War the make disappeared for good.

Alta

Geoffrey Taylor was already well-known as a manufacturer of tuning sets, especially for the Austin Seven, before he built his first sports car in 1928. There is nothing special about this at first glance, but the big difference between the cars made by Taylor and those made by many of the competitors was that he manufactured the engines

Passengers had to make themselves extremely small.

The light alloy engine was a gem. With its compressor and two overhead cam shafts it delivered no less than 180 bhp.

himself. Furthermore these were engines that were not to be sneezed at. The four cylinders had an aluminium engine block, a cylinder head with two overhead camshafts and two S.U. carburettors. The car was christened Alta and only very modest numbers were sold. They were successful in races. In 1937, the first Alta racing car appeared with independent four wheel suspension. When the 2.0 litre four-cylinder engine was fitted with a Rootes compressor, the racing driver had 180 genuine bhp at his disposal. In total, Alta only built 18 sports cars and 10 racing cars. Twelve of the sports cars were powered by a 1100 cc engine, two of them had a 1.5 litre engine and the remaining four had a 2.0 litre engine with in-built compressor.

This Alta from 1937 bears the chassis number 21. The car can be used as a sports as well as a racing car.

Alvis

Thomas George John started to build cars in Coventry in 1919. From 1921 onwards, these were sold under the name of Alvis. In contrast to most other manufacturers, he made virtually all of the parts for his cars himself. Several of these parts were so ingenious that he was able to take out patents on them. In 1922, Captain George Thomas Smith-Clarke joined the company as a technical director. In those days Alvis was already building cars of a very high quality, but in small quantities. In 1927, slightly more than 1,000 cars were produced for the first time, which resulted in the factory making a profit of £25,000.00. The company was not able to break this record until 1939. In 1925, Smith-Clarke introduced his plans for a front-wheel drive car. There was of course nothing new about a front-wheel drive car in itself, but in England the principle had, up to then, never been applied to a production car. The first car had an aluminium chassis. It had a 12/50-four cylinder engine that had

In 1925, Captain Smith-Clarke designed a front-wheel drive Alvis. The car was nicknamed the 'tadpole' because all of the heavy engine parts were fixed in front of or on top of the front axle.

been turned 180 degrees. The 1.5 litre engine had an overhead camshaft and delivered 50 bhp. In 1926, Alvis developed an eight-cylinder engine which was built into front wheel drive racing cars shortly after that. This model made its first appearance at the start of the Brooklands 200-mile race, in September 1926. The car unfortunately had to drop out of the

This TD 16.95 Silver Eagle was fitted with a 2+2 body. The last two passengers had to sit in the 'dickey seat'. In Germany these seats were referred to as 'Schwiegermuttersitz'.

Apart from sports and racing cars Alvis also built saloon cars, such as this one from 1927. Note the doors, all four of which opened in the safe direction.

The Silver Eagles could easily be recognised by the eagle on the radiator cap.

The first Twenty's had a six-cylinder 2511 cc engine delivering 87 bhp. In 1935 this overhead-valve engine was bored out to 2762 cc. This version delivered 98 bhp.

race. In May 1928, John decided to include the front-wheel drive car in the regular product range.

Because racing was still the best form of advertising, two of these cars were entered at Le Mans. The cars were powered by a 1.5 litre four-cylinder engine and were raced for 24 hours by the duos Harvey/Purdy and Davis/Dykes. And with success! The race was won by a 4.4 litre Bentley, but Alvis nevertheless ended in sixth and ninth place in the final classification. The first Alvis with a four-cylinder engine and front wheel drive appeared on the market in May 1928. These were specially designed for the sports car driver, who wanted to race at the weekend. The cars turned out to be

not at all suitable for everyday use. Because everything was built on top of another, any maintenance work on this car was very complicated. In order to, for example, replace the brake lining

Before the war, radiator mascots were commonplace. Rolls-Royce had its Flying Lady, Hispano-Suiza its stork and Alvis its little hare.

The Speeds Twenty was built between 1932 and 1936. The one in this picture was built in 1932.

This picture was taken in 1993 during the Klausen-Memorial mountain race. The driver of the 1932 12/60 TL apparently does not feel that winning the race is important.

A 1935 Alvis 4.3 Litre as a two-seater sports car. A car for 'tough' men (and women) who were not afraid to get wet.

on the front wheels, the entire engine had to be removed because the brake drums had been assembled as near as possible to the centre of the car. This definitely offered advantages on the racetrack but not in everyday use. In 1929, the effects of the world recession also became very noticeable in England. Alvis sold fewer saloon cars and was even forced to close the factory on Saturdays and Mondays. There was no money whatsoever for experiments in those days. In 1930, the front-wheel drive cars were only made to order. In the end, the factory only produced cars that sold well. In 1930, the product range consisted of four models, namely the TA 16/95 and the

The dashboard of the 4.3 Litre with the most important instrument, the rev counter, directly in front of the driver.

A 1936 Speed 25. The body might just as well have been placed on a Bentley or Jaguar chassis.

This Alvis is also a 4.3 Litre. The chassis was fitted with this 'civilised' body in 1939.

SA 16/95, also called the Silver Eagle, both with a 2148 cc six-cylinder engine, the FD 12/50 with a 1482 cc four-cylinder engine and the top of the range model, the FA 9/15 with a 1491 cc eight-in-line engine.

A rolling chassis of the latter model cost GB 975, £400 more than that of a TA. The FD was the sportiest model of the series. It could be used to break records and win races. In 1931, Alvis introduced a new and successful model, the Speed Twenty. The car was powered by the six-cylinder engine from the Silver Eagle, which with its three S.U. carburettors and two spark plugs delivered 87 bhp per cylinder. In 1937, the Speed 25 succeeded the Speed

Twenty. The engine in this model had been bored up to 3571 cc. With its 110 bhp the car was able to reach a top speed of more than 94 mph (150 kph).

The last pre-war models were the 4.3 Litre, a touring car with a 4387 cc six-cylinder engine, and the Silver Crest, which had a smaller 2762 cc six-cylinder engine under its long bonnet. Beautiful open touring cars were built on the chassis of the 4.3 Litre, as well as sporty saloons, which were similar to the Bentley and SS Jaguar available in those days.

A typical touring body with cut-out doors and room for four people. If really necessary, it was possible to fit side windows in the 4.3 Litre.

This 1936 Speed Twentyfive had a 3571 cc six-cylinder overhead valve engine. With its three S.U. carburettors the engine delivered no less than 110 bhp.

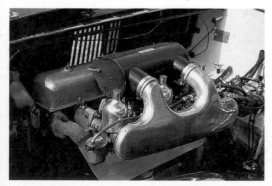

American LaFrance

In 1903 Truckson LaFrance, descendant of a French Huguenot who emigrated to America, founded the American LaFrance company (ALF). The first ALF fire engines were still pulled by horses, but in 1910 the first American LaFrance appeared with a Simplex petrol engine. During a demonstration ride the vehicle, laden with hoses and fire-fighters achieved an impressive speed of more than 50 (80 kph).

In 1910, ALF started to build its own engines. The following year the first sports car appeared, which was built on the shortened fire engine chassis. In September 1911, the car entered its first race in the city of Syracuse in the state of New York. It is not known how the car performed. This was due to the fact that the race was stopped prematurely, because a Knox racing car ran into the crowd, killing 11 spectators. This disaster made such an impression on Truckson LaFrance that he immediately stopped building racing cars. The only genuine ALF racing car can now be found in a museum somewhere near Cleveland.

Over the years, various ALF fire engines were nevertheless converted into racing cars. This just happened to be a cheap way of getting a fast and reliable sports car. The fire engines were generally well-maintained, had a low mileage and were inexpensive. The red ALF shown here could be admired on the English racing tracks in the fifties.

An ALF was not easy to drive, but its steering was relatively light, despite the tremendous weight pushing down on its front wheels. The brakes on the other hand required a great deal of muscle

This ALF was probably converted into a racing car in the fifties.

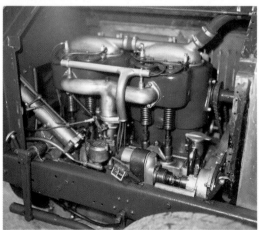

The engine comprising four cylinders with a total capacity of 10.5 litres. The valves can easily be adjusted.

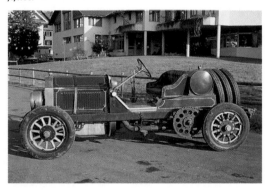

The transmission could be adjusted quite easily by replacing the gear wheels.

This ALF can reach a top speed of 81 mph (130 kph) on the motorway and could therefore still do well in today's traffic. The car is powered by a six-cylinder engine with a capacity of 14,500 cc.

power, because only the back wheels were fitted with brake drums. Experience was absolutely essential when using the unsynchronised three-speed gearbox and starting the engine was a laborious task. First of all, pressure had to be built up in the petrol tank using a hand pump. Next, the ignition had to be put on 'charge' and the choke had to be pulled out. Then the bonnet had to be opened and a little bit of petrol had to be poured into the cylinders with the aid of an oilcan. The coil ignition subsequently had to be switched on and the decompression switch pulled out, after which the engine could be cranked. And once the engine was running all of the various

In Switzerland the ALF is still frequently used in mountain races.

The dashboard of the six-cylinder ALF is undeniably comprehensive.

switches and handles had to be put back in their original position. The four-cylinder engine delivered 100 bhp at 2000 rpm. Thanks to the enormous torque it was easy to drive off in second or third gear. The white ALF in the picture was powered by a six-cylinder engine.

The car was specially built for long-distance races. This is shown by, among other things, the enormous petrol tank which holds 200 litres. Incidentally the carter contains 18 litres of oil and the radiator 40 litres of water! In 1911 there was no longer anything new about a cardan shaft, but manufacturers of cars with big and powerful engines in particular still preferred chain driven engines, and so did American LaFrance.

By changing the gear wheels a car could quite simply be changed for use on the public highway or on the track.

Amilcar

In 1919, the Le Zèbre car make got into financial difficulties. Grocer Emile Akar and his friend Joseph Lamy grabbed this opportunity to turn their hobby into a profession. They bought the factory and built one of the most beautiful cars of their day together with technicians Edmont Moyet and André Morcel. The former Le Zèbre dealers were so impressed with the new design that they supported the company financially with more than one million francs, to help get its production off the ground. In 1921, the first Amilcar of the type CC rolled out of the factory. However, they were soon able to increase production to five cars a day. The car had a 904 cc four-cylinder engine which delivered 18 bhp and had very low petrol consumption. In 1922,

The Amilcar in this picture was built in 1924 as a type CGS3. The '3' referred to its ability to transport three people.

Amilcar very soon switched to the production of passenger cars, including the G Tourer from 1926. The car was powered by a 1974 cc four-cylinder side valve engine delivering 25 bhp.

EAn Amilcar sports car was particularly popular among young people of the day. The fact that the car had no roof, side windows or doors, only made the model more popular.

this model was followed by the CS with a longer wheel base and a 1004 cc engine. This model proved to be highly suitable for use as a racing car. That same year two cars of the type CS took part in the 24 hour Le Mans race. They finished in third and fourth position in their class, behind two Salmsons. The Amilcar make only became really famous with the arrival of 1924 CGS. This car had brakes on all four of its wheels and was powered by a 1074 cc side valve engine delivering 28 bhp. The body of the two-seater was tapered at the end and offered room for a third passenger. The racing business was a good source of advertising in those days. In 1924 alone no more than 102 races were won! A year later Edmont Moyet built a racing car with a six-cylinder engine, the Amilcar CO. The 1096 cc engine, with a Rootes-compressor and two overhead camshafts, delivered 75 bhp at 6500 rpm. Not a single car factory has ever been able to survive from the racing business alone. The Amil car make is no exception. In 1923, therefore, the first passenger car was introduced. The type E car was powered by a 1485 cc four-cylinder engine. It was the first Amilcar with a differential

In 1928, the Italian count Luigi Castelbarco bought this Amilcar CGS with compressor. He subsequently raced in it for the rest of his life, until shortly before his death in 1992. In 1979, Castelbarco took part in a historic car race on the Nürburgring.

The six-cylinder engine of the CGS had a capacity of 1074 cc. With a Rootes-compressor the engine delivered 75 bhp, enough for a top speed of around 125 mph (200 kph).

The B38 'Compound' was meant to save the factory. The car was very interesting from a technical point of view. The chassis was made of aluminium and it was a front-wheel drive. The wheels had independent suspension. But sales of this model were disappointing. This picture shows a 1939 B38.

gear. Its successor, the type G, had a four seater body and won the Monte Carlo Rally in 1927.

At the end of the twenties, a lot of French car manufacturers got into financial difficulties because of the approaching world recession. There was a particular demand for closed cars in the medium-price range. The biggest supplier in this market segment was Citroën, with a production of 500 cars a day. Amilcar also tried to find its way into this market segment. The company stopped manufacturing the small cars on which the company's fame was based. In 1929 came the models L, with a 1188 cc engine, and CS8 with an eight-cylinder in-line

In 1929, the engine of the C8 had a capacity of 1810 cc. A year later the capacity was 1994 cc increasing yet again in 1933 to 2330 cc. All of these cars had an overhead camshaft, a double Solex-carburettor and magnetic ignition.

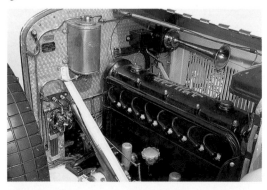

engine and an overhead camshaft. But the demand for both models was very limited.

The factory once again switched to the production of small cars of the type C, with a 621 cc engine. But it also turned out to be practically impossible to sell this model. In 1932, part of the factory had to be shut down. The last model was the N7 ('La Pégase') with a 2.1 litre Delahaye engine. But the retail price of this car proved to be too high, as a result of which the company had to stop production once more in 1937.

The Amilcar make was subsequently taken over by Hotchkiss. Money for the development of new models became available again. Jean Albert Grègoire designed the AB 38 'Compound', which seemed to be the spitting image of the Adler Trumpf Junior. The car had an aluminium chassis, but the 1200 cc engine was not powerful enough. As a result, sales were disappointing and fewer than 1000 of these cars were sold. Amilcar improved the model by putting a 1340 cc Hillman-engine into it. The production lines of the AB 38 were closed down as a result of the start of World War II.

The Tipo 22 was a beautiful car but came onto the market at the wrong time. The demand for expensive cars was limited and the market was being flooded with cars from Detroit.

Ansaldo

The Italian company Ansaldo was the biggest producer of heavy weapons in Southern Europe. Nearly of the Italian cannons used in World War I came from this factory in Genua. After the war the company had to switch to other products and it is for this reason that car production started in Turin in 1919.

The first model of the type Tipo 4C was a modern car with a 1847 cc four-cylinder engine with an overhead camshaft.On the outside the 4C looked very much like an old-fashioned American car. In 1922, the second model appeared, the 4CS, with a heavier 1981 cc engine, delivering 48 bhp. A year later the factory built the first six-cylinder engine into the Tipo

6A. In 1929, a sports car, the 15GS appeared, with a 1981-cc four-cylinder engine with two camshafts. This car delivered 60 bhp, enough to take the two-seater up to a top speed of 81 mph (130 kph). In 1929 Ansaldo also made its breakthrough onto the luxury car market with the beautiful Tipo 22, which was called Tipo 42 from 1934 onwards. This car had an eight-cylinder in-line engine under its long bonnet. This overhead valve engine delivered 86 bhp at 3500 rpm. Most of these cars were sold as rolling chassis. The buyer could subsequently go to the body-builder of his choice, such as Carrozzeria Bertone, Stabilimenti Farina, Asaro and Viotto. The cars had chassis with a 331 cm wheel base, big enough for a six or seven-seater body. But the timing at which these expensive models were introduced turned out to be wrong. The American industry was

The buyer of a 1930 Ansaldo was given two spare wheels because of the nails frequently shed by the many horses still using the roads of those days.

The 8-cylinder Tipo 22 had room for a family.

flooding Europe with inexpensive, big cars. And when the Wall Street crisis also became noticeable in Italy, sales dropped even further. The management in Genuadecided to close the car factory. The Ansaldo company was sold to O.M. in 1931, which in turn sold the make to Fiat in 1932. The cars still in stock and the warehouses full of

parts did not form part of the agreement. Ansaldo subsequently founded the Ansaldo-Ceva company, to sell the remaining stocks. This meant it was still possible to buy a 1930 model Ansaldo in 1936.

Aston Martin

Before World War I the company 'Bamford & Martin' had acquired quite a reputation for tuning up the engines of Singer-sports cars. In 1913 they built their own sports car by placing a Coventry Simplex engine in an Isotta Fraschini chassis. A simple body was built onto the chassis. It was not until after World War I that a second car left the workshop in London. This time they used their own chassis. In 1914, in a mountain race, this prototype beat its most important competitor, the Aston-Clinton. The second car was therefore given the name Aston Martin. This sports car was powered by a 1486 cc four-cylinder engine and was fast enough to win races. But not a lot of money was made. So funds were short when a new engine with one

The Ansaldo was a right-hand drive, just like all sporty Italian cars. This picture shows a car from 1922 with a four-cylinder engine.

An Aston Martin Inter from 1932. The car was available with two different wheel bases. The two-seater was 259 cm long while the 2+2 (picture) was 300 cm long. The 1495 cc engine delivered 70 bhp at 4750 rpm.

overhead camshaft and four valves per cylinder was built. This engine however had all sorts of things wrong with it. Just at the right moment Lionel Martin received financial backing from Count Louis Zborowski. This car lover had become famous for fitting racing cars with an aeroplane engine. He urged Marcel Gremillion to develop a new engine for Martin. This engine also had four valves per cylinder but now the whole thing was powered by two camshafts. The engine delivered 55 bhp and took the little sports car to a top speed of 94 mph (150 kph).

In the meantime, the production of sports cars with a side valve engine continued. In 1924, 50 cars of this type were ready for delivery. When Zborowski died in an accident while training for the Italian Grand Prix, the company lost an important source of income. Martin once again ended up in financial difficulties. He was forced to sell the business for just £3,600.

The new company 'Aston Martin Ltd.' was established in Feltham. The famous Italian technician Cesare Bertelli was one of the company's new directors. He was responsible for designing a new sports car. This car was powered by a 1.5 litre engine and was available with two different wheel bases. The long version was intended

In October 1932 Aston Martin introduced a new model, the 'Le Mans' at the London Motor Show. The model remained in production until December 1933. A total 130 of these cars were sold..

The back of a 1933 Aston Martin Le Mans. Look at the big petrol tank between the body and the spare wheel.

Aston Martin was less successful with saloon cars. The cars were too heavy for the small engines, looked too much like an MG or Jaguar and were far too expensive. This four-seater dates from 1937.

for saloon cars, while the shorter one was intended for sports cars. But this model did not sell well either. Even when an improved version was brought onto the market, production remained limited. In 1932 only 15 cars were produced.

The sports car performed well in races such as Le Mans. After Bentley, Aston Martin had in the meantime become the most famous English make of car. In 1934 the 'Ulster' was introduced, which was the first car to break the

When Bertelli left the company, his successor, Gordon Sutherland, had the famous Aston Martin engine bored up to a 2.0 litre. This engine was highly suitable for saloon cars, but was also built into two-seaters.
This 1937 Two Litre took part in the Mille Miglia in Italy in 1997.

The Aston Martin Ulster was available between 1934 and 1936. The car had a two-seater body and was more suitable for the racing track than the public highway. Only 21 of these cars were ever built.

magic 100 mile an hour barrier. In 1936 Bertelli left the company. His successor was R. Gordon Sutherland, who saw a bigger future in saloon cars. He had the 1.5 litre four cylinder engine bored up to 2.0 litre and subsequently placed it in a four door body.

The car was not a great success. The engine only delivered 98 bhp, hardly enough to get the heavy car up to a reasonable top speed. The model furthermore looked far too much like the considerably cheaper MG and SS Jaguar.

In 1929 Auburn there was a choice between six basic models, the model 76, the 6-80 with a six-cylinder engine and the models 88, 115, 8-90 and 120 with eight-cylinder line engines. This picture shows a 6-80 as a two-seater convertible with 'dickey seat'.

Auburn

This 1930 convertible offered room for two adults and two children. The body was built on a 6-85 chassis. The six-cylinder engine delivered 70 bhp.

In 1900, the brothers Frank and Morris Eckhart took over their father's carriage company. At the time the car was rapidly gaining in popularity. This is why the brothers decided to start concentrating on car production. First of all, a number of prototypes with one-cylinder engines and solid tyres were produced. As early as in 1903, the fiftieth car was ready for delivery. The cars were sold under the name of Auburn, after the small town in which they were built. In 1905, a model with a two-cylinder engine appeared. In 1910, four-cylinder engines were constructed and in 1912 the Auburn also became available with a six-cylinder engine. Compared to other makes of car the Auburn was nothing special either in terms of appearance or in terms of technology. While the other makes were doing extremely well, things went increasingly badly for Auburn. In 1924 the factory site was full of unsold cars and the bank was no longer prepared to finance the company. The brothers Eckhart went bankrupt and the company became the property of the bank. Bank director Ralph Bard did not, however, know enough about cars himself to be able to do anything with the factory. He asked Lobban Cord for advice. Cord was one of America's top car salesmen and had become a millionaire as a result. Ralph Bard offered Cord a generous salary for helping to get the Auburn make back on top. Cord, however, demanded 20% of the profit plus the right to buy

A two-seater convertible from the 8-105 series. In this series the customer was able to choose from a Speedster, a Brougham, a Sedan or a Phaeton. All models were powered by an eight-cylinder engine delivering 100 bhp.

This 8-100A sedan from 1933 had an eight-cylinder engine with a capacity of 3954 cc delivering 100 bhp. The car had a 323 cm wheel base.

shares at $20 each. Bard had nothing to lose and accepted the conditions. In 1924, Auburn employed 450 people. Cord had first of all ensured that the 700 unsold cars were taken care of. The window pillars were shortened so that the roof could be lowered. Next the cars were re-sprayed in striking colours.

The Auburns now no longer looked anything like their boring predecessors and were sold in no time. In 1925, Cord replaced the old four and six-cylinder engines with a brand new eight-cylinder in-line engine made by the firm Lycoming.

The Auburn 8-63 was a fast and sporty-looking car. The production figures shot up from 2,226 in 1924 to more than 22,000 in 1928. That same year Auburn made a net profit of $3.6 million. Cord received 20% of this, as a result of which his wealth increased by so much that he was able to buy an increasing number of shares at the agreed price of $20.

As a result of Auburn's excellent profits the share prices on Wall Street shot up. When the prices were high, Cord sold his shares, which caused the shares to plummet. Once the rate was low enough again, Cord bought back his own shares. Some years later this type of transaction was forbidden by law, but in the meantime Cord had built up an enormous fortune. In 1928, Auburn built one of the most beautiful cars of that year, the 8-115. The car was powered by an eight-cylinder in-line engine made by Lycoming. The 4.0 litre side valve engine delivered 115 bhp. The model became very popular as 'Speedster', especially as a result of the flared back (which was called a 'boattail' in America) and the low front window. The second series was fitted with a different carburettor, as a result of which it delivered 125 bhp.

In 1935 and 1936 Auburn built the 'Boattail Speedster' with compressor engine. This long eight-in-liner delivered no less than 150 bhp. The model had a top speed of more than 100 mph (160 kph).

In 1936 the Auburn was a relatively expensive car. An 8-852 convertible cost $1,225, or even $1,675 with a compressor engine (see picture). In comparison, in that same year a Ford V8 DeLuxe Roadster cost $560.

Between August 1928 and January 1929 almost 2,500 of these cars were sold. In 1929 this so-called 120-series became available in 7 different body shapes. But as a result of the approaching world-wide economic crisis producers of expensive cars, in particular, ran into difficulties. In 1930, the Auburn range was reduced to a mere four different models and in 1932 the range only consisted of two models, the 8-100 and the 8-1000-A, which were both powered by an eight-cylinder engine. The six-cylinder engine had disappeared from the product range altogether.

In 1932, Cord introduced an Auburn with a V12 engine. This Auburn 12-160 coupé cost a mere $975. This was cheaper than the retail price of an eight-cylinder Dodge. This nevertheless did not produce the expected result. In the first quarter of 1932 a limited

This picture clearly shows where the name 'boattail' came from. From this angle, too, the Speedster is a beautiful car. It is hardly surprising that many companies still build this model as a replica today.

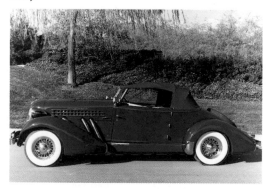

profit was achieved of only $7,959 with a production of 11,000 cars. At the end of 1932 losses totalled no less than $974,751. The most important reason for this was the fact the cars were too cheap.

An Auburn with a V12-engine just could not be any good at that price, the consumer assumed. Next, a new model with an eight-cylinder engine with compressor was brought onto the market.

This famous '851 Boattail Speedster' was sold with a further five different bodies. The same chassis was used for each of these. Production went up again by 20%, but the company was still not making a profit. In 1936 only 4,830 Auburns were sold. This was reason enough for Cord to close the factory that same year.

Audi

An Audi advertisement from the company's early days.

In 1909, Dr. August Horch got into an argument with some of the directors at his own factory in Zwickau. He left feeling angry and started a new company a couple of streets down. His son came up with the name for this company: Audi, the Latin translation of Horch ('listen'). It was therefore not so strange that the first Audi looked very much like the last Horch. The car had a 2.5 litre four-cylinder engine, with some interesting technical innovations. The engine had twin ignition with two spark plugs per cylinder, which were supplied by power by means of a magnet as well as by means of an ignition coil. Striking, too, was that the petrol was squeezed into the carburettor by the force of the exhaust fumes.

The most famous Audi from those first years was the 'Alpensieger', which was built between 1912 and 1921. The 3564 cc four-cylinder engine had enough power for the car to achieve a top speed of 62 mph (100 kph). During World War I, Audi built lorries for the German army, but immediately after the war the factory was able to present a new model, the Typ K, which in 1924 was succeeded by the Typ M.

After an Audi Typ C 14/35 won the Austrian Alps rally in 1911, the model was renamed the 'Alpensieger'. The model ended in the first three places in this rally three years in a row.

n 1932 Audi became part of the Auto Union. That same
year the Audi Front was introduced. The picture shows a
1934 four-door car of the type UW, of which almost
2,000 were built in 1933 and 1934.

The later model was a big car with a 4655 cc six-cylinder engine with an overhead camshaft delivering 70 bhp. The most important technical features were the hydraulic brakes and the hydraulic shock absorbers. The car was also fitted with a pump powered by the gearbox, with which the tyres could be inflated. When August Horch noticed that despite these novelties the car was unable to compete with the big

The UW 225, of which 2,600 were sold between 1935 and 1938, was powered by a 2257 cc Wanderer-engine. The engine delivered 55 bhp and was a front-wheel drive.

cars that Mercedes and Maybach were producing, he introduced an even more luxurious car, the 'Typ R Imperator'. This car was powered by an eight-cylinder engine with a capacity of 4872 cc delivering 100 bhp. Unfortunately, the demand for this expensive car was also limited. Business was going increasingly badly. This is why Dr. Horch could not refuse an offer made by Jörgen Rasmussen, the owner of DKW. In 1928 the factory changed hands. The first Audis built under the management of the Rasmussen, were the 'Zwickau' with an eight-cylinder engine and the 'Dresden' with a six-cylinder engine. These engines were not built by Audi but by the American firm Rickenbaker. This meant that the production costs were a lot lower and that Audi was able to offer its cars at a much more competitive price than before. A second attempt to make money using this same strategy failed however. Hardly any cars were sold of the type 5/30, an Audi with a DKW-chassis and a 1155 cc Peugeot

Between 1938 and 1940 Audi built its last pre-war cars of the type 920. This model had a 3281 cc six-cylinder Horch-engine delivering 75 bhp. The convertible version of the car, made by bodybuilder Gläser, weighed 1665 kg.

engine. In order to be in a better position to face the competition, the companies Horch, Wanderer, DKW and Audi decided to start working together in 1932 under the name Auto Union. Horch built the big cars, DKW the small ones, Wanderer the models in the middle range and Audi the 'special' cars. The first special model, the Audi Front, was powered by a six-cylinder engine that had been developed by Dr. Ferdinand Porsche. The car was also fitted with a front-wheel drive applied by DKW. In 1939, Audi introduced another expensive luxury car with a 3.3 litre six-cylinder engine and an overhead camshaft. During the war Audi did not produce any passenger cars. It was not until 1965 that Auto Union introduced another Audi.

In this picture some 'bigwigs' are getting out of their 1939 Audi UW 225 and into a three engine Junker 52, better known as 'Aunt Ju'.

Austin

Herbert Austin headed for Australia at the age of sixteen. He spent eight years over there working for different companies. His last employer was the firm Wolseley, which imported sheep shearing machines from its mother company in England. Austin did well in Australia, so well even, that the English offered him a job as a technical director in Birmingham. Here he built his first car in 1895. The ambitious Austin, however, ended up having a fight with his superiors in 1905. He left Wolseley and started his own company on 9 July 1905.

The first Austin from 1906 had an engine with four independent cylinders with a chain drive to the rear wheels. The cars were of an excellent quality. In 1907, Austin managed to sell 147 of them. In those days his company already employed more than 400 people. In 1908 a model with a six-cylinder engine appeared proving that

In 1910 the Austin Twenty HP Landaulette already looked like a real car. The driver was protected from rain and wind. The car was powered by a four-cylinder engine with a capacity of 3136 cc, delivering some 23 bhp at 1000 rpm.

The most famous Austin was undoubtedly the Seven, which was introduced in 1922. In those days the car cost £225, as much as a motorbike with sidecar.

Austin built a total of 290,924 Sevens. The first cars left the factory in July 1922.

The 696 cc engine was replaced by a four-cylinder 747 cc engine after only a few months.

he did not simply specialise in small cars. The 1914 Thirty may have had a four-cylinder engine, but its capacity was almost six litres. No cars were produced during World War I. The company did, however, produce some 8 million grenades and almost 2,000 planes.

Austin wrote car history with the Seven, which was introduced in 1922. The car was heavily criticised, just like the Citroën 2 CV would be 35 years later. But the model made the Austin make world famous. The first Seven was powered by a 696 cc engine. In the autumn of that same year a version with a 747 cc 13 bhp engine appeared. This model was also the first one to be fitted with brakes on all four wheels. The foot brake worked on the front

The Seven was also available as a sports car. The factory even had its own racing team in which Sir Herbert Austin also took part.
The cars had tuned up engines with one or two overhead camshafts and possibly a Rootes-compressor.

A 1930 sixteen HP. The six-cylinder engine had a capacity of 2249 cc. It was an excellent passenger car, being reliable and economical and offering enough room for the entire family.

wheels and the hand brake on the back wheels. The Austin Seven was built under licence in Germany by Dixi (later BMW), in Japan by Datsun, in Australia by Holden, in America by Bantam and in France by Rosengart.

The small Seven could not only be used as a family car but also as a sports car. Companies offering special tune-up kits and bodies shot up like mushrooms. In addition to the small Seven, the product range in 1928 also consisted of the bigger Twelve, Sixteen and Twenty with respectively a 1861 cc four-cylinder engine, a 2249 cc six-cylinder engine and a 3400 cc six-cylinder engine. In 1929, Austin introduced its own Seven racing car, whose engine was fitted with a compressor.

In 1933, the company launched the Ten. In 1934, the Austin customer was able to choose from no fewer than 50 different models! On 3 March 1939 the last Seven left the factory in Long-bridge. Up until then it had been the most popular small car in the world

The Austin Ten from 1937 was a luxurious car with leather seats. The 1128 cc four-cylinder engine delivered 28 bhp at 3400 rpm and the three top gears in the four-speed gearbox were synchronised. The Ten had a 2381 cm wheel base. Weighing 850 kg (1870 lb) the car achieved a top speed of 59 mph (95 kph).

With a bore/stroke ratio of 63.5 x 89 mm the engine of the 1933 Ten/Four had a cylinder capacity of 1125 cc. The car delivered 10 bhp. In England a rolling chassis cost £120 that year, while the car shown here went on sale at £168.

Baker

For a long time, supporters and opponents of electric, steam and petrol engines were at loggerheads with each other. Everyone was right to some extent when claiming that they had developed the right process. Similarly, a lot of experiments are still being carried out nowadays with fuels other than fossil fuels. The 'Baker Motor Vehicle Company' at Cleveland, Ohio, swore by cars equipped with electric

Baker tried to attract customers to his showroom by using beautiful advertisements. The car shown here looks a lot like a little carriage without a horse and basically it was not much more than that.

The Baker Electric had a number of significant drawbacks. Its range was limited because the batteries did not have enough capacity. Even today, more than a hundred years on, this is still the biggest problem facing an electric car.

engines. stinken "Those engines do not smell, do not make any noise and are cheap to maintain", the factory claimed. The drawbacks, such as the fact that these cars need an expensive battery and have a limited range, were conveniently ignored.

In 1899, Walter C. Baker and Fred R. White built their first car. That same year, the Belgian Camille Jenatzy broke the world speed record by achieving a speed of 65 mph (105 kph) in his 'Jamais Contente'. Jenatzy's car was powered by an electric engine, just like the first (and last) Baker. The Baker Electric was originally a small, lightweight two-seater. In 1910 and 1911, some bigger four-seaters were also built. These had to look like 'real' cars, so these cars had a long bonnet full of batteries. Baker tried to break the world speed record for motorcars several times. His cars, however, had to give up all the time before the top speed was achieved. On one occasion the car went into the crowd, killing two spectators. Baker managed to sell electric cars until 1916. Then the curtain fell for his company

Bantam

Not just big cars were built in America. People regularly tried to make their fortune by building a small car. The small Bantam, which was built in Butler, Pennsylvania, is a good example of this. In 1930, the 'American ustin Car Corporation' was founded. The company was to build the Austin Seven under licence. It was a purely American company, in which Herbert Austin held the position of 'honorary director'. He was to receive $7 for every Austin sold. The Austin Seven was originally a simple and cheap car. This model was very popular in Europe, but the Americans tried to turn it into a 'small American-type car'. New bodywork was designed by count Alexis de Saknoffsky, who was a famous designer in those days. The design did not in any way look like its European counterpart. It looked more like a miniature Chevrolet. The chassis was a direct copy of an Austin chassis. This model was also powered by an original 747 cc four-cylinder engine, which delivered 13 bhp. The factory did a great deal of advertising and managed to sell cars to, among others, Ernest Hemingway, Buster Keaton, and Al Johnson. The general public, however, preferred a real car, such as the A-Ford, which was also even $5 cheaper!

Less than 10,000 cars were sold in two years. This resulted in the company going bankrupt in its second year. The next owner did not last longer than two years either. In 1937, Roy Evans made a third attempt under the name of Bantam. The car looked like its predecessor in many respects, but it had changed so much technically that no more royalties had to be paid to Austin.

A Bantam estate car from 1940. If there were four people in it there was hardly any room left for luggage.

The Bantam was powered by a 716 cc light alloy engine delivering 20 bhp. Both the second and the third gear had been synchronised in the three-speed gearbox. The car was fitted with a rigid shaft at both the front and the rear.

The Bantam was also a small car. It had a length of 305 cm and a width of 143 cm, but had nevertheless been placed on the usual, big 16-inch wheels. In 1940, the cylinder capacity was increased to 800 cc and the capacity rose to 23 bhp.

That year, the car was available in various versions, namely a two-seater coupé, a convertible, an estate car, and a convertible sedan. In the latter version, the linen top continued to the boot lid, but the sides of the bodywork remained intact. Unfortunately, the small Bantam was not a great success.

Bantam is known as the inventor of the Jeep, even though Willys is not willing to admit this.

Bentley

When Bentley celebrated its fiftieth anniversary in 1969, 80-year-old W.O. Bentley, the founder of the company, was living in poverty. His car, a twelve-year-old Morris, had been given to him by members of the 'Bentley Owners Club'. Walter Owen Bentley, W.O. to his friends, was born in 1888. He trained to as an engineer, but started his career

41

One of the first cars built by W.O. Bentley was the Three Litre from 1922. It is easy to see that this car was only meant for racing.

A Three Litre from 1926. The linen top was left in the garage most of the time.

The Three Litre seen from behind. Note the 'boot lid' in the boat tail.

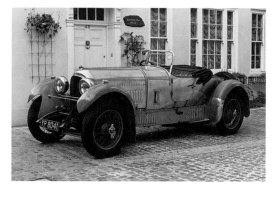

as a taxi driver in London in 1912. Shortly after that, he started up a garage business with his brother. The brothers had a dealership for the French make DFP (Doriet, Flandrin et Parant). In the early years, they prepared cars of this make for the racing business in order to make DFP more widely known. During World War I, Bentley was assigned to the Royal Air Force. Here he designed the radial engine, of which more than 30,000 were to be built by Humber. W.O. was fobbed off with a mere pittance for his design, but he was promoted to lieutenant. After the War, Walter Owen built his first Bentley together with Fred Burgess, whom

A Bentley always had plenty of instruments. This picture shows the dashboard of the Three Litre.

A 4.5 Litre with an open boat tail body. The leather bands across the bonnet and the small 'Brooklands' windows were supposed to make this model look like a racing car.

The 3.0 litre six-cylinder engine had an overhead camshaft and delivered 80 bhp. The 'Green Label' version had a tuned up engine that delivered 85 bhp. The car achieved a top speed of 100 mph (160 kph).

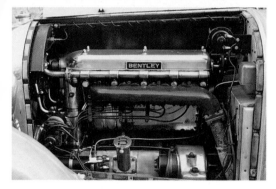

This 4.5 Litre is a Le Mans replica from 1928. This picture was taken at the 1997 Mille Miglia. The 4,398 six-cylinder engine delivered 182 bhp at 3,900 rpm. Note the Rootes-compressor in front of the radiator.

he had met at Humber. The first test-drives were carried out in 1919. The four-cylinder engine had a capacity of 3.0 litres, an overhead camshaft, four valves per cylinder and a double ignition. The open car was not much more than a chassis with an engine, two small bucket seats, and a giant fuel tank with two spare tyres on it. It had a top speed of 75 mph (120 kph). Bentley had been trying to draw attention to the DFP make before the War by entering DFPs in races and was now trying to do the same with his own car. This time his efforts proved successful. In the 1922 Tourist Trophy, the 3.0 litre Bentleys finished in second,

fourth, and fifth place, behind an 8.0 litre Sunbeam. The Vauxhall GP-cars with their 139 bhp engines stood absolutely no chance against the cars of the new and unknown make. In 1923, a 3.0 litre Bentley finished in fourth place at the 24-hour Le Mans race. The following year, the same car managed to win this heavy race. From 1923 onwards, Bentleys were fitted with brakes on all wheels, which was no luxury, as the cars weighed 1800 kg (3960 lb)! Sales were not as good as expected however. When the balance sheet was drawn up at the end of 1923, a mere total of 348 cars had been sold. As a result of this, W.O. Bentley got into financial difficulties for the first time. In 1924, a replica of the TT winner was introduced. This so-called 'Speed' could be recognised by its red radiator emblem, while the earlier models had an emblem with a blue background. To increase the potential number of customers,

W.O. built two new models in 1925. The '100 MPH' had a guaranteed top speed of 100 miles/hour. The second luxury model, the Speed Six, had to compete with Rolls-Royce. The 100 MPH was powered by a 92 bhp engine and could be recognised by the green emblem on the radiator. In 1927, a 100 MPH won the 24-hour Le Mans race.

The luxury car was fitted with a six-cylinder engine and had an engine capacity of no less than 6.6 litres. This car also had a blue emblem. The customer could choose to either have a

335 or 366 cm wheel base. The engine was so elastic that the driver could easily drive at a speed of 7.5 mph (12 kph) in fourth gear. The top speed was about 145 kph. Until 1930, Bentley managed to sell 373 cars of this model. In 1929, a Speed Six-convertible won the 24-hour Le Mans race at an

W.O. Bentley built this sports car for the famous racing driver Whitney Willard Straight. The 7,983 cc six-cylinder engine delivered 225 bhp to the rear wheels.

This 4.5 Litre sports car from 1930 was fitted with a compressor engine. Here the compressor had however tactfully been concealed.

average speed of 74 mph (118.5 kph). A Bentley with a 4.5 litre engine finished in second place. Both models managed to cross the finish line in Le Mans in winning positions the following two years as well. The 4.5 litre Bentley had incidentally won the 1927 Brooklands 500 at an average speed of 106 mph (170 kph). If the customer so wished the cars could be fitted with engines that were 'blown' with a compressor or turbocharger. Bentley himself, however, was not very happy with this slightly unreliable engine. In 1930, W.O. Bentley built

After Rolls-Royce had taken over W.O. Bentley's company the 'Derby Bentley' was born. This picture shows such a car from 1934 fitted with a 3.5 litre engine and bodywork by James Young.

a real dream car with the financial support of millionaire Woolf Barnato. The 7,983 cc six-cylinder engine delivered 220 bhp. With this car Bentley could easily compete with its competitor Rolls-Royce. In 1931, this model also became available with a 4.0 litre engine.

However, in order to save money this engine had not been fitted with an overhead camshaft and therefore was not really powerful enough. As a result no more than 50 of these cars were sold. The financial crisis on Wall Street also caused Barnato to lose a lot of money. He was no longer able to financially support Bentley and this in turn forced him to sell his company in 1931.

Arch-rival Rolls-Royce put in the highest bid and became the owner of the by then renowned make. Constructor W.O. Bentley was offered a job as a test driver. In 1935, he started working for Lagonda, where he once again built beautiful engines. The first Bentleys built by Rolls-Royce were known as 'Derby Bentleys', because they were built in the English city

This Bentley 4.25 Litre left the factory in November 1935. It was common in those days for the car to be sold as a rolling chassis. The owner had it fitted with a carriage by a bodywork builder afterwards.

Before World War II, the Thrupp & Maberly company was one of the most famous bodywork companies in England. One of their products was the Sedanca de Ville (1938), which was built on the chassis of a Bentley 4.25 Litre.

of the same name. The cars were not really true Bentleys. They lacked the sporty character of their predecessors. Up until 1936, a total of 1,191 of these cars had been sold. The successor of the Derby Bentley was fitted with a 4.25 litre engine instead of a 3.5 litre engine. Up until 1940, 1,241 cars of this model were built.

In 1940, two new models were launched, the Mark V and the Corniche. Seventeen Mark Vs were built. All of these cars were confiscated by the English government. The two Corniche sports coupes were destroyed by German Bombs in France.

Benz

It is not entirely clear who is entitled to claim the title of inventor of the car. According to the French, Edouard Delamare Deboutteville and Leon Malandin built the first car in February 1884. In the rest of the world it is generally agreed that this title should go to Carl Benz and Gottlieb Daimler (see Daimler). Benz built a three-wheeler poweredby a gas engine. The

The engine of the Benz was placed above the rear axle. The one-cylinder gas engine had a capacity of 954 cc and delivered a mere 0.75 bhp.

vehicle conducted its first test drives through the streets of Mannheim in the autumn of 1885. His invention was patented on 29 January 1886. The one-cylinder engine delivered 0.75 bhp at 400 rpm. The prototype of the three-wheeler achieved a top speed of 10 mph (16 kph). Over the course of time, the engine became increasingly bigger and more powerful. When the model was taken into production in 1893 under the name of Victoria, the 2.0 litre engine delivered 3 bhp. In 1899, Benz introduced his first four-wheel car. In this so-called 'Vis-à-Vis' the passengers were seated in the front, with their backs facing the direction of the traffic. The driver was seated in the rear with the control stick in the centre of the car. The first cars still

A replica of the three-wheeler from 1885. Carl Benz built a three-wheeler because he did not know yet how to control two front wheels at the same time.

The Benz 8/20 was built between 1913 and 1918. The first year, the car was sold to the public. After that, all cars were reserved for the army. The 1,950 cc engine delivered 20 bhp at 1,800 rpm. This four-metre-long car, which weighed 1660 kg (3652 lb) was capable of a top speed of 37 mph (60 kph).

looked very much like little carriages. In all cases the engine was placed above the rear axle. It took some years before the cars started to look more 'modern'. The Parsifal from 1903 was the first car to have the engine in the front, under a fine bonnet. The passengers were seated behind the engine in two lines. Carl Benz built several models. In the early years, the car was mainly a toy for the rich. That is why the number of cars built continued to be limited. Prior to 1902,

In 1899, Benz introduced the 'Vis-à-Vis'. In this model the 1,710 cc engine was still placed in the rear.

Benz also built fast cars with very big engines, for example this four-cylinder from 1908. Its engine had a capacity of 12,076 cc!

Benz nevertheless sold a total of 2,702 motorcars. In 1926, the company employed more than 5,000 people, who built 1,305 cars and 929 lorries that year. In 1926, Carl Benz and Gottlieb Daimler decided to merge their companies resulting in the Daimler-Benz make.

The Berliet VB from 1918 was powered by a 3.3 litre four-cylinder engine.

Berliet

The French make Berliet became famous largely as a result of its lorries, but this make also originally started by producing cars. In 1895, Marius Berliet built his first motorcar. It was powered by a one-cylinder engine, which was placed above the rear axle. Production got off the ground very slowly. After four years, Berliet had sold only six cars. In 1900, a first Berliet fitted with a two-cylinder engine was built.

In co-operation with constructor Pierre Desgouttes a model fitted with a four-cylinder engine delivering 12 bhp also came about that same year. In France Berliet sold almost 100 cars that year. The four-cylinder engine was so good that it was also built under licence in England, at Sunbeam. In 1906, the American ALCO company (American Locomotive Company) also showed an interest in Berliet-engines. The companies entered into an agreement that brought in $500,000 for Berliet. But perhaps even more important was the fact that the company was also commissioned to design a locomotive. Within a short period of time, the company became France's biggest manufacturer in this field. The motorcars were not forgotten, however. In 1907, Berliet was the seventh biggest motorcar manufacturer and the product range consisted of three basic models. Two of these were powered by four-cylinder engines with a capacity of 2,412 or 4,398 cc while the third model was powered by a six-cylinder engine with a capacity of no less than 9.5 litres. It is hardly surprising that demand for this third model was limited. During World War I, the factory only built lorries for the army. In 1919, the company started to build cars again. This time cars fitted with four-cylinder engines. In 1924, the engine was fitted with overhead valves for the first time. This four-cylinder

The impressive wooden steering wheel of the Berliet VB. The stand gas and ignition could be set using the levers underneath the steering wheel.

48

engine had a capacity of 1,159 cc. This model was not a great success. The general public was not very enthusiastic about the bigger version with a 4.0 litre engine either, despite the fact that this model was fitted with brakes on the front wheels, a four-speed gear box, and spoke wheels. In 1933, the factory could only offer two models. They were sold as model 944 and were powered by 1.6 or 2.0 litre engines. It became increasingly clear that Berliet was losing the battle with its competitors.

In 1936, the Dauphine was launched, a car with a 2.0 litre engine, aerodynamic bodywork, and independent front suspension. Demand for this model was limited too. In 1939, the company's board decided to focus exclusively on the production of lorries. In 1967, the company was taken over by Citroën.

Berna

Just like everywhere else in Europe small car factories were mushrooming up in Switzerland, too, before World War I. Most makes were very short-lived. Other companies switched over to the manufacture of buses and lorries, and by doing so managed to survive a great deal longer. Joseph Wyss' 'Schweizerische Automobil Fabrik Berna' in Bern, which was founded in 1902, was one of these companies. In 1906, the company changed its name into 'Motorwerke Berna AG'. Wyss designed the first cars.

They were powered by one-cylinder engines that delivered 5 bhp and were placed in the rear. The bodywork offered room for two or four persons. In 1903, the engine was placed in the

A Berna Vis-à-Vis Idéal type from 1902. The one-cylinder engine was still placed in the rear and delivered 5.25 bhp.

front of the chassis. The rear wheels were powered by heavy chains. Wyss was able to sell only nine of these so-called 'Unicums'.

Between 1905 and 1907, the factory at Olten only manufactured lorries. This, however, did not bring in enough money either. In 1907, Wyss had to sell his company. The new owner, the 22-year-old Locher, had another go at motorcars, but he eventually also went bankrupt.

The Tipo S9 was the last, pre-war model produced by Bianchi. The car was built between 1934 and 1939. This picture shows a car from 1939.

Bianchi

A lot of car companies originally started out by building bicycles. Edoardo Bianchi was no exception. In 1885, at the age of 20, he started a small bicycle factory in Milan. His bicycles were of a good quality and were very popular. In 1897, Bianchi built his first motorcycle and in the following year his first car. This car was basically nothing more than two bicycles placed side by side with a De Dion-engine between the rear-wheels. From 1905 onwards, a Bianchi fitted with a four-cylinder engine also became available. Production soared as a result of this model. In no time, more than 300 cars were leaving the factory per year. Most cars were powered by small engines. The Tipo 4, however, was a big coach that had a 8.5 litre four-cylinder engine that delivered 40 bhp at 1300 rpm. Its sports version, Tipo 5, was fitted with a 7,859 cc four-cylinder engine that delivered 70 bhp.

After World War I, production of the big cars was stopped and new models appeared, such as the S1 that had a 1.4 litre side-valve engine. Benito Mussolini drove a Bianchi S15. This model had a four-cylinder engine. In 1925, the engines were fitted with overhead valves as a result of this the cars not only became more economical but also more powerful. The Tipo 20 from 1925 was fitted with a 2.3 litre four-cylinder engine that delivered 58 bhp at 3,200 rpm. This model achieved a top speed of more than 62 mph (100 kph). Bianchi had specialised in the manufacture of small, cheap models for years. The company made a U-turn in 1928, however, and started to build big, expensive cars fitted with eight-cylinder in-line engines. Unfortunately, the company's timing was wrong, as the world was facing a recession. The M3 was, for example, fitted with an eight-cylinder in-line engine with a capacity of 2,732 cc that delivered 72 bhp. In 1931, the engine was re-bored to 2,904 cc as a result of which the Tipo S8 came about. The last car of this production series was fitted with a 2,950 cc overhead valve engine that delivered 95 bhp. The last pre-war model, the S9, was of the familiar, modest size once again. The car was powered by a 1,452 cc engine and had a 279 cm wheel base. Bianchi never made a great deal of money on his cars. If his company had not been building bicycles and motorcycles at the same time, it would most certainly have gone bankrupt. During World War II, Bianchi was the main supplier of motorcycles to the Italian army.

BMW

The BMW make had established a good reputation for itself with aircraft engines and motorcycles. In 1929, the company took over the Dixi factory. This company's product line included several models with small four-cylinder but also big six-cylinder engines. During the take-over by BMW the only car that was still being built, however, was the Austin Seven, which was being built under licence. BMW managed to sell about 20,000 of these cars. In 1932, the company introduced the first of its own designs. Originally the cars still looked in many respects like the old Dixis, but the 303 from 1933 marked the beginning of a new era. This car was fitted with a 1.2 litre six-cylinder engine and was available in several bodywork versions. More than 3,200 sports convertibles, for example, were sold. In 1934, the 303 was succeeded by the 309, the 315, and the 319. These models helped to boost production. In three years time, 6,000, 9,765, and 6,646 of these cars were sold respectively. The 309 was powered by a 845 cc four-cylinder engine, the 315 and 319 by six-cylinder overhead valve

BMW became famous by building aircraft engines and motorcycles. The Dixi make was not taken over until later.

This picture of a 319 was taken during the 1991 Mille Miglia.

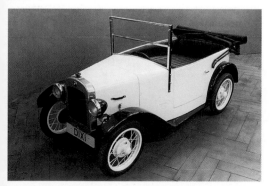

The 327/328 had the luxurious bodywork of the 327 and the powerful engine of the 328. This combination sold very well.

The 327/328 had the luxurious bodywork of the 327 and the powerful engine of the 328. This combination sold very well.

engines with a capacity of 1,490 cc and 1,911 cc. The cars were still relatively small with lengths ranging from 375 to 390 cm. The 326, however, took BMW into the bigger car sector. The model was introduced in February 1936. In contrast to its predecessors the 326 was a very sporty-looking car that was intended to compete with Mercedes-Benz. The 326 became a huge success. Between 1936 and 1941, almost 16,000 of these cars were sold. The six-cylinder engine had a capacity of 1,971 cc. The sports version, the 327, was fitted with the same engine, but this six-cylinder engine delivered 55 bhp instead of 50. The product range also included a real

The BMW 321 was launched in 1939. The model, which was built until 1941, was very popular with the German Wehrmacht.

The dashboard of the BMW 321. The indicator lever is visible in the top right corner.

The 326 took BMW into the same class as a Mercedes. The windscreen could be set ajar.

The 326 took BMW into the same class as a Mercedes. The windscreen could be set ajar.

BMW wrote racing history with a car of this type. Carrozzeria Touring in Milan built the bodywork.

sports car, the 328. With this model the 2.0 litre engine delivered 80 bhp to the rear wheels. The very sporty-looking 328 was highly suitable for everyday use, but was also capable of winning rallies and races. It was an extremely elegant car, which was almost too modern for its time. The headlights were built into the wings. The running boards were missing and so were the spoke wheels, which were common in those days.

The car was powered by a six-cylinder engine with three Solex carburettors and achieved top speeds of as much as 94 mph (150 kph). On 14 June 1936, the BMW 328 took part in the Eiffel race on the Nürburgring for the first time. The car was driven by Ernst

Henne, who had been racing BMW motorcycles for years. Henne won the race with an average speed of 63 mph (101 kph). It was to be the first of a long series of victories. In 1937 alone, the 328s won more than 200 races. In the following year they were very successful again. Among other things, a 328 won the difficult Mille Miglia and the 24-hour Le Mans race. Carrozzeria Touring had converted the 328 into a coupé especially for the latter race. Racing drivers Schaumburg-Lippe and Wencher won the 2.0 litre class with this car at an average speed of 83 mph (132.8 kph), a new class record. BMW built four cars in Eisenach especially for the 1940 Mille Miglia, which was called

The dashboard of a 328-Mille Miglia. The speedometer was of minor importance and was preferably read by the co-driver.

The bodywork of this car was built by Touring and consisted of a frame of thin steel tubes, covered with an aluminium sheet. The entire bodywork weighed only 80 kg (176 lb).

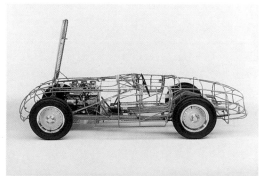

A BMW 335 at a rally in Italy in 1992.

BNC

The letters BNC stood for 'Bollack, Netter and Co.'. The small factory owned by these three gentlemen was situated at the Avenue de Paris 39, in the Levallois-Perret district. Between 1924 and 1931, mainly sports cars were built here. The fast two-seaters looked a lot like the cars made by Amilcar in that same period. The factory did not build its own engines and there was no reason to do so since the four-cylinder engines made by Ruby were cheap, reliable, strong, and economical. The cheap models were fitted with side valve engines, but overhead valve engines were also available. BNC never used really big engines. The

the Grand Prix of Brescia in those days. These were two coupés and two roadsters. The engines ran on a mixture of petrol and alcohol and delivered 135 bhp at 5,500 rpm. The cars finished in first, third, fifth, and sixth place in this race. The big winners were Huschke von Hanstein and Walter Bäumer, who achieved an average speed of 104.18 mph (166.7 kph)! After World War II, the BMW 328 continued to win numerous races. Production was stopped in 1940, but 328 engines continued to be built in England until the 1960s. The engines were successfully used by among others the makes Frazer Nash and Bristol.

The biggest pre-war BMWs were the 321 and the 335. These luxury models had a length of respectively 450 and 484 cm. The customer could choose between a 1,971 cc engine and a heavier 3,485 cc engine. The last six-cylinder engine delivered 90 bhp, which was enough for the car, which weighed 1,750-kg (3850 lb) to achieve a top speed of 90 mph (145 kph).

A BNC FCD type at the 1987 'Neige et Glace' rally. Note the anti-skid chains!

Characteristics for BNC was the radiator mounted at an angle. This car is from 1928.

cylinder capacity always fluctuated at around 1,000 cc. In 1926, a BNC was launched with a 1,100 cc S.C.A.P. engine, which was fitted with a Cozette compressor. The BNCs also participated in the 24-hour Le Mans race. Most of the cars that took part in that race were powered by a 1.5 litre Meadows engine. In 1929, a BNC was leading the race in his class, until the engine broke down a few hours before the finish. At the time, the car was in thirteenth place in the general rankings. In the late 1920s, BNC tried to penetrate a higher market sector. Enormous passenger cars were built that were fitted with eight-cylinder in-line engines made by Lycoming. There was, however, very little demand for this model. When the demand for ultra light sports cars started to drop as well, the company was forced to close down in 1931.

Brush

The small cars that were built by Frank Briscoe and Alan Brush between 1907 and 1911 were of a particularly good quality. Most of them were Runabouts, open two-seaters without roofs, doors, and windows that sold well mainly in the warmer parts of the United States. The one-cylinder engines delivered between 7 and 10 bhp.

In 1908, the make hit the headlines when Fred Trinkle drove from the east to the west coast of the United States in a Brush. En passant he climbed the Pikes Peak in Colorado in his little car. Only two cars had climbed this Peak before. The 'road' was only 37 kilometres long, but the drive took all day.

This Brush Runabout from 1910 was powered by a one-cylinder engine with a capacity of 1,340 cc. The gear box had two gears and a reverse.

BSA

BSA became famous mainly because of the light firearms and motorcycles the company produced. The company nevertheless also built cars. In 1907, the first cars left the 'Birmingham Small Arms Company' factory. The company built both small and big cars. As early as 1910, five different models were available.

One model that sold particularly well was the BSA 25/33. It was a splendid copy of the Itala, which had won the Peking to Paris race in 1907. When Daimler in Coventry got into financial difficulties, BSA decided to take over the company. The cars that were subsequently built in Birmingham looked more like a Daimler than a BSA. After World War I, Daimler stopped producing cars with four-cylinder

engines. In 1922, the BSA Ten HP was introduced. This small sports car was powered by a 1,080 cc two-cylinder engine. It was a cheap car that only had one door. The engine still had to be cranked.

Many English car makes started by building three-wheelers and later switched to 'real' cars. BSA did the same only the other way round. The Three-wheeler was not introduced until 1929. It was a front-wheel-drive car that offered room to two people and weighed a mere 406 kg (893 lb). The vehicle was powered by a 1,021 cc V-twin that delivered 21 bhp. It had a top speed of 62 mph (100 kph). The Three-wheeler performed particularly well at trials and mountain races. The model remained available until 1936. In 1935, BSA introduced a new sports car on four wheels, the Scout. The first

Scouts were fitted with a 1,075 cc four-cylinder engine. From 1937 onwards, the car also became available with a 1,203 cc side valve engine. In both cases the car was a front-wheel-drive, which was unusual for English cars in those days.

The Scout stayed in production until 1939. After the time, the factory once again started to specialise in firearms and motorcycles. BSA did not build any more cars after World War II.

Bucciali

The Bucciali was undoubtedly one of the strangest pre-war cars. It all started when the two brothers Paul-Albert and Angelo Bucciali wanted to buy a sports car. They were unable to find what they were looking for, however, and decided to build one themselves. The first models looked quite 'normal'. In 1922, they set up a small factory under the name of 'Bucciali Frères'. The first sports car that was built there was fitted with a 3.0 litre four-cylinder engine made by Ballot. In 1923, the brothers built front-wheel-drive sports cars with two-cylinder two-stroke

The Frenchman Jacques Saoutchik fitted the Buccialis with striking bodywork. This picture shows a TAV 30 from 1932.

engines. The model was introduced in Paris under the name of 'Buc'. Later, models fitted with V4-two-stroke engines and eight-in-line engines followed, but in most cases these were only prototypes. In the late 1920s and early 1930s, the most bizarre models were launched at the Paris Motor Show, such as the 1928 front-wheel-drive 'TAV 8' with its 4,398 cc eight-cylinder Continental-engine and 350 cm wheel base. The 1930 'Double Huit' also stood out. This model was fitted with a sixteen-cylinder engine consisting of two eight-in-line blocks that were placed next to each other on an aluminium oil carter. The cylinder capacity was 7,813 cc. The factory claimed that the overhead valve engine delivered 170 bhp.

In 1932, the Bucciali brothers launched the TAV 30. This car had a 409 cm wheel base. The biggest part of the car, however, was the bonnet. It was to be the last 'outrageous' model. After this Bucciali started to focus on more usual models, such as the Bucciali-Mathis. This car was powered by a 1,990 cc Mathis-engine. In total, only 151 cars of the Bucciali make were ever built, while no less than twenty different models were designed.

This 1930 Bucciali TAV 8 is very popular at the 'Pebble Beach Concours d'Elegance.'

Bugatti

Ettore Bugatti is often compared to Enzo Ferrari. Both men were born in Italy, were fond of horses and beautiful women, and tolerated no contradiction whatsoever. Bugatti insisted on being addressed as 'Le Patron' by both his relatives and employees. But what is perhaps the most important aspect of all is that both men managed to sign up the best technicians and racing drivers. Ettore Arco Isidoro Bugatti (1881-1947) was born in Milan.

His parents and brothers earned their living as artists. Ettore would most certainly have followed in their footsteps and would have become a sculptor if he had not been drawn to technology. At the age of nineteen, he built his own car, which earned him a medal at the 1901 Milan car exposition. Before setting up his own company in 1909, Bugatti worked for companies, such as Deutsch, Mathis, Dietrich, and Prinetti. His first models were not

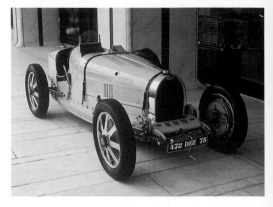

Bugatti won more than 2,000 races between 1909–1928, especially with the Type 35 like this one of the Czech driver Elisabeth Junek.

The four-cylinder engine of the Type 37 was available with or without compressor. This car, dating from 1925, is still often used for racing.

A Bugatti Type 35 at the 1993 Klausen Memorial-mountain race. Taking bends was hard work.

A Type 13 from 1912.

much better or more beautiful than his competitors'. The company only really made its name with the 1922 Type 35. It was undoubtedly one of the most beautiful cars of its time. Bugatti built many different models, but as in the case of Ferrari, their most interesting aspect could generally be found under the bonnet.

The four, eight, or sixteen-cylinder engines that were built in the factory at Molsheim all had one or two overhead camshafts. Almost all cars were rear-wheel drive cars. Only the Type 53 was a four-wheel drive.The Bugattis were way ahead of their time. The racing cars were almost unbeatable. In 1925 and 1926, they won more than a thousand

races. In 1927, they won even more than eight hundred! Bugatti sold most of the coaches as rolling chassis, but could also deliver complete cars. The enormous factory site at Molsheim not only housed the foundry but also special factories producing engines,

In addition to racing cars, there were also the Type 43-coupé and the 43A- convertible. This car is from 1933.

The Bugatti Type 41, or the Royale, is still rated as one of the most beautiful cars ever built. This car can be seen in the Schlumpf-museum at Mulhouse.

Bugatti not only built sports and racing cars. The four-cylinder engine of this 1927 Type 40 had a capacity of 1.5 litres.

The impressive engine of the Type 41. The crankshaft weighs 100 kg (220 lb) and turns in water-cooled bearings.

■ MOTEUR BUGATTI T41
(ROYALE)
8 CYL 12763 CM³ 3 SOUPAPES / CYL
200 à 250 CV à 1700 T/MN 9 PALIERS
1 ARBRE A CAMES EN TETE

chassis, and car bodies. Everybody agreed that Bugatti was able to build beautiful sports cars. But that was not all. With the launch of the Type 41, which was also referred to as the 'Royale', Bugatti openly competed with Rolls-Royce. This model was the crème de la crème of all cars. The chassis had a 425 cm wheel base and the enormous eight-cylinder in-line engine had a capacity of no less than 12,766 cc. At 1,000 rpm the car achieved a speed of 69 mph (110 kph) in third gear! The car had a statue of a white elephant on its radiator. The distance between the radiator and

The Type 53 was the only model with four-wheel drive. This car was not a great success and was very hard to drive. This picture shows former Bugatti racing driver René Dreyfuss demonstrating the car.

The engine of the Type 43 had a capacity of 4.9 litres, two overhead camshafts, and a compressor.

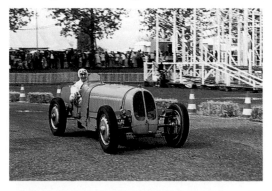

The Type 57 was the best sold Bugatti. More than 750 of these cars were sold. This two-seater from 1938 has a body built by Saoutchik.

The Type 57 was the best sold Bugatti. More than 750 of these cars were sold. This two-seater from 1938 has a body built by Saoutchik.

The Type 55 was powered by 2.3 litre eight-cylinder engine.

Fifty of these cars were sold.

Only seven Type 59 cars were sold between 1934 and 1936.

the windscreen was no less than 210 cm. The buyer was given a lifetime guarantee and the services were also free. Bugatti wanted to sell this car exclusively to kings and emperors, but unfortunately this target group was not really interested in the model. In total, only seven of these cars were built, among others for King Albert of Belgium and King Alfonso of Spain. In 1939, Bugatti's son Jean died in a car crash. Bugatti senior was heartbroken. When World War II broke out one month later, he left for Paris where he worked for the resistance. In 1947, the French government gave the factory

The brake drums and the wheels of this Bugatti formed a whole. Incidentally, the wheels were cast by Bugatti himself.

back to Bugatti, but he could not enjoy it for long. He died a few days later. His other son Roland Bugatti tried to restart the factory, but his efforts were in vain. In 1956, the renowned make disappeared from the market for good.

nobody wanted to buy the car. The company got into financial difficulties, but was saved by the Briscoe brothers. In return for this, they were appointed directors of the new 'Buick Motor Company'. This company, however, was not a great success either. On 1 November 1904, the 'Buick Motor Company' was sold to James H. Whiting, who appointed William Crapo Durant as president. He managed to turn Buick into a profitable company in no time. The same year, Durant founded 'General Motors', of which Buick formed the basis.

In 1904, Buick had sold no more than 21 cars. In 1905, the company sold 750 cars and in 1906, the year in which David Buick left the factory, it sold

The two-cylinder engine in this 1906 Buick delivered 22 bhp at 1,200 rpm.

Buick

David Dunbar Buick was a plumber by profession. He had discovered a way to connect porcelain to metal. This discovery was of great significance in particular for kitchen and bathroom appliances. Buick managed to sell the design for $100,000 and in 1901 he used this money to set up two new companies namely the 'Buick Auto Vim and Power Company' and the 'Buick Manufacturing Company'. Eugène C. Richard designed a two-cylinder overhead-valve engine for the latter company. The engine was built into the Buick F. Unfortunately,

In 1915, Buick exclusively built cars with four-cylinder and six-cylinder engines. All models were fitted with an electric starter.

1,400 cars. Production kept going up. In 1910, 6,500 employees built around 30,525 cars. The different models were powered by four-cylinder and six-cylinder engines. Demand remained steady. In 1926, more than 126,000 Buicks were sold. In 1929, all the Buicks were given new bodies and heavier engines. The four-cylinder engines now had capacities of 3.8 litres and the six-cylinder engines capacities of 5.1 litres. The standard versions of the Buick cost respectively $1,195 and $2,145. After 1931, only cars with eight-cylinder engines were sold. This eight-in-line overhead-valve engine was to remain virtually unchanged

A Buick from 1917. Note the rear wheel suspension above the foot board. In 1917, Walter P. Chrysler became president-director of General Motors.

The rear doors of the Buick Special from 1937 still opened 'the wrong way'.

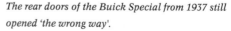

In 1996, this car was still owned by its original owner!

New York, 1973: a 1938 Buick still appears to be suitable for everyday use.

until 1953. Of course, far fewer motorcars were sold in America, too, during the world crisis. In 1931, 88,417 Buicks were sold and the following year this number dropped to 41,522. Smaller makes, such as Hudson, Studebaker, and Pontiac sold more cars, because they were able to offer less expensive cars fitted with four-cylinder and six-cylinder engines.

Buick found a solution to the problem in a cheaper car of the 40 type. In 1936, the cars were once again fitted with new bodies. The design was such a success that sales increased to 179,533 cars. A great deal of this success was also due to the new 5.2 litre eight-cylinder engine that delivered 120 bhp.

The eight-cylinder overhead valve engine of this Special from 1937 delivered 100 bhp at 3,200 rpm.

The models dating from 1937 and 1938 had an even more elegant design. In the meantime, the Buick make had moved up to fourth place on the list of American car manufacturers. Customers were being offered an increasingly wider range of models. In 1941, the company offered no less than 26 different bodies on five different chassis. That same year, Buick broke its own record by building 316,251 cars.

On 2 February 1942, the last pre-war Buick was built. Thereafter the production lines had to be used for the manufacture of tank and aircraft engines.

In 1932, customers were able to choose from two eight-cylinder engines with capacities of 4,470 and 5,650 cc. Note the holes in the bonnet through which hot air could escape.

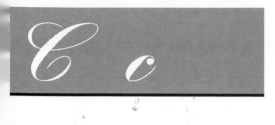

Cadillac

who in 1701 built the 'Ville d'Etroit' settlement. This village was later to become Detroit, where Henry Martin Leland started a small car factory in 1902. He called his company the 'Cadillac Automobile Company' in honour of the French explorer. In 1909, Cadillac became part of the General Motors company, where the

A Cadillac from 1906 in the basic design, without linen hood and without front windscreen.

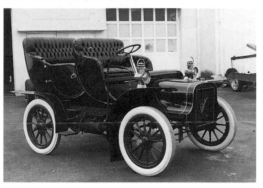

Car enthusiasts will be more than familiar with the names Henry Ford, Louis Chevrolet and Antoine de la Mothe Cadillac. But there are differences. The first couple of gentlemen built cars, but monsieur Cadillac was a French explorer

A Cadillac V12 roadster of the type 370A. The two-seater had a 'dickey seat' for the children and sufficient luggage space behind the little door in front of the rear wing.

The body with an extra window for the passengers on the back seat was called the 'Dual Cowl'. This convertible with a V8 engine was introduced in 1928.

In 1934, the cars already looked a great deal more modern. The radiator grill and the headlights were streamlined. The white-walled tyres were very fashionable in those days.

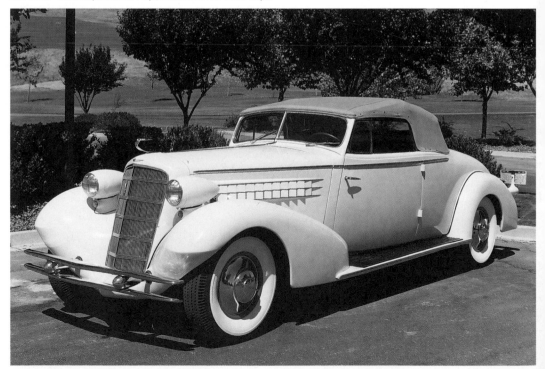

In 1912, tyres were still of a low quality and the roads were littered with nails from horseshoes. Two or more spare tyres would not go amiss in those days.

This Town Car dates from 1935 and has a V12-engine. The roof above the front seat could be opened and the rear compartment was sectioned off by a partition.

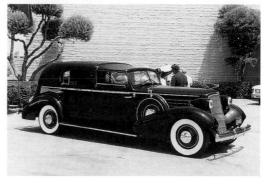

In the days when the competition was only offering cars with four-cylinder engines, Cadillac presented the V8 in 1914. From that year on they never produced a car with anything less. This type 53 dates from 1919.

'Opera Coupe' is what this 1936 model was called. It was a 2+2, but the space in the back was only suitable for children. At a price of $1,645 it was the cheapest Cadillac from that year.

make represented the most expensive class of cars. By then, Cadillacs had already built up a very good reputation. The make was very popular among the rich. The most beautiful bodies were frequently built on a rolling chassis. As far as the engines were concerned customers could choose from V8, a V12 or a V16. The Cadillac has been the most beautiful car produced in Detroit for close to one hundred years now. The make has always been ahead of its time in all areas, including the technical field. While the competition was still offering cars with a one or two cylinder engine, Cadillac introduced a four-cylinder engine. After 1914, the

factory never produced a car with less than eight cylinders. In 1912, the cars

In the years leading up to the war the streamlining of cars was becoming increasingly important. The picture here shows a 1935 Cadillac Aerodynamic with a V12-engine.

In 1937, the cheapest model with a V16 engine, the seven-seater sedan cost $7,350. In 1990 an enthusiast paid $2,500,000 for this car. The outstanding body is thought to be a design by Figoni & Falaschi.

The V8 in 1936 was 5784 cc, giving 115 bhp. The V12 was 6030 cc/135 bhp and the V16 was 7405 cc/165 bhp.

The Cadillac Series 62 Convertible Coupe from 1941 offered room for four people but the two passengers at the back did not have much of a view.

were already being fitted with electric lights. That same year the Cadillac was also the first car to have an electric starter motor, which abolished the need for cranking. Even though more than 20,000 Cadillacs were sold in 1918, the factory was still preoccupied with building fighter planes. Cadillac had been awarded the biggest government order of all time. The company had to build 40 planes a day! Cars were also built for the army. The first allied car to cross the Rhine on 18 November 1918 was a Cadillac. In 1922, the factory introduced a carburettor in which the petrol-air mixture was regulated by a thermostat. And in 1928 the cars were fitted with a synchronised gearbox. Safety glass and shock absorbers were introduced in 1929 and in 1930 the first car with a V16-engine roamed the streets of Detroit. This was followed in the same year by a car with a V12-engine. The beautiful overhead valve engines were to remain in production until 1940.

Celeritas

Wilhelm Stift owned a haberdashery shop in Vienna. We do not know whether he was able to make a living with this business. We do know, however, that he became a partner in a car factory in 1900. In 1901, he set up his own workshop, where he built a car under the name of Celeritas. The mini-car was powered by a French engine, a two-cylinder Buchet. It is not known how many cars Stift sold in total. He could not have sold more than a handful, because even Stift had not really taken to his own design. One day, when Stift saw the little car produced by the Gräf brothers, he realised that he had made a mistake. He joined the Gräf brothers and founded the 'Gräf und Stift' company in 1901.

The Celeritas was powered by a 635 cc air-cooled engine that delivered 12 bhp.

The drive of a Celeritas was not really reliable.

In 1901, the Celeritas already had a truly round steering wheel.

Charron

Fernand Charron was one of the first garage owners in Paris. In 1897, he became a Panhard et Levassor dealer. In 1901, Charron started a car factory together with two partners under the name of CGV. The car looked like the big Panhard and was particularly popular among the wealthier racing drivers. Charron had good contacts with these racing drivers. Charron himself was also a well-known racing driver and had won the first Gordon Bennett Race in 1900. In 1902, no fewer than 76 cars were sold. By 1905 this number had gone up to 265. That same year, the company employed 400 people. In 1906, CGV was sold to an

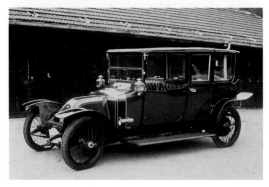

English company. Subsequently, the production of cars in France was stopped completely. A total of 753 cars were sold under the name of CGV. In 1907, Charron made cars under his own name for the first time. In 1908, however, the company was once again faced financial difficulties. Charron was forced to sell his company again. In the meantime, he had married car manufacturer Adolphe Clément's daughter and was able to take over his father-in-law's car factory. It is not known how it happened, but in 1910, Charron was once again working in his original garage at the Avenue de la Grande Armée in Paris. In 1912, he introduced the so-called 'Alda', but this model was not successful either. In the meantime, the production at the Charron-factory had simply continued. In 1909, the Q, QR, and the L were launched. These models, which were fitted with two-cylinder and four-cylinder engines, remained in production until World War I. In 1919, the RGM and the PGM followed. The former was fitted with a four-cylinder engine that delivered 12 bhp, the latter with a four-cylinder engine that delivered 15 bhp. The factory mainly built small cars. In 1926, customers could choose from four models fitted with a 1,057 cc, a 1,368 cc, and a 3,405 cc four-cylinder engine and a 2,771 cc six-cylinder overhead valve engine. These models did not sell very well either. The last Charron was sold in 1930.

Chenard & Walcker

The first car produced under the name of Chenard & Walcker was intoduced at the Paris Motor Show in 1901. It was a small car with a 1,160 cc two-cylinder side valve engine. Ernest Chenard set up a small bicycle factory in 1888. In 1898, Henry Walcker became a partner in the company. Two years later, in 1900, they switched over to the production of motorcars. The first model, a three-wheeler with a De Dion-engine, was a fiasco, but from 1901 onwards the situation improved.

In 1905, Chenard & Walcker only built cars with four-cylinder engines. This car had a 3,021 cc four-cylinder engine.

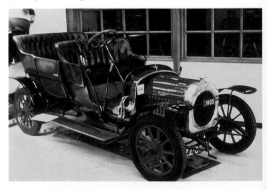

The way in which the real wheels were driven, each with its own cardan shaft, was interesting. This system was to be used until the 1920s. In 1909, the company was able to offer five different models. The least expensive version was powered by a 945 cc one-cylinder engine, the most expensive one by a 5,881 cc four-cylinder engine. The cars were not very sporty-looking. This changed in 1922, when the factory introduced a model with a four-cylinder

The characteristic front view of the Chenard & Walcker

engine with an overhead camshaft. The engine had a capacity of 3.0 litres, dry-sump lubrication, and delivered 90 bhp. It was the kind of car that was able to win races! In 1923, Chenard & Walcker finished in first and second place in the 24-hour Le Mans race. In 1924, a real racing car with an eight-cylinder engine was introduced.

This so-called X-type was powered by a 3,942cc eight-in-line engine that delivered 130 bhp. The factory team of Chenard & Walcker was very successful, resulting in a lot of free publicity. The cars in the 1,100 cc class were fitted with special, heavy bodies. The four-cylinder engines were fitted with overhead camshafts, just like all racing cars made by Chenard & Walcker, and delivered 55 bhp. If a compressor was fixed on the engine the car could achieve a top speed of 106 mph (170 kph).

After 1928, no more races were run, as a result of which the make rapidly became less widely known. In 1927, Chenard & Walcker merged with Delahaye, Unic, and Donnet. The joint venture was to last until 1932. The main point of the merger was to meet the competition of cheap American imported cars. The main outcome of the merger, however, was that all of the models looked very much alike and that demand was limited. In 1932, Chenard & Walcker withdrew from the group. By then, the company's reputation had already suffered a great deal.

Consequently, it took several years before the company became profitable again. The Aigle 8, which was powered by a 3,565 cc V8-engine, was the most successful car. This model was sold until 1936. Its successor was fitted with a 3,610 cc Ford V8-engine. After World War II, the company limited its production to lorries.

Chevrolet

Every founder of every car make has his own history. The development and launch of a car make often worked out well, but sometimes it did not. The latter was the case for Louis Chevrolet. Chevrolet was born on 25 December 1878 at La Chaux-de-Fonds, in the western part of

This Chevrolet from 1926 was powered by a four-cylinder overhead valve engine.

A 1926 Chevrolet did not have a boot yet, but it did have a luggage rack.

A Chevrolet from 1929 at a Concours d'Elegance at the racing circuit of Zandvoort in 1981.

Switzerland. At the age of 21, he left for Beaune in France, where he worked as a bicycle repairer. From there he travelled on to Paris, Canada, and subsequently New York. In the latter city he worked as a mechanic in a Fiat garage. In France he had taken part in bicycle races. In America he did the same with his boss' cars. Among other things, he won a car race on the Morris Park racing circuit, in the state of New York. William C. Durant, who founded General Motors, employed Louis Chevrolet and his brother Arthur Chevrolet, who had also arrived in America. With financial support from Durant, Louis Chevrolet set up his own company in an empty Buick-factory. In 1909, he built a six-cylinder engine, which in 1911 was followed by a first

In 1932, the cars were fitted with synchronised gearboxes. That same year, the spare wheel was fixed to the side of the car.

motorcar. The car was not a great success. In 1912, only 2,999 Chevrolets were sold. And then fate struck. Chevrolet had a fight with Durant and left his factory. He died a poor and lonely man on 6 June 1941. It must have hurt to see how General Motors turned 'his' factory into the biggest in the world. As early as 1919, Durant sold 190,000 cars. In 1941, the last pre-war year of production, Chevrolet even sold more than a million cars!

Louis Chevrolet was no longer allowed to use his name for a car make. The only time Louis came into contact with Chevrolet after all of this was when he worked as a mechanic in one of Durant's factories. There is, incidentally, a striking parallel with Buick. When Durant took over the Buick factories, he made the same deal with David D. Buick who also died a poor and

The Roadster was the least expensive Chevrolet. In 1931 it cost $475. The model could seat two people in the car and two in the 'dickey seat'.

unknown man. Louis Chevrolet had once hoped to be allowed to build a beautiful, expensive car. His partner Durant, however, had other plans. He wanted to cross Ford and was looking for a cheap car that could compete with the T-Ford. The result was the 490, a car with a small four-cylinder overhead

In 1937, Chevrolet introduced the Suburban. Strangely enough the big car was fitted with only two doors and a backdoor.

A Special DeLuxe Convertible from 1941, which cost only $949 in those days. Nevertheless only 15,296 of these cars were sold.

It was quite common for a convertible to have a 'dickey seat', but coupés rarely had one.

The two-door sedan was the best sold Chevrolet in 1933. 162,629 of these cars were sold.

In 1931, Chevrolet sold 623,901 cars.
This picture shows a car of the production series from that year.

valve engine, which in 1916 was sold for $490 (a T-Ford was just as expensive, but offered considerably less). Durant was right. In the first year of production, 63,000 of these cars were sold. The following year, Chevrolet was the fourth major car make in America in terms of sales figures. In 1918, the make became part of the General Motors concern. In 1924, William S. Knudsen became the president and general manager of Chevrolet. He later went on to become the president of General Motors.

In 1929, the 'Cast Iron Wonder', a six-cylinder engine that was to remain virtually unchanged until 1953, was designed under his supervision. In 1934, the 'Knee Action' front-wheel-

This Chevrolet Special Deluxe was built in 1941.

suspension' was another technical tour de force. The same year, the one-millionth car left the factory. In 1936, the make celebrated its 25th anniversary. The factory proudly claimed that it had been the world's biggest car manufacturer eight times over the last decade. In 1940, Chevrolet sold more than one million cars over a period of ten months. In that year, a Master DeLuxe Town Sedan cost $728, which was more than Durant was asking for his Chevrolet 490 in 1915, but considerably less than the $2,150 that Louis Chevrolet received for his first cars in 1912.

This two-seater coupé was built in 1934.

Robust and reliable...

Chrysler

Walter Percy Chrysler (1875-1940) was a real 'self-made man'. He was born on a farm but was more interested in technology than cows. He got himself a job as a locomotive cleaner at the 'Union Pacific Railroad'. Via a job as a mechanic he managed to work his way up to become the director of 'American Locomotive'. In 1905, he bought his first car, which was a Locomobile, a make that he was to remain faithful to until 1912. That same year he joined General Motors, where he worked his way up to president and general director of Buick. He left the company after an argument with Billy Durant. He was assigned the task of getting the insolvent Willys-Overland company back on its feet. He was not going to do this for free. Chrysler earned $1,000,000 a year, but on the other hand his intervention was a success. After a couple of years, Willys was profitable again. Chrysler was subsequently given the same assignment at Maxwell. This car manufacturer was also in the red, until Chrysler reorganised things. In 1924, the company made a profit of $4 million. When Chrysler left the company he took three young engineers with him, namely Fred Zeder, Carl Breer, and Owen Skelton. Within a couple of months, they had built a car that bore the name of Chrysler on its radiator. The prototype looked so good that Chrysler managed to get a five-million-dollar loan.

In 1924, he laid the foundation stone of his empire with this money. In 1924, the first Chrysler was introduced to the public. People responded enthusiastically. It was powered by a six-cylinder engine with a high compressor ratio of

The dashboard of the Seventy. Over to the far left you can see the speedometer, which has the mileometer and the trip recorder below it.

In 1926, Chrysler was able to offer three standard models. The Seventy was the least expensive six-cylinder. It is shown here as a five-seater.

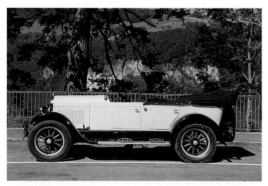

In the 1928 calendar year, Chrysler sold 160,670 cars, which was a new yearly record. This picture shows a two-seater roadster with 'dickey seat' from that same year.

The Chrysler Imperial was the company's showpiece. The model could easily compete with the Cadillac of General Motors and the Lincoln of Ford. This picture shows an Imperial from 1931.

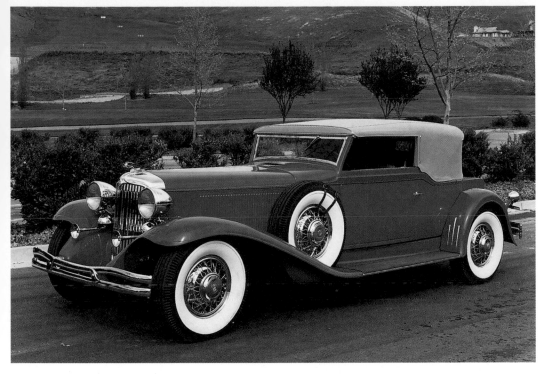

4.7:1. The car was fitted with all kinds of technical gadgets, such as an air filter on the carburettor, an oil filter with an exchangeable filter part, aluminium pistons, and a seven-bearing crankshaft that runs on seven bearings. Moreover, the car had four hydraulic brakes, which was an unknown luxury in those days. That first year, Chrysler managed to sell no fewer than 32,000 cars, which was more than Oldsmobile, Hupmobile, and Nash combined production. In 1926, Chrysler was already able to offer three models, one with a 3.0 litre four-cylinder engine, and two with a six-in-line engine. The latter

At the 1931 New York Motor Show, Chrysler introduced the so-called CM production series.
These models had entirely new bodies. The car in this picture cost $970 then.

The front seats of the Imperial Eighty from 1928 were undoubtedly much more comfortable!

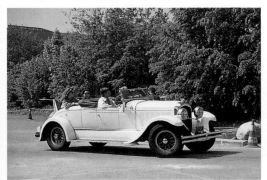

This Chrysler from 1932 was fitted with a 3,750 cc six-cylinder engine that delivered 83 bhp to the rear wheels.

The Royal Six was the best sold model in 1937. A total of 62,408 of the Touring Sedans shown here were sold.

1932 Chrysler Imperial Le Baron with V-shaped windscreen.

In 1935, the 'Airflow' was launched. The model was too far ahead of its time to sell well.

The Thunderbolt was designed by Alex Tremulis and Ralph Roberts in 1940. The car was really designed for car exhibitions rather than the public highway. As a result, production was limited to six cars.

The boot of the Airflow was rather small...

scraper in the world was built. This so-called 'Chrysler-Building' was 319 metres high and had 77 storeys. The Chryslers did not enjoy their sky scraper or their new house on Long Island for long. In 1938, Chrysler had a heart attack, which he survived, but which left him an invalid. Some months later, his wife Della died. On 18 August 1940, Walter Percy Chrysler also passed away. The following words were written on his tombstone: 'He proved that this is a land of unlimited opportunities'.

models were the Chrysler 70 and the Chrysler Imperial, which had a 4.7 litre engine and cost no less than $3,000. That year, 162,242 cars left the Chrysler factory. In 1928, Chrysler took over the Dodge brothers' company. When he also founded the Plymouth and De Soto makes, he became a much feared competitor of Ford and General Motors. His success was so big that Chrysler himself was barely affected by the recession. On the contrary, 1929 was a record year and 1933 was even better! Walter Chrysler and his wife Della had two sons and two daughters, but none of their children or their children's partners were interested in their father (-in-law)'s factory. Chrysler subsequently decided to sell his shares on the stock market. He used some of the money to buy a piece of land in Manhattan, where the highest sky

Citroën

On 5 July 1935, André Citroën died a poor man, abandoned by his friends. Not long before he died, he had invited 6,500 guests to the opening of his new factory. The new super car was to be built in this new factory. The banks, however, decided to stop their funding before the car got over its initial teething problems. Citroën's company

In 1919, Citroën built the 'Coupé Docteur' on the chassis of the 10 HP Type A. The car had a length of 400 cm and was powered by a 1,327 cc engine.

In 1921, the big news at the Paris motor show was the Citroën Trèfle, which was also known as 'the cloverleaf'. The car got its name because of the pointed rear that accommodated a third passenger.
This Trèfle is from 1924.

A Citroën C4 from 1928. The four-cylinder engine had a capacity of 1,628 cc.
It delivered 30 bhp at 3,000 rpm.

In 1929, the factory built a first six-cylinder engine into the Citroën Six. The 2,442 cc engine delivered 45 bhp at /3,000 rpm.
The car achieved a top speed of 65 mph (105 kph).

A C6 from 1930 as a four-seater convertible.

In the 1930 model year, the AC 4 was given a new body. The four-cylinder engine had a capacity of 1,628 cc.

subsequently went bankrupt in December 1934. Tyre manufacturer Michelin, however, paid off the 150 million francs debt and made the company world-famous with the Traction Avant. Up until 1957, 759,111 of these cars were sold. André Citroën's parents were rich. His Dutch grandfather, Roelof Limoenman, had his name changed into Citroen. And when his son, Levi Bernard, set up business in Paris as a diamond dealer, the dots appeared on the e. André Citroën studied technology in Paris. In 1898, he received the title 'engineer'. He set up a factory producing gear wheels with corner-gears after a patent by a Polish uncle. These gear wheels were later to become his trademark. In 1908, he took over the bankrupt Mors car factory, which he managed to

In 1938, this Citroën type 11 BL was introduced. That year, the model cost FFR 32,000.

The 11 BL was a 2+2. The two persons in the rear had to sit in the dickey seat.

A typical Citroën-interior. The light switch and the horn were attached to the steering column. The chrome gear lever was located in the dashboard.

revive. During a visit to America, he was introduced to the concept of mass production. Citroën was the first to introduce such a system into Europe. This happened during World War I, when he had signed a contract with the French government to produce 50,000 grenades a day. Specifically for this purpose Citroën built a new factory at the Quai de Javel, where the first Citroën-passenger cars were also built after the War. In 1921, more than 10,000 cars had been built. In 1924, Citroën was also the first car manufacturer to build a body made completely from steel. He was the first to found an insurance company exclusively for Citroën drivers. He had the streets in

In 1932, the C4G was the most expensive and luxurious model.

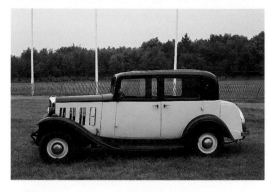

some parts of Paris fitted with electric street lightning and had his own name written in tens of thousands of light bulbs on the Eiffel Tower in 1925. Citroën funded expeditions through Africa and Asia. His motorcars broke numerous records, the 'Petite Rosalie', for example, which in 1933 non-stop covered a distance of 300,000 kilometres. That same year, Citroën

In 1933, the Petite Rosalie covered a distance of 300,000 kilometres at the racing circuit of Montlhéry. The average speed was 58 mph (93 kph). During this race, Citroën beat no less than 299 records!

This C4G Familiale cost FFR 31,000 in 1933.

The Traction Avant made Citroën famous outside Europe as well. This car dates from 1936.

started working on his dream car, the Traction Avant. The model was fitted with a self-supporting body, front-wheel drive and an automatic gearbox. This gearbox, however, proved to be useless. At the very last moment, a regular (Citroën) gearbox had to be fitted into the car. The banks were no longer prepared to invest any more money in the cars and Citroën sold cars before they had been sufficiently tested.

Guarantee claims came in by the dozen. The company went bankrupt andCitroën was forced to leave his enormous villa in Deauville. If the banks had only been more patient...

Clément-Bayard

The French company Clément-Bayard was situated at the Boulevard de la Saussaye 57 in Neuilly. Between 1899 and 1922, three-wheelers and cars were built there. Like so many others, Gustave Adolphe Clément (1855-1928) originally started out by building bicycles and motorcycles. His first car was a three-wheeler with a De Dion-engine, but it was not long before he switched over to real motorcars. His models were fitted with one, two or four-cylinder engines. General Pierre du Terrail, Seigneur de Bayard, had defeated the English army in 1521 and this proud general became the logo of Clément's cars. In 1903, Clément was

even officially granted permission by the French government to change his name into Clément-Bayard. Some super cars with 12,963 cc six-cylinder overhead camshaft engines were built for the 1908 French Grand Prix. The engines delivered 138 bhp at 1,450 rpm and their top speed was no less than 106 mph (170 kph). Three of these cars took part in the race, but the race was

A 1911 AC6 type Clément. The car had a six-cylinder engine with a capacity of 3.3 litres.

A 1913 Clement-Bayard.

won by Christian Lautenschlager in a Mercedes with a cylinder capacity of 12,831 cc. The Cléments finished in ninth, twenty-seventh, and thirtieth place. The accident in which Albert Clément's, the boss's son, died could not stop the team from finishing the race.

The following year, a second attempt was made to beat Mercedes, but Mercedes won despite the fact that the top speed had been increased to 119 mph (190 kph). After World War I, a few inconspicuous models were introduced. In 1922, the company was taken over by Citroën.

Clyno

In 1900, cousins Frank and Alwyn Smith started to build motorcycles in Wolverhampton. During World War I, a great deal of money was made with the production of motorcycles with sidecars for the army. In 1922, the 'Clyno Engineering Company Ltd' built its first motorcar. The small cars were powered by 1,368 cc four-cylinder engines made by Coventry Climax. In the first year of production, 623 Clynos were made. The cars were fast and reliable. The company invested a great deal of money in racing and in 1924, a Clyno won a race at the Brooklands circuit with an average speed of 70 mph (113 kph).

The cars that were built after 1924 could be fitted with brakes on all four wheels, if so requested. In addition, customers were given the choice of different bodies. Business was going well. In 1925, 4,849 cars were built and this number was to increase even more. In 1926, the factory built 350 cars a week, a number that was only equalled by Austin and Morris. The directors, however, wanted more. A big new factory was built and several new

This 1926 Clyno seated three people, two on the front seat and a third in the rear.

models were introduced, but all of this was paid for with borrowed money. In 1929, the product range consisted of four models, namely the 12/35 in a standard or luxury version, the Nine and the Century. All of the models were powered by 951 or 1,593 cc four-cylinder engines. The cheap Century cost £100, the expensive 12/35 DeLuxe £150. The cars sold well, but they were priced so low that the company hardly made any money on them. In 1928, competitor Morris reduced its prices.

Clyno had to follow suit, but it was at the expense of quality. The Coventry Climax-engines were, for example, replaced by less expensive, home-made four-cylinder engines. For insiders it was therefore hardly surprising that the company had to file for bankruptcy in 1929. Over the years, the factory had sold a total of more than 40,000 cars.

Cord

Errett Loban Cord (1894-1974) undoubtedly lived a varied life. He went bankrupt several times, the first time at the age of only 25, but eventually he managed to work his way up from car salesman to become one of the most important American car manufacturers. Cord's career was typically American, although he never worked as a kitchen hand. In 1924, he took over the insolvent car make Auburn.

He managed to get the company back on its feet. Two years later, he bought the famous Duesenberg make. In 1929, Cord introduced the first car under his

Cord sold this car as the Cord 812 Beverly Sedan. The compressor engine delivered 170 bhp at 3,500 rpm.

The Cord L.19 was the first American front-wheel drive production car.

The eight-cylinder in-line engine of the L.29 originally had a capacity of 5,893 cc.

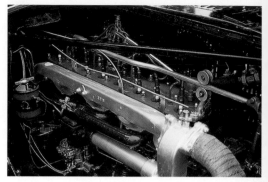

The L.29 was available in different versions or as a rolling chassis. This picture shows a seven-seater limousine.

own name, the Cord L.29. Despite the fact that the car was largely built using Auburn parts, it was nevertheless a special design. Cord had bought several patents from Harry Miller, the famous advocate of front-wheel drive cars. The Cord L.29 was the first American production model to have front-wheel drive. The long bonnet concealed a Lycoming eight-in-line engine (Cord also owned the Lycoming engine factory).

The car was launched at the New York Motor Show, where it caused a lot of commotion. Unfortunately the timing was wrong. Only two months later, Wall Street crashed. The result was a drop in demand for expensive cars in particular. Cord had counted on selling

10,000 cars a year, but when the production of the L.29 was stopped in 1932, only 5,010 cars had been built. The very expensive Duesenberg was also not easy to sell. In 1933, the Auburn make alone recorded a loss of more than $2.3 million. But Cord did not give up. On the principle that it was a case of 'all or nothing' he had a new model built in 1936. This Cord 810 was to be so exceptional and appealing that every rich American would want to own one.

In July 1935, Cord commissioned his employees to design the car. Gordon Buehrig designed the bodywork, which was so beautiful and exceptional that he received an award for it from the 'Museum of Modern Art' in New York in 1952! The model was, of course, a front-wheel drive, but this time a V8-

The Cord 812 Sportsman Convertible.

The impressive dashboard of the 812.

In 1936, Cord introduced the 810 and 812, but unfortunately these models were not a great success either.

The headlights of the Cord 812 Sportsman Convertible could be operated via a switch on the dashboard.

engine had been built into it. In 1937, the model was also available as a Cord 812. In this version the engine was fitted with a Schwitzer Cummins-compressor, which initially delivered 170 bhp, but later 195 bhp. The car with compressor engine could be easily recognised by its chrome exhaust pipes, which came out of the side of the bonnet. Both models were unfortunately plagued by a series of technical problems. A total of 3,200 cars of the types 810 and 812 were sold, but the make became immortal despite this small number. Replicas are still being built. Cord's empire, which among other things consisted of the Checker car factory and an airline company, collapsed in 1937. Cord left for California via England, where he established himself as a real estate agent. He was successful in this business as well. The well-known 'Fortune' magazine rated him as one of the fifty wealthiest Americans. When he died on 2 January 1974, he was estimated to be worth about $17 million.

Cottin et Desgouttes

"The route from Paris to Beauvais, Abbeville, Saint-Riquier, Eu, Le Tréport, Dieppe, Cany, Fécamp, Etretat, Le Havre, Rouen and back is 580 km long. With four people in the car plus their luggage we achieved a top speed of 90 kph (56 mph). The average speed over the entire distance was 65 kph (40 mph). We covered the 18 km between Rouen and Pont-de-l'Arche in 15 minutes, which meant an average speed of 72 kph (45 mph). We used 17 litres of petrol and 1.5 litres of oil per 100 kilometres." This is how the famous car reporter Charles Faroux described his journey in a Cottin et Descouttes in 1913. At the time, these road tests were still something special. The technical information he mentioned in his article was of great importance to potential buyers. For example, he stated that the car in the picture was powered by a four-cylinder engine with a bore/stroke ratio of 100 x 160 mm. The Cottin et Descouttes had a wheel base of 380 cm and according to the factory weighed 950 kg (2090 lb). A Bosch magnet controlled the ignition, which could be adjusted with a lever attached to the steering wheel. A water pump controlled the circulation A Bosch magnet controlled the ignition, which could be adjusted with a lever attached to the steering wheel. A water pump controlled the circulation of the cooling-water and there was a fan behind the radiator. The clutch consisted

This Cottin et Descouttes from 1912 seated six people. The factory called the body a 'Torpedo'.

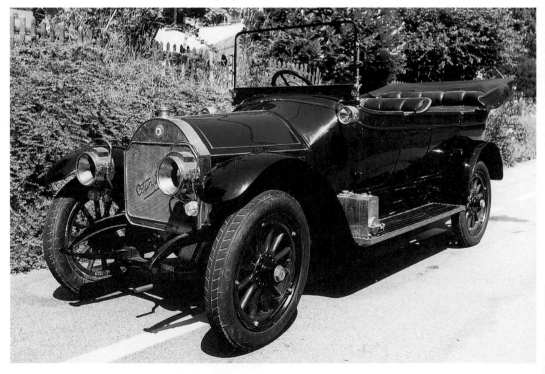

of a number of plates and the car was fitted with a cardan shaft and a foot brake on the rear wheels. The 70 litre petrol tank was located in the rear of the car. The Cottin et Descouttes cars were built in Lyon. The first model was introduced in Paris in 1905. The factory built simple, but reliable four-cylinder and six-cylinder engines. The engine, which was built into the 12 CV in 1922, was a technical tour de force. This four-cylinder engine had no less than three overhead valves per cylinder. The cylinder capacity was 3.0 litres. From 1930 onwards, the company only built models with six-cylinder engines and independent front-wheel suspension. In 1931, the make disappeared from the market for good.

Cyklon

Three-wheelers played an important role in the development of the car. The first Morgans and the vans made by Tempo in the 1950s were famous and popular. And Karl Benz, too, started with a three-wheeler. However, the three-wheeler made by Cyklon, the Cyclonette, was something really special. The engine was located above the single front wheel, a construction which the factory also used for motorcycles. The monsters were built by the 'Cyclonwerke AG' at Charlottenburg close to Berlin. And in 1902, they even became successful. The first three-wheelers were powered by a 450 cc one-cylinder two-stroke engine that delivered 3.5 bhp. Later on, twins were also built with 1,290 cc engines that delivered 6 bhp. In 1922, these were followed by ones with a four-cylinder engine. The later model was available until 1923. In 1920, the first four-wheeler was built, the Cyklon Schebera, which had a 1,225 cc four-cylinder engine that was located in the front. The 1926 Cyklon 9/40 was fitted with a 2,340 cc six-cylinder side valve engine. Unfortunately, the factory did not survive the recession. It had to close its doors in 1931.

Daimler, Germany

This Daimler 'motor coach' was powered by a single-cylinder engine with 462 cc. It delivered 1.1 bhp at 700 rpm, giving a top speed of 10 mph (16 kph).

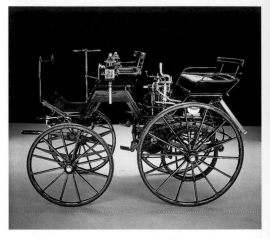

In 1883, Gottlieb Daimler introduced his first petrol engine. Two years later, this engine, with its relatively high speed (900 rpm) was built into a bicycle. Daimler's friend and colleague Wilhelm Maybach drove this vehicle from Cannstatt to Untertürkheim.

Initially, the engine delivered only 0.5 bhp, but once it had been boosted to 1 bhp Maybach built it into a small coach. At approximately the same time, Karl Benz made his first test drive with his motorised three-wheeler. In 1889, Daimler introduced his 'Stahlradwagen' ('steel-wheeled car') at the motor show in Paris. This vehicle is considered to be the first Daimler 'car'. The first models still had the engine positioned above the rear axle, but by the time of the Phoenix, which dates from 1897, it had been moved to the front. Two years later, the first Daimler with a

Maybach's engine delivered 1 bhp.

The front and rear were not significantly different.

Gottlieb Daimler with his son Adolf in 1886.

Gottlieb Daimler mit seinem Daimler-Wagen 1886.

Daimler, England

By 1896, cars were already a fairly common sight in mainland Europe, and in France they were even being raced. In England, however, the situation was totally different. Cars were only permitted on the public roads under very stringent conditions. At least two people had to be in the car and someone had to walk ahead with a red flag to warn people and livestock of the approaching danger.

The maximum speed outside built-up areas was 3,7 mph (6 kph) (the man with the flag could not walk much faster than this anyway) and in the town 1,85 mph (3 kph). Despite these restrictions, Daimler signed a contract with Frederick R. Simms in 1896 for the supply of engines. When these arrived in England, he sold them, together with his company to trader Harry J. Lawson for £35,000. This led in 1896 to the establishment of the

four-cylinder engine was introduced. Emile Jellinek, a rich businessman from Nice, bought one of these cars, but found the power too limited. He contacted Daimler, they became friends and he later became a director of the company and importer for France, Austria and the USA.

The cars ordered by Jellinek were named after his daughter, Mercédès. From 1902, all passenger cars were sold under the name Mercedes. Lorries and busses kept the Daimler name.

This Daimler, with its silver bodywork, became known as 'The Star of India'. The car was built in 1924 for the Maharaja of Rewa. He used the car primarily for hunting. The seats on the rear mudguards were for the beaters.

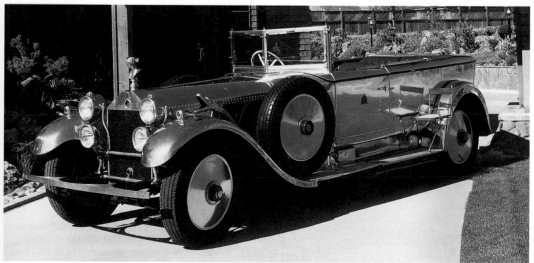

'Daimler Motor Company Ltd.' in Coventry. The first car was introduced one year later. The engine came from Germany, but the chassis was a copy of a French Panhard & Levassor. This Daimler was the first car to be built in England. Shortly afterwards, the Prince of Wales bought his first Daimler. This was the beginning of a long relationship between the Royal Family and the Daimler make. The factory in England also developed its own engines. By 1903, the customer could choose from twelve different power sources. The two or four-cylinder engines had capacities from 1.1 to 4.5 litres. As with virtually all makes of car at this time, Daimler also invested in racing. In 1900, thirteen Daimlers took part in a 1000 mile race. And all of them completed the race without any problems occurring.

In addition to cars, Daimler also produced buses and ships' engines. From 1910, only very expensive cars with four and six-cylinder engines and capacities of between 2614 and 9421 cc were produced. The same year, Daimler merged with BSA. From this point, the company was known as 'Daimler Company Ltd.' During the First World War, a lot of money was made building cars, tractors, heavy cannon and armoured vehicles for the army. In 1916, these 'tanks' played an important part in the battle of the Somme.

During the 'Roaring Twenties', money was no object. Daimler built cars with V12 engines according to a design by Laurence H. Pomeroy. Once again, the first order for these 'Double Six' Daimlers came from the Royal Family. Initially, the engines had a capacity of 7136 cc. In 1928, a noise-less sleeve valve engine with 3744 cc was on offer. In 1931, the car make Lanchester was

In 1927, the engine of the Double Six had a capacity of 7136 cc. This delivered 150 bhp at 2500 rpm.

The bodywork on this Double Six was made by bodywork builder Hooper for King George V and Queen Mary.

This Daimler ES-24 from 1938 was powered by a 3317 cc six-cylinder engine. This model was produced between 1936 and 1940.

incorporated into the BSA-Daimler concern. The Lanchester bridged the gap between the expensive Daimler and the cheap BSA. In 1934, Daimler built its first eight-cylinder sleeve valve engine.

One year later, the 'Straight Eight', an eight-in-line engine, was introduced. Immediately after the start of the Second World War, Daimler switched to the production of military vehicles. For this reason, the factory was bombed as early as August 1940 by German aircraft. And this was not the last such attack. Between November 1940 and April 1941 a total of 170 bombs fell on the factory. Despite the fact that 70% of the factory complex was destroyed, production was never ceased.

This Dalgleish-Gullane dates from 1908.

Dalgleish-Gullane

Never heard of it? Little wonder, as the company 'Haddington Motor Engineering' built only a handful of two-seaters under this name in 1907 and 1908. The French De Dion engine powered the rear wheels through a cardan shaft. Something special in those days.

In 1927, Darmont gave this three-wheeler the lovely name 'Etoile de France'.

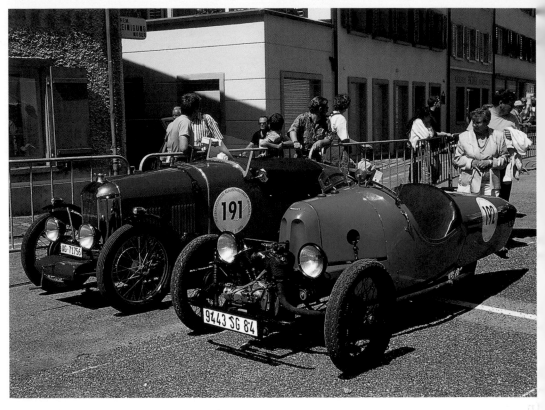

Darmont

Roger Darmont started a small factory in Courbevoie, France. He built the first English Morgan here under licence. The first three-wheelers were sold in 1924. The air-cooled V-2 engine was placed in front of the front axle. A water-cooled twin was also available, and even a compressor engine, intended for racing. In 1936, Darmont introduced his first four-wheeler, but this sports car was not really suited to everyday

The four-seater from 1936 was powered by the same twin as the three-wheeler.

No windows, no roof, not even a boot... what else could you do with this car but race it?

use. The linen hood and side windows were missing from this model.

Datsun

It now seems incredible, but before the war, there were very few cars in Japan. In 1908, only twenty were driving around in Tokyo, and three in Yokohama. In 1911, Masujiro Hashimoto completed his engineer's training in America. Once back in Japan, he founded the 'Kwaishinsha Motor Car Works'. In six months, he built a first car for his friends Kenjiro **D**en, Rokuro **A**oyama and Meitaru **T**akeuchi. The first model was called the DAT from the initial letters of the surnames of the first owners. In 1914, a second version was produced and in 1915 a small series of the DAT 31 was on sale. The DAT 41 from 1916 was powered by a 20 bhp engine, giving a top speed of 25 mph (40 kph). The market for cars was very limited, however, as only the rich could afford them. In 1925, the company changed its name to 'DAT Motor Car Co.' and several months later to 'DAT Automobile Manufacturing Co.' The company also moved

from Tokyo to Osaka. In 1931, DAT became a part of the 'Tobato Imono' concern. The first model produced was even smaller than its predecessors and was christened Datson (son of DAT). In Japanese, however, the word 'son' means something like 'ruin'. So it was decided to change the spelling to Datsun.

In 1934, Tabato Imono merged with the 'Nihon Sangyo Company'. The new company was named 'Jdosha Seizo Corporation'. The cars were produced under the name 'Nissan Motor Company Ltd.' Initially, these small cars were still called Datsun. They looked a lot like the Austin Seven and were available as a sedan, coupé or convertible. In 1936, a larger model was introduced under the name Nissan.

The Nissan 70 was a luxury car with an 85 bhp, six-cylinder engine. It looked a lot like the American Graham-Paige. However, the car was incredibly expensive, meaning that only the government and the army could afford to purchase a few. In 1938, Nissan stopped producing cars. From then on, the company only built lorries for the Japanese army.

The Datsun had a four-cylinder engine with a capacity of 747 cc. This model was introduced in 1932.

De Bazelaire

The De Bazelaire car plant was established in the Rue Gager-Gabillot in Paris. The make existed from 1907 to 1928. Most of the cars were intended for racing. At this time, all Grand Prix cars had a second seat for a mechanic who would ride along.

So all that was needed to make these into passenger cars was to bolt on mudguards. De Bazelaire made its debut in July 1908 during the Coupe de l'Auto race. The cars on the starting grid for this race were powered by an engine consisting of two cylinder blocks.

The engine had a capacity of 1460 cc and delivered 22 bhp at 1800 rpm. This gave the cars a top speed of 59 mph (95 kph). As brakes were only fitted on the rear wheels, De Bazelaires were not easy to steer. From 1910, models

with a six-cylinder engine were also built. The intake valves were in the cylinder head and the outlet valves in the cast-iron engine block. After the First World War, the factory took to using the 2.1 litre S.C.A.P. engine, but this brought them little fame.

This De Bazelaire took place in the 1983 Lausanne Grand Prix.

A De Bazelaire 10CV from 1910. In fact, this was not much more than a chassis with an engine and two seats. The two spare wheels were certainly no unnecessary luxury in those days.

This Décauville from 1900 is in the automobile museum in castle Aalholm in Nysted, Denmark.

well. During the first year (1898) 107 were supplied. By 1904, this number had risen to 350. From 1905, the company began specialising in larger models with a four-cylinder engine. The customer could choose from engines ranging from 2.7 to 9.2 litres. Unfortunately, demand for cars fell dramatically, and the company was forced to close it gates in 1910.

De Dion-Bouton

Décauville

The Décauville make was already famous for locomotives when the company set out on its automobile adventure in 1898. Instead of starting from scratch, a design by Messrs Joseph Guédon and Gustave Cornilleau was purchased for 250,000 French francs. Cornilleau was also taken on as chief engineer. The car had a peculiar structure, featuring not only independent suspension, but also two engines. The single-cylinder engines by De Dion-Bouton were placed one behind the other in the chassis. The car sold

In 1883, Count Albert de Dion, Georges Bouton and his brother-in-law Trépardoux built a vehicle powered by a steam engine. The three-wheeler had a top speed of almost 37 mph (60 kph). Although the partners built steam cars until 1904, experiments were carried out with petrol engines as early as 1893. In 1894, Trépardoux developed the famed De Dion rear axle. But when a decision was made to

A De Dion-Bouton of the Q Popular type from 1903. The single-cylinder had a capacity of 700 cc, which delivered six bhp.

IAround the turn of the century, the 'Vis-à-Vis' was a much-used concept. This picture shows a De Dion-Bouton from 1899.

This picture shows that De Dion-Bouton also made big cars. This model, from 1905, has a four-cylinder engine with 5320 cc, capable of delivering 40 bhp at 1400 rpm.

The make always had a racing car in its range, for example this one from 1914. The drum behind the driver is the petrol tank.

Despite its weight of 1820 kg (4004 lb), in 1905 this car produced a top speed of 37 mph (60 kph).
The foot-brake worked on the cardan shaft and the handbrake on the rear wheels.

If you hunt, you are somebody, and if you are somebody, you drive a De Dion-Bouton...

switch to petrol engines for good, he left the company. Messrs De Dion and Bouton went on to build petrol engines in all shapes and sizes. Massive twelve-cylinder engines, for example, but also small single-cylinders with a respectable 2,000 rpm. These smaller engines in particular brought the company international fame. From 1896, these were used by more than 140 different car factories. In 1899, the first four-wheeler was built. From 1902, the vehicles started to increasingly resemble real cars. The engines were now placed in the front and the steering handle made way for a real, round steering

wheel. De Dion-Bouton built racing cars and both small and large passenger cars. By the standards of the time in question, quite a number of the latter in particular were sold. In 1900, more than 1,200 cars had been supplied, and the following year the number reached 1,800.

At this time, the company already employed some 2,000 people. The friends also performed pioneering work in the area of V8 engines. They succeeded in incorporating the first V8 engine in a car. In 1914, the customer could choose from cars with various cylinder capacities. The biggest engine had a capacity of 14.8 litres. In 1923, the last of the cars with a V8 engine left the factory. These made way for models with marvellous four-cylinder overhead-valve engines. In 1930, the last passenger car left the Puteaux works. Lorries were produced until 1950, when the company finally shut down for good.

Delage

The cars made by Louis Delage (1874-1947) are certainly some of the most beautiful built in France before the war. Delage began his career as an engineer at Peugeot, where he became head of development. In 1905, he decided to go it alone. Together with engineer Augustin Legros, he started a small workshop in Levallois-Perret in Paris.

One of the first Delage passenger cars was the AE type.
The car was powered by a four-cylinder
De Dion-Bouton engine.

The DI, here in the form of a seven-seater from 1924, was
produced between 1923 and 1928. The four-cylinder
engine had a capacity of 2120 cc.

Initially, the company made parts for various car factories, but the company's first own car was not slow to appear. The 'Voiturette' took second place in a race in 1906. This produced so much publicity that orders flooded in. The factory moved to a larger plant, where the number of staff quickly grew to 80. They built racing cars, as well as small and large passenger cars. When in 1913 two Delages finished first and second in the French Grand Prix, sales soared even higher. By this time, the factory was selling 150 rolling chassis a month. The company continued to expand until, in 1918, it employed almost 3,000 people. The cars that won the Grand Prix in 1913 were very special from a technical point of view. They had brakes on all four wheels and

an engine with a double overhead camshaft that not only opened the valves, but also closed them.

After the war, Delage introduced a new model, the CO. This model was powered by a six-cylinder side-valve engine. The CO-2 had the same engine, but with overhead valves. Taking this excellently selling model as a basis, a

Grand Prix car was developed that reached a top speed of 125 mph (200 kph). In 1924, the factory introduced the GL (Grand Luxe). This wonderful car had a six-cylinder engine and 5954 cc, an overhead camshaft and delivered 100 bhp at 2400 rpm. The GL was a big, fast car.

It had a wheel base of 385 cm and a top speed of 94 mph (150 kph), a speed unheard of at the time. For the racing version of the GL, the engine was boosted to 185 bhp, giving a top speed of 143 mph (230 kph). In 1924, the DIS was introduced, a relatively cheap car with a four-cylinder overhead-valve engine.

In 1925, the DISS sports model followed. The DM, from 1927, was powered by a six-cylinder engine. The sports version was known as the DMS. Many technical innovations that were later

The crème-de-la-crème: a D8SS Super Sport. This one is from 1934. The bodywork is by Fernandez and Darrin.

fitted in passenger cars were born in Delage's racing department. For example, under the auspices of the engineer Planchon, a V-12 engine with two compressors was developed. This engine delivered no less than 190 bhp! Racing drivers such as Robert Benoist and Albert Divo were able with such cars to win many prestigious races:

Delage racing car from 1914.

1913	French Grand Prix	1st, 2nd and 5th
1914	Indianapolis 500 miles	1st
1924	European Grand Prix	2nd, 3rd and 6th
1925	French Grand Prix	1st and 2nd
	Spanish Grand Prix	1st, 2nd and 3rd
1926	European Grand Prix	2nd
	Spanish Grand Prix	3rd
	English Grand Prix	1st and 3rd
1927	French Grand Prix	1st and 3rd
	Spanish Grand Prix	1st and 3rd
	English Grand Prix	1st, 2nd and 3rd

One of the most beautiful cars ever built by Delage was introduced at the Paris motor show in 1929. The D8 had a 4.1 litre, eight-in-line engine. The bodywork builders went on to realise the most marvellous creations.

A popular pastime during this period was the Concours d'Elegance, in which ladies allowed themselves and their cars to be admired. The D8 made a great impression during this parade in particular. However, it was not only

The D8 was powered by a 4.0 litre eight-in-line engine that delivered 102 hp. This model was one of the best in France at the time.

Bodywork builder Henry Chapron built this colossal body on the chassis of a DR 70 from 1930. The engine was a six-cylinder with 2517 cc.

the car's exterior that came in for praise. In 1931, a D8S broke several records at the Montlhéry circuit. For example, 1,000 kilometres was completed at an average speed of 110 mph (176 kph). The D8S had the same 4,064 cc eight-cylinder engine as the D8, but was boosted from 100 to 125 bhp. In the D8SS, introduced in 1931, the engine

even delivered 140 bhp, whereby the car attained the fabled speed of 100 mph (160 kph). The cars in this series were the top of the factory range. After this peak of achievement, unfortunately, things started to go downhill. Investments in racing had to be restricted for financial reasons. What the make in

Letourneur and Marchand built the 'Aerosport Coupé' on the chassis of a D8-120.

The Delage D6/75 was introduced in 1939, but was in reality a Delahaye. This last pre-war model contained a six-cylinder overhead-valve engine with 2797 cc.

fact lacked was a simple model that would sell well. In addition, Louis Delage maintained a lifestyle that consumed enormous amounts of cash. He lived in a castle and liked to entertain hundreds of guests. In 1933, Delage tried to alter the policy, but it was already too late. He built a number of cheaper models with four and six-cylinder engines, but in 1935 he was forced to sell the company to his hated rival Delahaye.

Louis Delage received a small pension, under the condition that he never show his face in his factory again. He had already had to sell his castle, and this automotive pioneer died, impoverished and forgotten in 1947. In the meantime, his factory continued to function but now Delahayes were being built under the Delage name. The era of the 'real' Delage had come to an end.

Delahaye

Emile Delahaye built machines for the brick production industry and had long dreamed of producing his own car. It was only in 1896 that he finally took steps towards making this dream a reality. In that year, he built two automobiles that took part in the race from Paris to Marseilles and back. As driving was only possible during the daylight hours, the race took ten days. The Delahayes did not win a single stage, but did reach the finish which was quite an achievement in itself. The cars had two-cylinder engines constructed by Delahaye himself. The wooden wheels were fitted with pneumatic tires. Delahaye continued to build racing cars, although the production of passenger cars became increasingly important. The engines grew in cylinder capacity and acquired extra bhp. In 1904, the customer could choose from various different engines, namely two two-cylinder engines delivering 8 and 12 bhp and four-cylinder engines that delivered 16 bhp. The four-cylinder consisted of two two-cylinder blocks. By now, the factory's own racing team had been disbanded. A decision was taken to concentrate fully on perfecting passenger cars, and with some considerable success. The cars had a reputation for reliability, a more important factor in those days than a low price. After the

First World War, Delahaye introduced some enormous cars onto the market. One model, for instance, had a 4.3 litre, six-cylinder engine and a 368 cm wheel base. In comparison a VW Golf from 1997 has a wheel base of 248 cm. But the small Delahaye make found it increasingly difficult to compete against Citroën, Renault and Peugeot. In 1927, therefore, the company concluded a cooperation agreement with Chenard & Walcker, Donnet and Unic. Over the course of time, however, the same parts were increasingly used, meaning that the peculiar characteristics of each make were gradually eroded. In 1930, the Delahaye range consisted of models with small 1.5 litre four-cylinder engines by Chenard &

A Delahaye from 1911. At this time, Emile Delahaye had already been dead for five years.
This model was developed under the supervision of his successor, Charles Weiffenbach.

This Delahaye 32A from 1912 contained a four-cylinder engine with a capacity of 2.0 litres. •
The bore/stroke ratio was 75 x 110 mm.

The 32A, seen from the front. "If the run-up is long enough, it can do 41 mph (65 kph)", the owner claimed.

In 1937, Figoni & Falashi built the bodywork for this 135MS.

Walcker, 1.8 litre overhead-valve engines and four-cylinder overhead-valve engines with a capacity of 2.7 litres. The top-of-the-range model was a car with a 2.5 or 2.9 litre overhead-valve engine. In 1932, the partnership was split up. In 1933, Delahaye introduced a number of new models at the Paris motor show. These cars were called 'Super Luxe'. They were powered by two new engines. A four-cylinder with 2,150 cc delivering 55 bhp at 3800 rpm and a six-cylinder overhead-valve engine with 3,227 cc delivering 90 bhp. The cars had the same chassis with a wheel base of 286, 295 or 315 cm. In 1935, Delahaye took over the Delage make. The sporty Delages were subsequently

The dashboard of the 135MS. Note the gear-change handle of the Cotal gearbox, to the left of the steering wheel.

With its three carburettors and 3557 cc cylinder capacity, the engine of the 135MS could deliver 130 bhp.

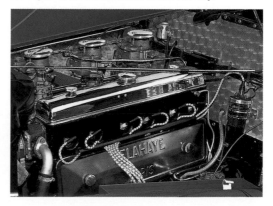

The chassis of the Delahaye 135MS formed the basis for the most bizarre bodywork, such as this from 1939.

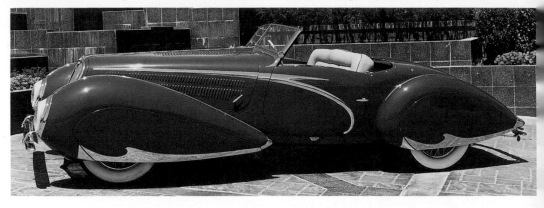

sold as Delahayes, including the 18 CV, built on a chassis shortened to 286 cm and powered by an engine with three carburettors. These models formed the basis of the most well-known pre-war and post-war Delahayes, the 135 series. These models incorporated a six-cylinder overhead-valve engine, which in the 135M delivered 110 bhp and in the sporty 135MS 130 bhp. The cars had a wheel base of 295 cm and reached top speeds of 94 to 109 mph (150 to 175 kph). These models were to remain in production until 1952. Considerably fewer type 145 and 165 models were built. The former was intended specifically for racing, the second for the public road. They were powered by a V12 engine with 4490 cc, which in the racing car delivered no less than 235

bhp. This car could reach a top speed of 156 mph (250 kph). The touring car had to make do with 'only' 160 bhp, giving it a top speed of 118 mph (190 kph).

Delamare-Deboutteville

Several replicas were quickly built and were ready just in time to celebrate the 100th anniversary of the car in 1984.

This 135M was fitted with new bodywork by bodywork builder VandenPlas.

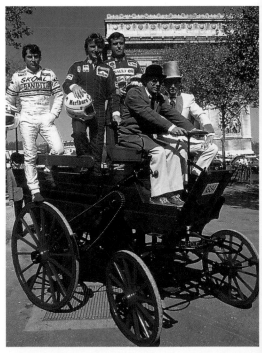

Car shows were organised all over France, even in the Grand Palais.

100 ANS D'AUTOMOBILE FRANÇAISE

GRAND PALAIS - JUIN - JUILLET - AOUT 1984

Although almost everyone in the world agrees that Messrs Daimler and Benz built the first cars in 1886, the French are of a different opinion. They celebrated the 100th anniversary of the car in 1984. The funny thing is, the French had only found out a few years previously that they had invented the car. A document from 1884 had come to light in which a Mr Edouard Delamare-Deboutteville described how he had built a car and driven around in it. And, to make the whole thing a bit more official, he had registered his invention on 12 February 1884 under patent number 160267. Furthermore, the French claimed that it was not Daimler and Benz who laid the foundation for the automotive industry, but Panhard & Levassor and Peugeot, who had offered cars for sale as early as 1890 and 1891.

The fact is that France was the first country to organise a car race, in 1895. France also organised the world's first car show, in 1898. Whatever the facts of the matter, several replicas were quickly built of the first car and introduced at all kinds of events.

A few years before the celebrations for the turn of the century, the French discovered the drawings of the first car.

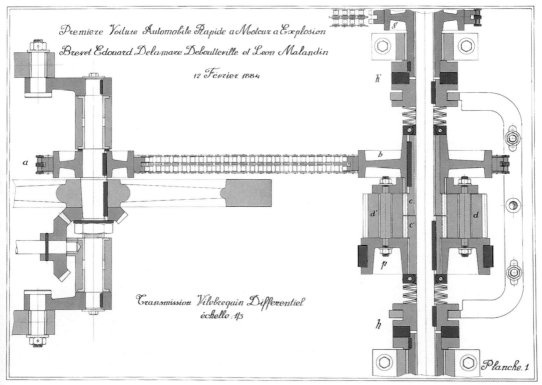

De Soto

When, on 30 November 1960, De Soto had produced precisely 2,024,629 cars, the production line suddenly fell silent. There was no longer a demand for cars in that price bracket. If Walter P. Chrysler had still been alive it would perhaps not have come to this. He had founded the make on 4 August 1928. The De Soto was named after the Spanish explorer Hernando De Soto, who had, among other things, been governor of Cuba in the 16th century. With this new make, Chrysler wanted to enter into competition with the arch rivals Oldsmobile, Nash and Pontiac. Initially, this was quite a success. But because the De Sotos were often fitted with the same bodywork as Plymouths and Dodges, the make lost its individual character. The first De Sotos were introduced in the summer of 1928. It seemed like this was the car the world had been waiting for. During the first twelve months, no less than 81,065 were sold. The very first De Soto already had a six-cylinder engine and in 1930 the CF type was on sale with an eight-cylinder engine. This car

At the same time Chrysler introduced the Airflow, a De Soto of the same type appeared. This 'imitation' actually outsold the original.

In 1932, it was possible to order the De Soto with an eight-in-line engine. But in that year, only 3,730 cars of this type were sold.

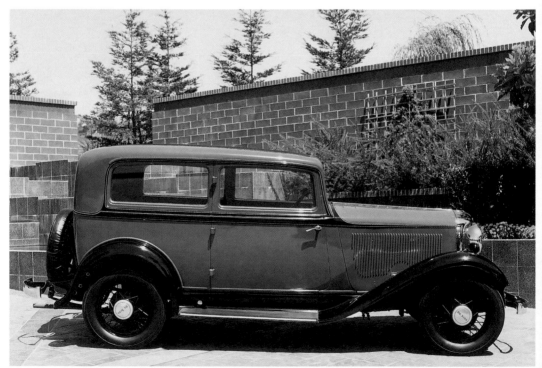

The De Soto convertible from 1929 still had wooden spoked wheels, although it had brakes on all four wheels.

In 1941, the last pre-war year of production, De Soto produced 99,999 cars. One of these was this Sportsman Club Coupe.

shared its chassis and engine with a Dodge from the same year. The CF was succeeded in 1932 by the De Soto SC, which had a new six-cylinder engine. When Chrysler introduced the Airflow models in 1934, there was also a De Soto of the same model. This streamlined car was not a great success, but nevertheless more De Soto Airflows were sold that year than Chryslers (15,000 as opposed to 11,000).

The De Soto make was established to fill the gap between the expensive Chrysler and the cheap Plymouth. But when Walter Chrysler took over the Dodge make, this became a competitor of the De Soto. For a long time, the De

This car, from 1938, had an extra long wheel base of 302 cm. The car could accommodate seven adult passengers and their luggage.

Sotos were cheaper than Dodges, but this principle was abandoned in 1934. The last pre-war cars rolled off the production line on 9 February 1942.

This coupé from 1938 could carry three passengers. At $870, it was the cheapest De Soto.

Detroit Electric

Around the turn of the century, constructor's opinions were divided. Some continued to believe in the steam engine, while others saw more potential in the more modern petrol or electric engine. In 1899, engineer Camille Jenatzi broke the speed record with his

At this time, the Detroit Electric was so well-known that it was even put on a postage stamp.

Grandma Duck's car?

vehicle, powered by an electric engine. This 'Jamais Contente' reached a top speed of 62 mph (100 kph). One of the constructors' camps shouted in relief, "We told you so!" The technicians of the 'Detroit Electric' company were certainly members of this camp. This company introduced the first electric cars in 1907. A total of 14,000 were sold. The principle was defended until 1929. Customers liked their non-smelling, completely silent cars. They were also easy to operate. They had two handles, one of which was for steering, the other to increase or decrease the speed. But although production of the Detroit Electric continued for a long time, the car had no future. The operating range of 100 kilometres was far too limited. And the car weighed some 2,300 kilos because of the massive built-in batteries.

No, a Detroit Electric from 1929.

The dashboard of the Detroit.

Electrical cars have not been forgotten, however. In fact, today they are more relevant than ever before. But as long as battery technology remains where it is, the experiments have little chance of success.

D.F.P. in 1908, when the Parant brothers joined. The factory supplied cheap cars with one or four-cylinder engines. From 1912, W.O. Bentley and his brother represented the make in England. Bentley used the D.F.P. in races, which proved to be an effective means of advertising. A lot of cars were exported to England.

After the First World War, Bentley became increasingly involved with his own cars. D.F.P. slowly but surely disappeared from the English market. In France, however, sales continued, but profits fell. In 1926, the directors decided to close the factory in Courbevoie.

D.F.P.

The D.F.P. make is named after the founders of the company: Auguste Doriot, Ludovic Flandrin and Alexandre and Jules-René Parant. Doriot and Flandrin had worked for Peugeot for a long time before they decided to set up their own company in 1906. Their first products were sold under the name Doriot-Flandrin. The company's name was changed to

One of the first D.F.P. cars.

DKW

Jörgen Skafte Rasmussen (1878-1964) was born in Denmark. At the age of eighteen he left for Germany, where he studied at various universities. He completed his study of engineering in Zwickau. Rasmussen remained in Germany and started a machine engineering plant where he built motorcycles. DKW motorcycles were cheap and good. During the '20s and '30s, the Dame became the largest producer of motorcycles in the world

In 1926, DKW built its first car, called 'der Kleine Bergsteiger' ('the little mountaineer'). It was a strange design. The two passengers sat one behind the other. The car had an open, self-supporting body. The engine drove the

111

A type 15 roadster from 1928. Contrary to the later, more well-known DKWs, this model still had rear-wheel drive.

DKW also built sporty cars. This roadster has the chassis of a DKW Front from 1932.

With a top speed of 47 mph (75 kph), the DKW Front Sport from 1931 was not really a racing car, but very nice to look at..

The bodywork of this F1 roadster was made from plywood, covered in a kind of synthetic leather.

A DKW FA 600 F1 from 1931. The bodywork was one of the best-selling 'faux cabriolets'.

left-hand rear wheel with a chain. Two years later, DKW tried again with a 'real' car, in which the passengers could sit next to one another. In this P type, the engine was at the front, under the bonnet. The drive was provided by a stuttering two-cylinder two-stroke engine with 584 cc and delivering 15 bhp. The engine used in the sports car version of the PS type delivered 18 bhp. The PS was one of the very few sports cars Rasmussen built. Despite the fact that his cars were highly suitable for sporting purposes, he continued to build passenger cars.

DKW cars were built in various different factories. The large DKWs were built between 1930 and 1940 in the factory in Spandau. As with the first models, these cars had rear-wheel

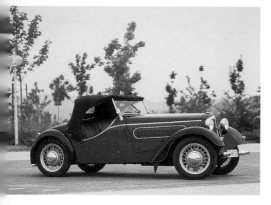

This two-seater was sold in 1936 and 1937 as the DKW F-5-K 700, Front Luxus Sport. The 692 cc twin delivered 20 bhp and the top speed was 56 mph (90 kph).

IIn this 'Schwebeklasse', the rear wheels are powered by a V4 two-stroke engine. In 1934 and 1935, the cylinder capacity was 990 cc and in 1936 and 1937 1054 cc.

The bodywork of the convertibles was produced by Baur or Horch, including that of this DKW F8 from 1939.

This advertising poster for DKW is clearly from the late '20s or '30s.

DAS NEUE DKW-AUTO

drive. This time, however, the engine was a four-cylinder two-stroke. The make acquired fame however with the small DKW with front-wheel drive and a two-cylinder engine and after the war with a three-cylinder, two-stroke engine. These small cars were produced in the Audi factory.

The wooden bodywork came from Berlin, the engines from Zschopau. The cars were available in three price categories, as the DKW Front, Reichs-klasse and Meisterklasse. Although the bodywork was different, the models all had the same chassis and 584 cc two-cylinder two-stroke engine. With their oil-petrol mixture of 1 to 25, these cars could be recognised at a great distance by the stinking blue cloud emerging from the exhaust pipe. In 1933, the cylinder capacity was increased to 692 cc. Delivering 20 bhp, the DKW now had a top speed of 53 mph (85 kph). During the '30s, the world economic crisis almost meant the end of Rasmus-

sen. For this reason, on 1 November 1931 he set up the 'Auto Union', together with Horch, Audi and Wanderer. Just two years later, however, he was sacked from his company by the bank. He still owned a small factory manufacturing refrigerators and a company that produced cars of the Framo brand in limited quantities.

After 1945, however, these factories were in the Russian sector of Germany. They were expropriated and Rasmussen returned to Denmark, where he died in 1964.
Relatively large numbers of DKWs from before the war have survived in Germany, as the Wehrmacht never requisitioned them.

Although in 1926 cars with steel disk wheels were sold, the buyers of more expensive models and convertibles preferred the wooden spoked wheels.

their own and in 1914 the first finished product left the small factory in Hamtramck. In a number of respects, this first car was way ahead of its time.

For example, it had completely steel bodywork, while other makes were still using wood in the doors and side panels. It also had a 12-volt system, while most other makes still had 6-volt batteries.

The power came from a four-cylinder side-valve engine. The model hardly changed until 1926, except for a gradual lengthening of the wheel base from 270 to a final 295 cm. During the first full

Dodge

John and Horace Dodge owned a machine engineering plant making motorcycles and gearboxes for Ford and Oldsmobile. In 1913, they started building a car of

This Dodge was assembled by Saurer (renowned for its lorries and busses) in Switzerland in 1937.

The cars from model year 1927 really had all the trimmings. Alongside a mileometer, there was also an amperemeter in the dashboard. The cars also had an electric horn, a tool bag and a rear-view mirror. And all for just $795.

Windscreens were only fitted at an angle from 1932. In 1929, they still stood vertically, as in this Victory Six from that year.

year of production, 1915, a total in excess of 45,000 Dodges were sold. The car was and remains a great success. In 1920, sales rocketed to 141,000 vehicles. In that year, Dodge was the second-largest car producer in the United States. Only Ford sold

more cars. Unfortunately, the Dodge brothers did not survive to experience this pleasant state of affairs, both dying in quick succession in 1920 of flu. Their heirs sold their shares in 1925 to a bank in New York, for the astronomical amount at the time of 146 million dollars. Three years later, on 31 July 1928, Walter P. Chrysler took over the factories from the bank for

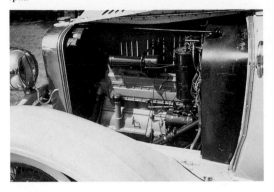

In 1929, the six-cylinder engine delivered 63 bhp at 3000 rpm.

Another Swiss product: a Dodge from 1939 with bodywork by Hermann Graber.

In 1936, the D2 was Dodge's flagship. This four-door, five-seater convertible cost almost $1000, while a Business Coupe could be yours for as little as $640.

The production year 1942 ended in February. One of the reasons why only 1,185 Custom Convertible Coupes were sold.

a cool $170 million. At that time, Dodge was one of the largest car manufacturers in the world, selling more than 146,000 cars in 1927 alone. Under the leadership of Chrysler, sales of Dodges rose even further.

In 1928, almost all models were powered by a six-cylinder engine and all four wheels had hydraulic brakes. The more expensive models even featured a radio.

In 1930, the cars were sold for the first time under the name 'Dodge' rather than 'Dodge Brothers'. The years of crisis also had a terrible effect on Dodge. In 1929, 124,557 cars were still sold, but by 1932 this had dropped to 30,216. In 1933, however, a recovery was already under way and sales rose to exceed 108,000.

Between 1930 and 1934, the customer could choose between a six-cylinder or an eight-cylinder engine. Between 1936 and 1953, all cars had a six-cylinder engine.

Donnet-Zédel

In 1901, Zürcher and Lüthi of Switzerland started a factory making motorcycle engines. These were sold under the name Zédel. In 1906, the

Donnet also built several racing cars, such as this one from 1926.

pair built their first car under the same name. The factory did not produce many cars. When the First World War broke out in 1914, a total of between 300 and 400 cars had been sold. In 1918, the Zédel make was taken over by another Swiss, Donnet.

From then on, the cars were sold under the name Donnet-Zédel. In 1927, Donnet's factory relocated to Nanterre, and the make just became known as Donnet.

The last car rolled off the production line in 1933. In 1935, the company was sold to Simca.

Most of the cars built under the names Zédel, Donnet-Zédel and Donnet were powered by four-cylinder engines. The Zédel had a capacity of 3168 cc, the Donnet-Zédel 1100 or 2120 cc. One of

In 1924, Donnet-Zédel sold two different models, the G and C types.

the most remarkable models was a Donnet with a 2540 cc six-cylinder side-valve engine.

Duesenberg

Friedrich Samuel (1876-1932) and August (1880-1955) Duesenberg were born in Germany but grew up in America. Despite the fact that the brothers had received no technical training, they were remarkably talented in this area. They built bicycles, motorcycles and in 1904 even a racing car. They received financial support from the lawyer Edward R. Mason, after whom the car was also named. The Mason was powered by a two-cylinder boxer engine. Unfortunately, the company was forced to close down soon afterwards. The Duesenbergs continued alone. The same year, they introduced a new racing car, this time with a four-cylinder engine with

The best bodywork builders in the world fought for the right to build a Duesenberg. This Roadster was provided with a superstructure by Walter M. Murphy in 1929.

The Duesenberg was a big car. This Type J had a wheel base of 390 cm. The eight-in-line engine had 6882 cc and delivered 210 bhp.

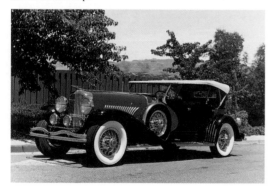

This Duesenberg SJ also came from Murphy's bodywork factory.

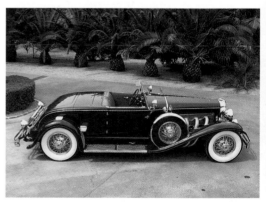

two overhead camshafts and four valves per cylinder. The car was extremely fast and laid the foundation for the good name quickly acquired by the 'Duesenberg Motor Corporation'. During the First World War, the company produced 400 Bugatti aircraft engines under licence for the US Air Force and in 1920 the first passenger car emerged from the Indianapolis factory. This was a two-seater Model A roadster with a 4.2 line eight-in-line engine. It was built until 1926. In 1927, Errett Loban Cord bought the Duesenberg factory. The brothers were now able to concentrate fully on building cars, and the results were amaing. The most marvellous designs

Clark Gable was a loyal Duesenberg customer. At one time, he even had four cars.
This is his Duesenberg JN from 1935.

This picture shows Clark Gable's car from a different angle.
The bodywork was produced by Rollstone.

A Duesenberg from 1934 with Sedanca-de-Ville bodywork. The driver had to sit outside.

The SJ's interior was fairly simple, with the exception of the complete dashboard.

The JN's engine delivered 210 bhp.

A Duesenberg Phaeton from 1935.

were produced. In 1927, forexample, the Duesenberg J was introduced. This model was powered by an eight-cylinder 6.8 litre engine with two camshafts and four valves per cylinder. The engine delivered no less than 265 bhp. And what about the SJ from 1932. This car had the same eight-in-line engine, but now also a compressor, meaning a top speed of 125 mph (200 kph) could be reached. The collapse of Errett Cord's empire in 1937 also meant

The SJ in this picture spent more than 50 years in a garage.

Charles Rolls took a number of test drives in this Dufaux in the vicinity of Geneva. The car can now be admired at the Schlumpf Museum in Mulhouse.

curtains for the Duesenberg Corporation. In total, 480 cars were sold under this brand name. They were tailor-made for film stars such as Gary Cooper, Mae West and Clark Gable.

At the time, Duesenberg was the most expensive, but certainly most special, make of car in America.

Dufaux

The brothers Charles and Frédéric Dufaux became interested in racing at an early age and as young men in their twenties were looking for a car in which to win the famous Gordon Bennett race. This was no easy task in those days, however, and this led to them to build their own racing car. The model consisted of little more than a chassis, an engine and two bucket seats.

The eight-in-line engine had no less than 12,760 cc and delivered 80 bhp at 1300 rpm. The brothers won a race in Geneva over a distance of one kilometre at an average speed of 72 mph (115 kph).

The eight-cylinder engine delivered 80 bhp and had a cylinder capacity of 12,760 cc.

The Dufaux from Lucerne was built in 1904 and reached a top speed of 87 mph (140 kph).

120

Despite its amazing cubic capacity of 12,761 cc, the eight-cylinder delivered 'only' 80 bhp at 1300 rpm.

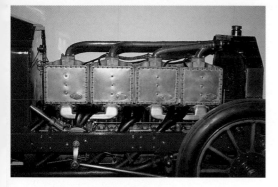

The Dufaux petrol tank was made of brass.

This Dufaux is owned by the 'Verkehrshaus der Schweiz', a small museum in Lucerne. The model was powered by a 12.7 litre engine.

At a second race in Paris, the duo took second place. The car had in fact been driven by road from Switzerland to Paris in less than ten hours. A subsequent model was given a four-cylinder engine, this time with 26,400 cc.

The massive engine delivered more than 150 bhp. In this car, Frédéric Dufaux broke a world record on 13 November 1905. At a speed of 98 mph (156 kph), he completed a kilometre in just 23 seconds.

In 1906, a number of cars with smaller four-cylinder engines were built. However, an eight-cylinder with 120 bhp was also included in the range. At a hill climb near Marchairuz in 1906 no less than three Dufaux took place in the starting line-up. These were two eight-cylinders with 12,760 cc and 14,449 cc and a four-cylinder with 4,400 cc. The brothers called a halt to their terribly expensive hobby in 1907.

DuPont

The DuPont make is not really known these days. Nevertheless, these were marvellous cars, of which some 537 were built. The first of these, the A model, was made in the factory in Wilmingdon in 1919. Constructor Paul

This Dual-Cowl Phaeton from 1931 had a chassis with a wheel base of 370 cm.

DuPont developed a four-cylinder side-valve engine with a capacity of slightly more than 4.0 litres specially for this car. He soon realised that it was much cheaper to use an existing engine, so this one experiment remained unique. DuPont's cars were of an especially high quality. They could easily compete with competitors such as Duesenberg, Packard or Lincoln. In 1921, the model B was introduced. This model still contained a four-cylinder engine, but in the model C from 1924 this was replaced by a six-cylinder engine by Herschell-Spillman. A total of 48 of these cars were sold. In 1927, the C was succeeded by the model D. The last DuPonts, model H, had an eight-cylinder engine made by Continental.

These cars were no longer made in the factory in Wilmingdon, but in the Indian motorcycle factory in Springfield. This company had been taken over by DuPont shortly before. Unfortunately, the DuPont make did not survive the crisis of the '30s. In February 1933, a bankruptcy petition was submitted.

Durant

William Durant (1861-1947), one of the founders of the General Motors concern, built cars under his own name from 1921 onwards. However, these models were not really anything special, although they sold quite well. As early as in 1923, the 100,000th car rolled off the production line. The first Durants were powered by a four-cylinder overhead-valve engine designed by the company itself, although the customer also had the option of a six-cylinder

In 1928, the Durants were given new four and six-cylinder engines. The four-cylinders were fitted in a chassis with a wheel base of 271 cm and the six-cylinders in chassis of 277, 284 or 302 cm.

Ansted engine. In 1928, all the models were fitted with new engines. By 1929, the range consisted of four basic models, namely the 4-40, containing a 36 bhp four-cylinder engine and the 6-60, 6-66 and 6-70 containing a six-cylinder engine delivering 43, 47 and 65 bhp respectively. In spite of the completeness of the range, however, sales were disappointing. The approaching crisis naturally played a considerable role in this. In 1929, 47,716 cars were sold. By 1930, this number had fallen to 21,440 and in 1931 only 7,229 cars found customers ready to buy. When, in 1932, only 1,135 cars could be produced, Durant was forced to sell his company.

The Durant 6-60 from 1929 had a wheel base of 277 cm. The six-cylinder engine delivered 43 bhp.

Egg

Before the Second World War, some fifty manufacturers were embarking upon an automobile adventure in Switzerland alone. Some of these companies existed only for a few days, but others survived for considerably longer. One of the latter was Rudolf Egg. Engineer Rudolf Egg (1866-1939) built a car for his own use in 1893.

In 1896, he concluded an agreement with the wealthy Mr Egli. From that moment, the company of Egg & Egli was in business. The first production car made by the company was a three-wheeler powered by a De Dion engine. This car was so good it was quickly being built under licence by various other Swiss companies. In 1899, the factory produced its first four-wheeler. This car still strongly resembled a coach, as the rear wheels were larger than the front ones. In 1904, Egg moved from Zürich to Wollishofen. From that moment on, the company was known as 'Motorwagenfabriek Excelsior'. The first models bore a strong resemblance, both in terms of bodywork and technology, to the Oldsmobile Curved Dash.

Egg went on to build several other models and was also involved in the development of the first Swiss aircraft engines. After the First World War, however, he wound up the company and became a Renault dealer in Zürich.

Essex

The first Essex was built in 1918 in the old Studebaker factory on Franklin Avenue in Detroit. The Essex make

The Egg company also built 'Vis-à-Vis'. This picture shows a small car of this type from 1898. The engine was above the rear axle and the petrol tank at the front.

This Egg was built in 1919, the last year of production by the company. The car was powered by a four-cylinder engine produced in-house.

This Essex Super Six from 1928 had a six-cylinder engine with 2637 cc, delivering 55 bhp. Bumpers, mileometer and water thermometer could be supplied at an extra charge.

was part of the 'Hudson Motor Car Company'. The first cars were powered by a four-cylinder engine. The model was not particularly attractive to behold, but was of good quality. In 1919 on the Cincinnati circuit, an Essex completed a distance of no less than 4,859 kilometres in fifty hours. In the '20s, closed cars were something of a rarity. When in 1922 Essex offered such a model for only an extra $300, production figures soared. Naturally, the Essex make benefited from technical developments at the Hudson parent company. For example, all cars supplied after 1928 had four hydraulic brakes. Alongside the trusty four-cylinder, the customer could also choose a six-cylinder engine. In that year, Essex sold 229,887 cars, while Hudson only sold 52,316. In 1929, the Hudson-Essex combination held third place in the list of American automobile producers. That year, a record number of 300,962 cars were sold. Of these, Essex accounted for no less than 227, 653. However, Chevrolet was now also in a position to offer a cheap six-cylinder, and although Essex

The same model for which the customer could choose steel or wooden spokes.

still advertised with the slogan 'King of the Sixes', the company lost more and more ground. The management tried to embellish the make's image by breaking records. For example, in 1932 an Essex drove from Los Angeles to New York City in sixty hours and twenty minutes, but unfortunately this made little impression. In 1933, the make disappeared from the market, to be replaced by the Terraplane.

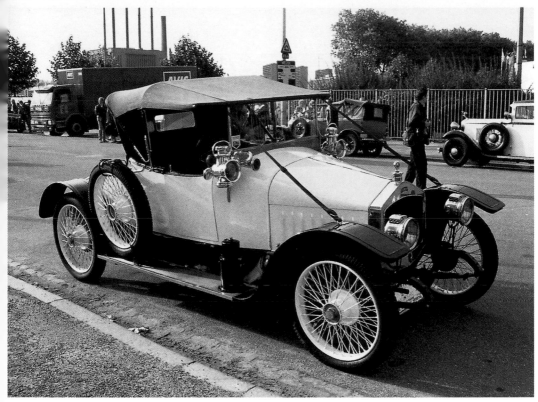

Excelsior

Engineer Arthus de Coninck founded the 'Compagnie Nationale Excelsior' in Brussels in 1903. The first cars were built in 1904 and had one, two or four-cylinder Aster engines. The models were not that special however. It was only in 1907 that the make really made the headlines with the Adex, powered by a six-cylinder side-valve engine with a capacity in excess of nine litres. This car's chassis could easily be modified for Grand Prix racing. In 1912, an Excelsior took second place in the French Grand Prix. And when the Belgian royal family ordered an Excelsior, the advertising value of this proved considerable. A second version of the Adex appeared in 1920, with a smaller 4767 cc, six-cylinder engine with an overhead camshaft. The Adex laid the foundation for one of the most beautiful cars ever made by Excelsior, the Albert I Excelsior. This model was powered by a six-cylinder engine with a capacity of 5346 cc. The twin-camshaft engine could also be supplied with three carburettors. In this case, the engine could deliver some 100 bhp.

The Albert I was the most beautiful, but also the last, Excelsior. In 1929, the make was sold to its competitor, Imperia. Until 1932, the company was called Imperia-Excelsior, but from that year the name Excelsior was dropped from the nameplate.

Favier

Talk about rarities… According to most car enthusiasts, the 'Atelier Favier' on the Avenue de la Gare in Tullins, France, never built a car, but there must have been at least one, a Favier type F. According to the documents, the car, with chassis number 14, was built in 1924. The Favier was powered by a small four-cylinder side-valve engine.

The nameplate is certainly original, the switches are from a car from the 1950s.

The proof of its existence: the Favier from 1924.

Fiat

In café Burello, not far from the station of Porta Nuova in Turin, a group of friends, among them Giovanni Agnelli, speculated on the production of cars. Ten years later, on 1 July 1889, the 'Società Anonima Fabbrica Italiana de Automobili Torino', or F.I.A.T. for short, was established. The first car was built the same year. It was a 'Vis-à-Vis' with four wheels and a small linen hood. The two-cylinder engine had 679 cc and delivered 3.5 bhp. In 1901, Fiat produced its first model with a four-cylinder engine. The engine was in the front of the car, under a real bonnet.

The capacity was 3770 cc and the 16 bhp generated were transmitted to the rear wheels by chains. Fiat has been building racing cars right from the start. The Fiat 6 HP Corsa was introduced in 1900. This model achieved a top speed of no less than 38 mph (60 kph). The Corsa won various races, many with

Fiat Brevetti Tipo from 1907. The Tipo had a wheel base of 307 cm and was powered by a four-cylinder engine with a capacity of 3052 cc and delivering 25 bhp.

The Fiat 500 was affectionately known as 'Topolino' in Italy. Despite its length of only 322 cm, the model offered space for the whole family.

IIn 1910, the customer could choose from six different models. The capacity of the engines varied from 1846 to 9017 cc. The picture shows a Fiat 12/15 HP with an 1846 cc engine.

The 501 was the first post-war model. Between 1919 and 1926, some 45,000 were sold.

the factory driver Vincenzo Lancia. The racing cars were two-seaters, with a small space for the mechanic. In addition to racing cars, passenger cars such as the small Voiturette and the massive S.76 from 1911 were made. The latter was powered by a four-cylinder engine with a capacity of 28,353 cc delivering some 300 bhp.

In 1927, Fiat built its first and last monoposto, the 806 Corsa. In 1927, a car of this model won the Milan Grand Prix. From a technical viewpoint, the design was very special. The twelve-in-line engine had a capacity of only 1484 cc. The engine, which consisted of two six-cylinder engine blocks,

In 1911, this Fiat S 74 Corsa won the American Grand Prix. A total of seven were built.
The engine, a four-cylinder with 14,137 cc, delivered 190 bhp at 1600 rpm.

The bodywork for the open-topped version of the 501 was designed by lawyer Carlo Cavalli.

with a Rootes compressor and three overhead camshafts, delivered 187 bhp at 8500 rpm. It was the last racing car Fiat ever built. After 1927, the company produced only passenger cars. One of these was the model 503, some 42,000

The last of the real racing cars, the 806. At a top speed of 156 mph (250 kph), Pierto Bordino won the last race for Fiat.

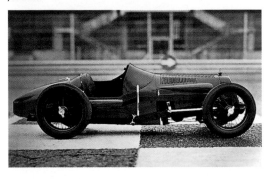

A scaled-down American? The Fiat 514 from 1929 was the first model to have hydraulic shock-absorbers.

The Fiat 508 Balilla was one of the best-selling Italian cars. The model was introduced in 1934.

of which were sold in 1926 and 1927. The Fiat 514 was also a big success. This model was powered by a 1438 cc four-cylinder side-valve engine that delivered 28 bhp.The customer could choose from different types of body-work. Between 1929 and 1932, 36,970 of these cars were sold. In 1932, the Fiat 508 Balilla was launched at the car show in Milan. This was to be the model anyone could have. It was a small, cheap car with a 995 cc engine.

The Balilla Sport, an open-topped two-seater with an engine boosted to 36 bhp, was added to the range for sports car enthusiasts. In 1936, Fiat introduced the

A sports version of the 508 Balilla was also available. The picture shows a 508 S 'Coppa d'Oro' built between 1932 and 1937.

The Ardita had a choice of several engines. In 1933 it was supplied with either 1758 or 1944 cc four-cylinder engines. A 2516 cc six-cylinder engine was also available between 1934 and 1936 (see photo).

first of its series of midget cars: the Fiat 500. This model became a milestone in automotive history. This small two-seater (which was nevertheless big enough for a whole Italian family with dog and baggage) had a 569 cc, water-cooled side-valve engine. It was popularly known as the 'Topolino' or 'little mouse'. The model was built virtually without modification until 1955.

A Balilla 508 S Coupe Aërodynamica. The picture was taken during the Mille Miglia in 1991.

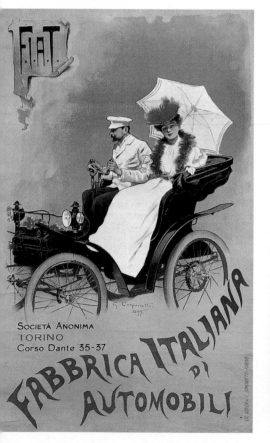

These advertising posters from the '30s are as popular now as the cars have always been.

F.N.

In total, Belgium has had some 140 makes of car produced within its borders. In most cases, the first model never even made it beyond the proto-type stage, but there were also factories, such as the 'Fabrique National d'Armes de Guerre', or F.N. for short, which lasted a great deal longer. In 1895, F.N. produced mainly bicycles, although the first 954 cc Voiturette was produced in 1897. Before the war, F.N. built 26 different models. Most of these were powered by a four-cylinder engine with a capacity of between 1300 and 2300 cc. From a technical viewpoint, the make remained a few steps ahead of its competitors. For instance, the first F.N.

Advertisement by F.N. from 1905.

At the end of the last century, F.N. was still an arms manufacturer. The nameplate on the radiator is a reminder of this.

Between 1928 and 1930, F.N. produced some 2,000 cars. The F.N. pictured here is from 1929.

Shortly before the First World War, the F.N. 1250 was introduced. A total of 444 of this model were sold. The 1250 was powered by a 1328 cc four-cylinder engine.

cheap American cars. Many European makes, including F.N., lost out in the fierce competition. The last F.N. passenger car was produced in the factory in Herstal close to Liège in 1935. From that point, the company specialised in the production of lorries and busses.

Ford Germany

On 1 April 1926, the first Model T Ford emerged from the German Ford factory in Berlin. In August 1928, this was replaced by the famed Model A Ford, built until 1934.

The Model A Ford was succeeded by the Ford Rheinland. Technically speaking, this model hardly differed from its predecessor, however. The Rheinland was powered by a 3285 cc four-cylinder engine, delivering 50 bhp to the 17-inch rear wheels. In 1930, Ford moved from Berlin to Cologne. Henry Ford and Konrad Adenauer, Mayor of Cologne at the time, together laid the first stone for the new factory. Various models were assembled in Cologne, such as the small Ford Köln, the German version of the English Ford Y. Initially, the Köln was built

already had a round steering wheel, although this was still placed centrally in the car. In 1902, the wheel was placed at an angle for the first time. As with virtually all pre-war car manufacturers, F.N. also built sports and racing cars. In 1930, the first model with an eight-cylinder, eight-in-line engine was produced. Three cars of this type were entered for the 24-hour race in Spa in 1932. The cars finished in fourth, fifth and sixth places, behind three Alfa Romeos. The F.N. driven by George and Mathot completed a distance of 2,323 kilometres at an average speed of 61 mph (96.830 kph). In addition, F.N. won the 'Coupe du Roi', the prize for the best works team. During the '30s, the European market was flooded with

using English parts, but a convertible developed in Germany was also included in the range. The Köln's four-cylinder engine had a capacity of 921 cc and delivered 21 bhp at 3500 rpm. Of this model, a total of 11,121 cars were sold up to 1936. In 1935, the Ford

Apart from the engine and gearbox, the Ford Taunus was an all-German design.

Köln was superseded by the much more modern Eifel. For this model, the Köln's engine was enlarged to 1172 cc. The Eifel was a great success. Until 1939, no less than 61,495 were produced. In 1939, the Eifel was replaced by the Ford Taunus, the first model to be completely developed and produced in Germany. The engine and gearbox of the Taunus came from the Ford Eifel, but the chassis and bodywork were all new.

It was not only in America that Ford acquired fame for its cheap V8 engines. More than 15,000 cars were fitted with such engines in Germany. The models looked American, but were designed and built in Germany.

This Eifel was supplied in 1938. Up to 1937, this model had had 17-inch spoked wheels. Thereafter, steel wheels with a 16-inch diameter were used.

The Ford Taunus was available until 1952.

Ford England

Henry Ford opened a factory to produce Model T Fords in Manchester, England, in 1911. This was intended to reduce the production and transport costs. The model became a resounding success in England too. When the conveyor belt finally stopped in 1925, more than 250,000 Model T Fords had already been built in England.

In 1920, the British government had introduced a new tax system. From then on, the engine size determined the amount of tax payable.This was a problem for the Model A Ford in particular, as this was powered by a heavier 3285 cc engine. For this reason, the Ford AF was built specially for the English market in the city of Cork in southern Ireland. This model was powered by a 2.0 litre engine.

Unfortunately, the AF proved not to be a worthy competitor for the small Morrises and Austins. The Ford Motor Company therefore decided in 1932 to design a completely new model. A new factory was built in Dagenham specifically for the production of this Model Y, or Model Eight. The four-cylinder side-valve engine had a capacity of 933 cc.

The Ford Y looked like a smaller version of the Model A Ford.

In 1934, the Ten appeared, with a 1172 cc engine. Shortly before the war, these models were re-christened the Ford Anglia and Ford Prefect, and they were sold under these names shortly after the war as well. In 1932, the famous Ford V8 was introduced in America. The first English model to feature this 3622 cc side-valve engine appeared just one year later. With two-door bodywork, the car cost £230, a lot of money compared with the £120 for a Ford Y.

The V8 engine was also produced in France, where it was incorporated into the Ford Matford. After the war, this model with a V8 engine was named the Ford Pilot in England.

When the Ford Ten was presented, it was given the label 'De Luxe'. From that moment onwards, the Ford Eight was known as the 'Popular'.

In 1939, the Ford Ten was re-christened the Prefect. This is a four-seater convertible from that year.

Ford USA

Henry Ford (1863-1947) was born on a farm in Springwell. In 1879, he moved to Detroit. He started out in life as an assistant in a workshop, but by the beginning of the '90s he had a management position with the 'Edison Illuminating Company'. In 1892, Ford

The interior of the open-topped Prefect. Note the steel tube under the dashboard, which reinforced the bodywork.

designed his first car. However, it was several years before he quit the day job and, on 16 June 1903, founded the 'Ford Motor Company', together with a number of friends. On 1 October 1908, the first Model T Ford was introduced. This model would go on to be produced, practically unchanged, for almost nineteen years and in total more than 15 million cars were to be sold. The Model T Ford was certainly not the best American car, but it was the cheapest and the most reliable. From 1913, production of the Model T took place in an extremely modern manner. The chassis was pulled through the factory on a long rope. The various parts were fitted to the chassis as it passed. Using this 'conveyor belt' system meant that cars could be produced cheaply and quickly. In 1914, a Model T Ford emerged from the factory every 40 seconds and in 1925 it was possible to deliver more than 9,000 in one day. The last Model T Ford came off the production line on 31 May 1927. Its chassis number was 15,176,888. Henry Ford bought out his former colleagues for more than one hundred million dollars. The Model T Ford was succeeded by the Model A Ford, but Henry Ford mistimed its introduction. The first Model A Ford could only be delivered six months later, on 2

The Model T Ford was available with various types of bodywork. This is a two-seater coupé.

A Model A Ford 'Town Sedan' from 1929.

In 1927, a Model T Ford cost $380 in America. That same year, 81,181 of these cars were sold.

This 2+2 was built on the chassis of a Model A Ford from 1931.

December 1927. In the meantime, the Ford dealers had to sit back and watch as their customers defected to the competition. Despite the fact that the Model A Ford was much more modern than its predecessor, this model was not nearly as popular. Competitor Chevrolet was already producing a car with a six-cylinder engine, while the Model A Ford only had four cylinders.

This time, however, Ford was quick to respond. On 31 March 1932, he introduced the first model with a V8 engine. But what was much more important, the car in a four-door limousine version cost the same as a Model A Ford. And in the Tourer version, the new model was even $35 cheaper, at $ 545 instead of $580. The V8 engine was designed by Henry's son, Edsel. Unfortunately,

Ford has always been the biggest supplier of estate cars. This Woody appeared on the market in 1932.

The V8 side-valve engine in this 1936 split rear door estate delivered 85 bhp at 3800 rpm.

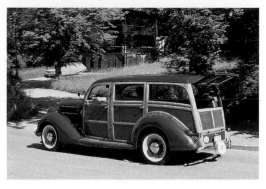

IIn 1935, the customer could choose from no less than fifteen different bodywork types. This two-door convertible with 'dickey seat' was one of the options.

In 1938, Ford sold 791,812 passenger cars, including this five-seater convertible.

Edsel Ford died in 1943 at the age of 49. Henry Ford once again took over the management of the company. In 1945, he was succeeded by his eldest

The rear window could be opened with a zipper. So the passengers in the back needn't feel shut out.

In 1941, all Fords were given new bodywork. Another new development that year was the choice for the customer of an eight or six-cylinder engine.

grandchild, Henry Ford II. Two years later, at the age of 82, the founder of this legendary motor company died.

In 1910, the Franklin Tourer cost $1,850. The same year, a Model T Ford cost only $950.

Franklin

In 1901, engineer John Wilkinson built a small car with an air-cooled engine, but unfortunately failed to sell his brain-child. Just as he had almost given the whole thing up, however, he met Herbert H. Franklin. Franklin was so impressed by the design that he convinced Wilkinson to produce the cars under the name Franklin. In 1902, the first car produced under this name was sold. After this, sales figures climbed steadily. At first, mainly small,

Franklin used exclusively air-cooled engines. The V12 was no exception.

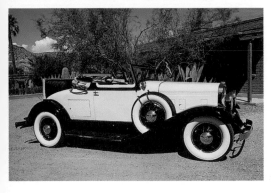

Aviation pioneer Charles Lindbergh was a loyal Franklin customer. The Franklin Airman series was introduced in 1928 in honour of this fact. The picture shows Amelia Earhart's Airman from 1931. Earhart made a solo flight across the Atlantic Ocean in 1932.

This Franklin was supplied in 1932 as the 'Series 16-A Custom Bodied Phaeton'. The air-cooled engine delivered 100 bhp.

open-topped two-seaters were produced, but these were quickly followed by larger passenger cars. All models were powered by air-cooled overhead-valve engines. In 1906, Franklin introduced the first model with a six-cylinder engine, and these too sold well. In 1919, Franklin improved upon its own production record selling almost 9,000 cars. Until 1928, all Franklins still had a wooden chassis. This was replaced by steel in 1929. The same year, almost 14,000 cars were built, a record that would stand for all time. Due to the impact of the world crisis, less than 2,000 cars were pro-

duced in 1932. In 1933, the make introduced a car with a V12 engine, the sedan version of which cost $3,885. Even this design, however, was unable to stave off disaster. All the cars had to be sold at a loss, and the banks quickly choked off the money supply. The company closed its doors for good in 1934.

Frazer-Nash

H.R. Godfrey and Captain Archie Frazer-Nash started a factory for small sports cars or 'cycle cars' in 1910. The cars were sold under the name G.N. When demand for this form of transport declined, the partners sold off their company in 1923. Frazer-Nash decided to start anew, however. He sold the first car under his own name as early as 1924. This was once again a sports car, but larger than the old G.N. However, this model also amounted to little more than a chassis with an

This picture shows Averil Scott-Moncrieff driving her Frazer-Nash on the circuit at Zandvoort. She had come over from England for the race, and her husband Bunty removed the mudguards and headlights for the occasion.

A lot of Frazer-Nash cars were used for racing. This shows John Charles' car on the Monthléry circuit.

still made sports cars, but from 1934 the majority of the income came from the import and assembly of BMW sports and passenger cars. Virtually every BMW model was available in England as a Frazer-Nash BMW. The BMW 328 in particular was very popular. In 1934, the last of the chain-driven cars left the factory in Isleworth.

They had now become really outdated, and were even more expensive than the more modern BMWs.

engine and two bucket seats. As the rear wheels were driven by chains, drivers of these cars quickly became known as the 'Chain Gang'. Frazer-Nash never built an engine of his own.

But then, why should he? He could take his pick from the cheap four or six-cylinder engines by Anzani, Meadows or Blackburne. In 1927, Frazer-Nash sold his company to the Aldington brothers. This led to the emergence of the A.F.N. make (Aldington-Frazer-Nash). The company

A.F.N. only imported 66 cars of this type. This was third from last, with chassis number 56,140.

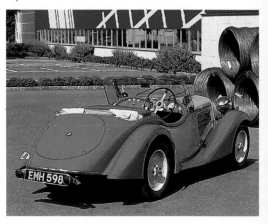

Once the A.F.N. make started to import BMWs, they were able to supply marvellous sports cars such as this Frazer-Nash BMW 319 from 1936.

The 2.0 litre six-cylinder engine delivered 45 bhp at 3750 rpm, giving a top speed of 72 mph (115 kph).

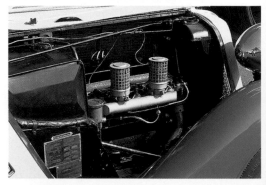

Georges Irat

Frenchman Georges Irat only started out on his automotive adventure in 1921. He built small cars that were sporty enough to win rallies and races, while also being real family cars. All models were powered by four-cylinder overhead-valve engines of his own make. Furthermore, all of the cars had power-assisted brakes, something new in those days. The sports cars turned out to be highly suited to long-distance races. They consequently took their places in the starting line-up of the Le Mans 24-hour race in 1923, 1924 and 1926.

In 1927, Irat introduced a larger model with a 3.0 litre six-cylinder engine. Owing to increased competition, however, this model never enjoyed the success of the smaller two litre cars. In order to reduce the price, during the '30s Irat sold cars with a six or eight-cylinder engine by Lycoming, but these did not sell well either. Irat therefore decided to once again devote more attention to smaller models. In 1935, a sports car with a 954 or 1100 cc Ruby engine and four-wheel drive was introduced. Although this model looked a lot like an MG or Morgan, it never became as popular as its famous competitors. These were sold almost exclusively in France. Once some 1,000 of the sports cars with a Ruby engine

Irat sold approximately 1,000 of these sports cars. This model was powered by a four-cylinder Ruby engine. This car is from 1937.

This Georges Irat from 1927 has a surprisingly low windscreen.

The impressive 'dashboard' of the Richard, with lots of gleaming brass.

had been sold, Irat switched to the engine and drive of the Citroën Légère. After the Second World War, the Irat make disappeared from the market altogether.

Georges Richard

In 1893, brothers George and Max Richard started a small bicycle factory. Two years later, they built their first car there. Initially, only prototypes were produced, with both petrol and electric engines. It was not until 1899 that they introduced their first production car. Although the model had the appearance of a Benz, it was in fact a Belgian Vivinus built under licence. In 1900, a second model appeared, the Poney. In the first year, 423 of these cars were sold. The Poney was powered by chains to the rear wheels. From 1901 onwards, a George Richard was also available with a cardan shaft. In 1902, Richard hired the famous designer Henri Brassier.

Subsequent models were then sold under the name Richard-Brassier. The cars were larger than Richard's Voiturettes and were powered by two or four-cylinder engines. In 1905, Georges Richard left the company. He went on to establish the Unic make, while the Richard-Brassiers continued to be sold under the name Brassier.

George Richard's cars had a tubular chassis and were powered by a single-cylinder engine.

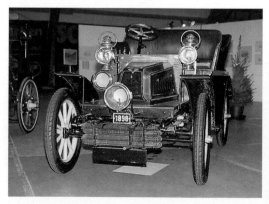

Gladiator

In 1891, the two friends Jean Aucocq and Alexandre Darracq started a bicycle factory in Pré Saint-Gervais. The first car was built here in 1898. A short time later, Darracq left thecompany. He was succeeded by Adolphe Clément and the engineer Marius Barbadou. In 1903, Clément started his own factory, while Barbadou joined Benz the same year. At this time, Gladiator built cars with single, two, four and six-cylinder engines. The family cars turned out to be well suited to the long-distance races that were

Gladiator also built Grand Prix cars, such as this one from 1904. The four-cylinder engine had a capacity of 9000 cc and delivered 90 bhp. The top speed was 94 mph (150 kph) at a fuel consumption of 25 litres/100 km.

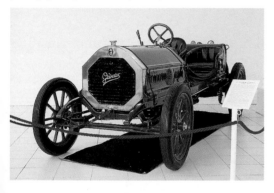

This Gladiator is also from 1904. This family model seated six.

very popular in France. In 1909, the Gladiator make was sold to Messrs Vinot and Deguingand. From then on, the models bore a distinct resemblance to those of the Vinot make. Sales were disappointing, however. In 1920, radical cutbacks had to be made. The Gladiator make had to be abandoned and, six years later, the same fate befell the Vinot make.

G.N.

The name Cyclecar is a combination of the words 'motor**cycle**' and 'motor**car**'. The small, narrow Cyclecars combined the price of a motorcycle with the comfort of a car. Such vehicles were very popular before and immediately after the First World War, particularly in England and France. Factories making Cyclecars sprung up everywhere. Messrs H.R. Godfrey and Archie Frazer-Nash also produced these vehicles. Godfrey had the know-how and Frazer-Nash the financial resources and production space. The first G.N.s were built in a shed behind his mother's house in Hendon. Initially, the cars were intended primarily for racing, but this did not mean you could not drive them to the office. The car was extremely light. The powerful engine drove the rear wheels with heavy chains. The steering system was really something special. The front wheels were controlled by cables; the engine had to be started with a rope. It was only in 1922 that the cars were fitted with a starting handle beneath the radiator. The same year, a model with doors was introduced. These innovations failed to tempt customers into the showroom, however. The era

The G.N. was a typical Cyclecar. As it was particularly slender, it could fit into just about any shed. Nevertheless, this model did offer a certain amount of 'luxury'. This vehicle dates from 1919.

of the Cyclecar had definitely passed. People preferred to buy an Austin or a Model T Ford, which offered greater comfort at a lower price. Godfrey and Frazer-Nash sold their company in 1923. From then on, Frazer-Nash built sports cars under his own name and Godfrey founded the H.R.G. make together with Halford and Robbins.

Gordini

Italians Ettore Bugatti and Amadeo Gordini had a great impact on the history of the French car industry. Gordini was born on 23 June 1899 in Bozzano near Bologna, the son of a horse trader. By the age of eleven, he was already working in a garage. On his twenty-fifth birthday, he moved to

The Schlumpf Museum in Mulhouse has a virtually complete collection of Gordinis. This Simca-Gordini Cinq is from 1937.

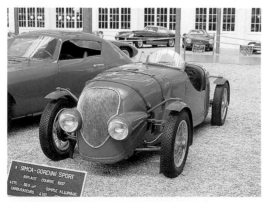

In 1939, five Gordinis started the Le Mans 24-hour race. The cars finished in 10th, 13th, 19th and 20th place in the general class and won the 750 and 1100 cc classes.

Paris, where he got a job with the importer of Hispano-Suiza. Two years later, he started his own workshop. He repaired Fiats and became increasingly interested in racing. He participated in various rallies with tuned-up Fiats. His cars often took part in the Le Mans and regularly won their class. This did not bring in much money, however.

Gordini was therefore happy when he was able to conclude an agreement with Simca. The most famous result of this was the renowned Simca-Gordini. This model was based on the small Simca Cinq and the cars proved to be fast and reliable. In 1938, no less than six Simca-Gordinis lined up for the start of the Le Mans race. The 568 cc engine delivered some 26 bhp. In 1957, Gordini joined Renault. Here, he was responsible for the equally famous Renault-Gordinis. Gordini built all manner of cars, including even Grand Prix cars. But it was primarily these expensive cars that were his ruination. He could not compete with the much wealthier competition. Gordini was finally forced

to sell his company to Fritz Schlumpf. He died a lonely death in Paris on 25 May 1979.

Graham-Paige

In 1908, the three brothers Joseph, Robert and Ray Graham ran a garage repairing lorries. By 1925, the

From 1929, the cars were sold under the name Graham-Paige. One striking feature was the parking lights, located under the windscreen.

The Graham Special Touring Sedan was a very special car in 1938. The luggage space was now in, rather than behind, the car.

The three-seater Special Six was the cheapest Graham in 1938. The car cost only $940 and could even be delivered with a compressor.

A new front was not enough to save the make in 1940. Even this Graham Hollywood Convertible found hardly any takers.

In 1939, this Sedan could also be supplied with a compressor. The prices for a DeLuxe were $993 and $1,130 respectively.

workshop had become the largest producer of lorries in the world. The brothers decided to sell the company in 1927. With the proceeds, they bought the bankrupt 'Paige-Detroit Motor Car Company'. The first Graham-Paige was introduced in 1928 at the New York car show.

The car proved a great success with more than 58,000 being sold in the first year. In 1930, the make's name was changed to Graham. The same year, the range included various models with six and eight-cylinder engines. The customer could choose from sporty two-seaters or dignified Town Cars, which really needed to be driven by a

chauffeur. In 1934, the Custom Eight appeared, featuring a compressor engine that delivered 135 bhp at 4000 rpm. These eight-cylinder engines were last fitted in 1935, when the factory introduced a new six-cylinder engine. The 1936 range included three series, namely the Crusader Six, the Cavalier and the Supercharger Series 110. The same year, a total of 16,439 cars were sold, but two years later this number had fallen to 4,139. In 1938, Graham had only two series on offer, namely the Special Six and the Supercharged Six.

Each series consisted of three models, the Business Coupe, the six-seater Combination Coupe and the six-seater Sedan. There was very little appreciation for the new design however. The front of the car in particular was regarded by many as horrendously ugly. Furthermore, there were plenty of other makes available that year. Demand for the Graham make declined even further. The company altered the design, but even this measure could not prevent sales figures from dropping to just 1,856 in 1940. The make disappeared from the market for good in 1941.

Grégoire

This Grégoire from 1912 was powered by a 2113 cc four-cylinder engine. The two spark plugs per cylinder and the two Solex carburettors were interesting features.

In 1903, the French company 'Automobiles Grégoire' predominately manufactured car engines, but in 1904 the company's first car was introduced. The design was not really special, but the make was immediately recognisable by its pear-shaped radiator. The company made cars with single, two and four cylinder engines.

In 1911, a six-cylinder engine and a four-cylinder sleeve-valve engine were added to the range. The Grégoire make never sold in vast quantities. In 1913, for example, only 500 cars were produced by the factory on the Boulevard Devaux in Poissy. In comparison, Peugeot sold some 5,000 cars that year. After the First World War, Grégoire introduced its first car with a modern overhead-valve engine. Although the engine was only a 2.3 litre, this sporty car could reach a top speed of 62 mph (100 kph). The financial results were disappointing however. By 1923, Grégoire was only producing engines for the Bignan make. The factory closed down for good in 1924.

The pear-shaped radiator was characteristic of all Grégoires. This car from 1912 can immediately be recognised as a Grégoire thanks to this distinctive feature.

ℋ h

Haase

The American company 'Northwestern Furniture Company' of Milwaukee built a few cars between 1902 and 1904. These were given the name Haase, after the director of the company. Only some fifteen such cars were sold in total. All models had the same two-seater bodywork. The two-cylinder engine was located under the seat and drove the rear wheels using chains. The radiator was at the front of the car. The Haase was steered by means of a handle, rather than a wheel.

This Haase from 1903 was never a real speed king. The top speed was approximately 3,7 mph (6 kph).

Hanomag

The 'Hannoverische Maschinenbau AG', or Hanomag for short, was founded in 1835 by Georg Egestorff.

A side view of the 'Kommisbrot'.

A 2/10 as racing car. In order to save weight, this car had cane bodywork.

The company built engines, steam boilers and locomotives. In 1925, the company produced its first car. At that time, Hanomag employed some 5,000

The Hanomag 4/23 was produced between 1931 and 1934. The 1097 cc four-cylinder side-valve engine delivered 23 bhp.

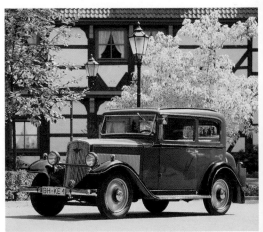

people. The first cars were small and cheap. This meant that, unlike other car manufacturers, Hanomag was not hit so hard by the looming economic crisis. The very first car was called the 2/10 PS. It was a very simple design by Fidelis Böhler. In order to save weight, Böhler dispensed with the mudguards and running-boards. This created the

The Rekord was the most successful Hanomag. The diesel version was particularly popular. This convertible has bodywork by Ambi-Budd.

first car with a pontoon bodywork. The 502 cc single-cylinder side-valve engine was located in front of the rear axle and delivered 10 bhp at 2500 rpm. As the entire car weighed less than 280 kg, (616 lb), it could reach a top speed of 37 mph (60 kph).

The 'Kommisbrot' (soldier's loaf), as the car was known because of its shape, was a big hit. No less than 15,775 were sold during a three- year period. The successor to the 'Kommisbrot', the 3/16 PS from 1926, looked more like a real car, but was less successful, with only 9,300 being produced.

Hanomag has, with great success, always stuck to building small cars. For example, 19,188 Rekords were sold between 1934 and 1938. Of these 1,074 were powered by a diesel engine which was very unusual in those days. The Sturm, from 1934, was a more luxurious model, but had little success. This car was powered by a 1152 cc six-cylinder overhead-valve engine delivering 50 bhp.

When production ceased in 1939, only 4,885 had been sold. Hanomag continued building passenger cars until 1941. The post-war comeback failed.

Hansa

At the beginning of this century, two friends, Dr Robert Allmers and Dr August Sprockhorst, built cars for their own use, and in 1905 went on to make this a commercial operation. They founded the 'Hansa Automobilgesellschaft', which in 1914 led to 'Hansa Automobilwerke AG'. The cars built by the company before the First World War were until 1908 powered by a single-cylinder engine by De Dion-Bouton. Subsequent models had four-cylinder engines and cardan shafts instead of being chain-driven. During the First World War, Hansa built predominately lorries for the German army, and production after the war

The dashboard of a Hansa 1700. The ignition key also operated the lights.

The Hansa 1100 and 1700 were the most successful models. These cars had the same bodywork; the difference was under the bonnet.

started slowly. For this reason, it was decided in 1920 to merge with the automobile companies Lloyd, NAG and Brennabor. This created the 'Gemeinschaft Deutscher Automobilfabriken', or GDA. Even this cooperation was not enough to prevent Hansa's capitulation in 1929 however. Engineer Carl Borgward, whose company occupied premises opposite the Hansa factory, took over the bankrupt company.

In 1931, Borgward incorporated the makes Goliath, Hansa and Lloyd into a single company. Goliath produced lorries and the other two makes passenger cars. With the exception of the small models referred to above, Hansa

The Hansa 1700 had a six-cylinder six-in-line engine with a capacity of 1634 cc. This overhead-valve engine delivered 40 bhp at 3800 rpm.

also attempted to produce larger cars. For example, in 1927 the Hansa Typ A6 and A8 were introduced. Both models were powered by American Continental engines. The A6 had a 3262 cc six-cylinder engine, and the A8 an eight-in-line engine with a capacity of 3996 cc. The engines were relatively cheap, meaning that both models could be competitively priced.

This did not however automatically lead to large sales. In total, only something in the region of 1,000 cars with an American engine were produced. The company had greater success with the Hansa 1100. Between 1934 and 1939 a little more than 20,000 of these cars were sold. The Hansa 1700, an 1100 with a bigger engine, was also fairly successful and approximately 6,000 were produced.
The last Hansa passenger car was made in 1939.

Hinstin

The Hinstin may resemble a Bugatti externally, but the comparison stops there. The Hinstin was built between 1920 and 1926 by Jacques Hinstin, a

A Hinstin from 1920 during a race for historical cars at the Nürburgring in 1979.

Grégoire dealer from Maubeuge. The company did not produce engines or gearboxes itself, but purchased these from well-known manufacturers such as C.I.M.E., Altos and Ruby. Thanks to his good contacts with Grégoire, Hinstin was able to sell his cars in England through the Grégoire dealer network. In England, the cars were known as 'Little Greg'.

Hispano-Suiza

Although this make's name translates as 'Spain-Switzerland', no car of this name was ever produced in Switzerland. The special name was created by engineer Marc Birkigt, who emigrated in 1899 at the age of twenty-one from

The 'flying ostrich', the Hispano-Suiza emblem, with the Spanish and Swiss flags beneath.

Baron de Rothschild acquired this J12 in 1934. Between 1931 and 1938 only 120 cars were fitted with the V12 engine.

The most beautiful creations originated in France, such as this H6B from 1925. The model had a 6597 cc engine that delivered 135 bhp.

Geneva to Barcelona. In 1904, together with J. Castro, he founded the 'Hispano-Suiza de Automobiles'. Their first car was the 14 HP. This model was powered by a four-cylinder engine. And beneath the bonnet of its successor, the 20 HP, droned a 3.8 litre six-cylinder engine.

In 1906, the young company introduced two new models. These cars were beautifully finished and particularly popular with the 'upper ten'. The Spanish court also ordered a number of Hispano-Suizas. King Alfonso XIII was a particular fan of the make. The Alfonso model, a car with a 3.6 litre four-cylinder engine, was even named

after him. Hispano-Suiza exported a lot of cars, particularly to France. In order to avoid the steep import duty, in 1911 Birkigt relocated part of his production facilities to Levallois on the Seine. This factory went on to produce one of the make's most beautiful creations. The H6 from 1919 could compete on even terms with a Rolls-Royce, Isotta Fraschini or Mercedes-Benz. During the First World War, the company switched to the production of aircraft engines. The experiences brought by this switch were later applied in the production of cars. The H6 had a 6597 cc six-cylinder engine with an overhead camshaft, double ignition and brakes

The H6C was the last model in the famous series. The engine had a capacity of 7983 cc.
The car in the picture was provided with bodywork by Franay in 1932.

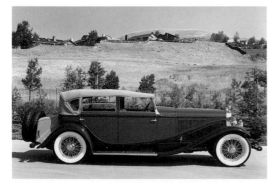

A Hispano-Suiza J12 T68bis from 1932. The 'Dual Cowl' bodywork was made by Henry Binder in Paris.
Beneath the bonnet lurked a V12 with a capacity of 11,310 cc.

After King Alfonso XIII had ordered a sports car, he gave the factory permission to call the model Alfonso.

on all four wheels. The model was produced until 1932. Another top model was the J12 (1931-1938). This car was powered by a 9424 cc V12 engine. The engine delivered an incredible 220 bhp at a low 3000 rpm. The last series had a 11,310 cc engine that delivered 252 bhp at 2800 rpm.

This engine also had an overhead camshaft for each row of cylinders. These cars were extremely expensive and were therefore harder and harder to sell as the economic crisis bit deeper. The factory in Spain also made cheaper cars with four and six-cylinder engines. The French factory followed this

example in 1933. The model was called the K6. This car was powered by a six-cylinder overhead-valve engine, without overhead camshaft, with a capacity of 5184 cc. 1938, Hispano-Suiza decided to cease production of passenger cars in France. The concern instead concentrated on the production of aircraft engines and special cannon.

In Spain, cars were produced until 1943. The company then became part of the ENASA group, which also included the sports car make Pegaso. In total, some 8,600 Hispano-Suizas were built, 6,000 in France and 2,600 in Spain. Marc Birkigt died in 1953 in his country house in Versoit, on Lake Geneva.

Horch

August Horch was born in Germany in 1868. At the age of thirteen, he got a job in his father's smithy. After receiving a basic foundation, he worked as an apprentice at various companies in eastern Europe and followed a technical training course in Germany between 1887 and 1891. Upon completing his studies, he worked briefly as a technical draughtsman in a machine engineering plant in Leipzig. The talented Horch was quickly spotted by Karl Benz, who offered him a job in his factory in Mannheim. Horch became so fascinated by cars that he decided to start his own company in 1899. Just one year later, the first prototype emerged from his small

A total of eighteen of the Horch 10/12 PS were built. The model was introduced in 1901. This Tonneau is from 1904.

The Horch 8 type 420 was only built in 1931 and 1932. The eight-cylinder engine had a capacity of 4.5 litres.

The interior of a Horch 853A contains a lot of wood and leather. It took a great deal of strength to drive this car.

The 853A, this one is a works convertible from 1937, contained an eight-in-line engine with a capacity of 5.0 litres.

This 853A was confiscated by the Russian army and has since been driving around in Russia.

workshop. The vehicle was way ahead of its time in technical terms. The two-cylinder engine was placed at the front, rather than the rear. And the rear wheels were powered by a cardan shaft instead of chains. In 1904, the first Horch with a four-cylinder engine was introduced and this was even followed in 1908 by a model with a six-cylinder engine.

In 1909, August Horch left the company following an argument with his fellow directors. He then continued independently with the new make, Audi. In spite of the departure of its founder, the Horch make continued to exist. The factory made cars with big 6.4 litre engines or small four-cylinders with capacities of around 1600 cc. In 1914, these cars could be fitted with electric lights or an electrical starter motor at a considerable extra cost. None of the Horch models was ever built in large quantities. After the First World War, a total of less than 35,000 cars had been sold. Most of these left the factory as a rolling chassis to be provided with bodywork by a specialised bodywork builder. In October 1926, the Horch 8 was introduced. This car would go down in history as the first German production car. The Horch 8 was powered by a marvellous eight-cylinder engine, developed by the company in house. The engine had a cylinder head with two overhead camshafts, a

The bodywork company Voll & Ruhrbeck provided the superstructure for this Horch 853.

'Ladies and gentlemen, pay attention, here you see the most beautiful car ever produced...'

capacity of 3132 cc and delivered 60 bhp at 3200 rpm. As with virtually all makes, the Horch engines got heavier over time:

The Horch 855 Special Roadster was the top-of-the-range model. Film stars liked to have their picture taken in one. A total of only seven of these cars were built.

year of manufacture	engine capacity	horsepower
1927	3378 cc	65 hp
1928	3950 cc	80 hp
1931	4517 cc	90 hp
1935	4944 cc	100 hp

Between 1931 and 1933, a V12 engine was also included in the range. With a capacity of 6021 cc and delivering almost 120 bhp at 3200 rpm, a top speed could be obtained of some

153

75 mph (120 kph). This vehicle, that weighed almost two tonnes, consumed at least 30 litres of petrol for every 100

'A giant among passenger cars.'

kilometres travelled. From 1933, the factory restricted itself to the 'smaller' eight cylinders with engine sizes between 3.0 and 4.0 litres. The most beautiful models date from this period, and were very popular with the Nazis. Between 1935 and 1940, the 850, 853 and 855 models were fitted with a 5.0 litre, eight-cylinder engine. The 851 model was specially made for German diplomats and officers. The 851 could be delivered as a Pullman Limousine with four-door bodywork, or as a four-

This Horch 8 type 780 was also available as a sports convertible in 1932 and 1933.

door convertible. During the Second World War, Horch built (inbetween bombardments) mainly off-road vehicles and light armoured vehicles for the Wehrmacht. After 1945, the make finally vanished from the market.

Hotchkiss

The two cannons in the Hotchkiss logo reveal that the company also made weapons. Benjamin Berkeley Hotchkiss was born in Watertown, Connecticut in 1826. After trade school, he went to work in Colonel Samuel Colt's arms factory, where he helped design the famous Colt revolver. In 1855, Benny Hotchkiss started a company with his brother, Andrew, producing cannon and cannonballs. These weapons were exported, mainly to Mexico and Japan. The brothers benefited enormously from outbreak of the American Civil War.

In 1867, Benjamin Hotchkiss opened a branch in the French town of Aveyron. This company primarily made ammunition for the French army, but a new machine gun was also invented. Hotchkiss died in France in 1885. His successor, Vincent Benet, started to produce car parts. The valves,

The 1930 Hotchkiss looked like an American car from that year.

A lot of cars were sold to bodywork makers as rolling chassis. This AM 680 was provided with bodywork by the Graber company in Switzerland in 1935.

crankshafts, pistons and connecting rods were sold to companies such as Panhard & Levassor and Charron. Whole engines were even built for the Clayette make. In 1903, Hotchkiss built its first car. This vehicle, which looked remarkably like a Mercedes, was powered by a 50 bhp four-cylinder engine which drove the rear wheels using chains.

Racing and Grand Prix cars followed, such as the E type from 1904. This model had a four-cylinder engine with a capacity of 17.8 litres, delivering 80 bhp at 950 rpm. In 1909, the factory built its first type Y passenger car.

The Hotchkiss AM2 was introduced on 25 September 1925. The four-cylinder engine had a capacity of 2413 cc.

A typical Hotchkiss from the early '30s. Robust, reliable, slightly American... but not exactly exciting.

A Hotchkiss type 486 from 1936. This car had a top speed of 69 mph (110 kph).
The four-cylinder engine had 2312 cc, the wheel base was 292 cm.

The small four-cylinder engine had capacities of 2.2 and later 2.4 litres. During the First World War, the company concentrated totally on arms manufacture. As soon as the armistice had been signed, however, cars once again started rolling out of the factory in St. Denis. One highly successful model was the Hotchkiss AM from 1922. Between 1919 and 1939, Hotchkiss built no less than thirty-one different models. Sixteen of these were powered by a four-cylinder, the rest by a six-cylinder, engine. The best-selling AM 680, for example, had a six-cylinder engine with 3015 cc. After the First World War, Hotchkiss stopped making racing cars, although the

models offered were sporty and fast enough to win rallies. The famous Monte Carlo rally was won by a Hotchkiss in 1932, 1933, 1934 and 1939, for example. 1939 was the last year of passenger car production.

After this date, the factory switched to tank and aircraft engine production. Shortly after the war, the Hotchkiss make disappeared from the market.

The dashboard of a H.R.G. had more instruments than a light aircraft.

H.R.G.

Independent suspension and hydraulic brakes were unnecessary luxuries for the H.R.G. driver.

Although no more than 241 H.R.G.s were built, the make made history in England. The factory was founded in Kingston-on-Thames in 1935 by technician E.A. Halford, mechanic Guy Robins and designer H.R. Godfrey. Godfrey's designs included the G.N. sports cars. H.R.G. built sports cars without suspension or any other comforts, but they were very fast. The long bonnet concealed an engine by Singer or Meadows. In the spring of

1936, a first prototype appeared, and by the end of that year five cars had already been delivered. The pre-war models did not yet have hydraulic brakes and the cars had rigid front and rear axles until well into the '50s.

There was never a broad range to choose from, as the following production figures indicate:

Model	1.5 litre, serie A	1.5 litre, serie W	1100 S
1935	1		
1936	5		
1937	10	1	
1938		8	1
1939		1	7
Total	16	10	8

The remaining 207 cars were produced after the Second World War. A last prototype of the H.R.G. make appeared in 1966.

During the First World War, Hudson built cars for the army. General John Joseph Pershing, Supreme Commander of the American army, toured the battlefields of France in this Super Six.

In 1909, Hudson sold this roadster under the name 'Strong, Speedy, Roomy and Stylish'.

Hudson

A good start is half the battle, and friends Roy Chapin and Howard Coffin certainly got off to a good start. Their first Hudson left their factory in Detroit on 3 July 1909 and within a period of just twelve months they had sold more than 4,000 cars. Never before had so many of a new model of car been sold in such a short time. Joseph Hudson also had reason to be satisfied. After all, he had put up the finance for the whole enterprise. The 'Hudson Motor Car Company' built cars with four and six-cylinder engines. At that time, racing was extremely important for the reputation of a make of car. In 1916, for instance, a Hudson Super Six was the first American car to drive from New York to San Francisco and back, and three years later a Hudson finished ninth in the murderous Indianapolis 500 mile race. In 1918, Hudson introduced the Essex make.

In 1917, the Hudson make was still active in racing. The company had its own racing department and its own works team. The cars were very successful. World records were broken and numerous races won.

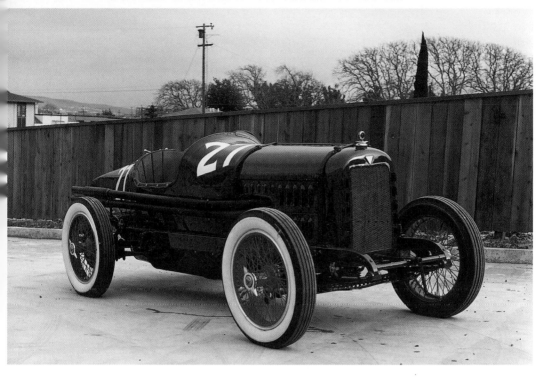

The factory could now offer a car in all price classes, although Hudson had its ups and downs like any car manufacturer. 1916 was a top year, and

The cars from model year 1929 had wheel bases of 286 or 353 cm. The customer could choose from an amazing fourteen different types of bodywork. These models were called 'The Greater Hudson' instead of 'Super Six'.

25,772 cars were sold during that year. In 1918, on the other hand, only 12,526 were sold. By 1925, Hudson occupied third place in the list of American automobile manufacturers, behind Chevrolet and Ford. Sales in that year reached 109,840 cars, all of which were powered by a six-cylinder engine, the 'Super Six'. In 1929, all the American car manufacturers together produced five million cars.

That year, Hudson broke its own record with a production of 71,179 cars. In 1930, the first Hudson with an eight-cylinder engine appeared. These cars were sold under the name 'Hudson Great Eight' and were available with two different wheel bases and no less than eleven different types of bodywork. The same year, another 36,674 Hudsons were sold. Over the next few years, however, sales declined drama-

This Hudson Big Six from 1940 can be seen in the Jysk Automobile Museum in Gjern, Denmark.

Hudson sold rolling chassis to various bodywork builders. The picture shows a Hudson from 1935 with a body by Gangloff.

tically as a result of the world economic crisis. It was not until 1938 that the volume of production achieved in 1930 could be bettered.

Year	Quantity	Year	Quantity
1931	17,487	1937	19,848
1932	7,777	1938	51,078
1933	2,401	1939	82,161
1934	27,130	1940	87,900
1935	29,476	1941	79,529
1936	25,409	1942	40,661

The depression dealt Hudson a heavy blow. It was cold comfort that the entire American automotive industry was suffering the same problems. After the eight-in-line engine was introduced in 1930, no more six-cylinder engines were built. A mistake? Probably, as a Super Six was reintroduced into the range in 1932. The same year, Hudson established the make Terraplane and the competitor to the new Ford V8. The new make sold well and was responsible for virtually the Hudson Corporation's entire result.

Hupmobile

Robert Craig Hupp had already worked for Ford and Oldsmobile when, in 1908, he built his own car. It was a small, open-topped sports car. Hupp introduced this car a year later at the car show in Detroit as the 'Hupmobile'. During the initial years, the 'Hupp Motor Car Company' did well. In 1909 alone, 1,618 cars emerged from the factory on Milwaukee Avenue in Detroit, and by 1910 this number had risen to 5,340 and by 1911 to 6,079. The first cars were powered by a four-cylinder engine. In 1925, the model E-1 appeared, with an eight-in-line engine.

In 1926, this model was succeeded by the A-1, which had a six-cylinder side-valve engine. In 1930, the factory offered three basic models, namely the model S with a 70 bhp six-cylinder engine, the model C with a 100 bhp eight-cylinder engine and the 'H', which boasted an eight-cylinder engine delivering 133 bhp. The last model had a 318 cm wheel base and 19-inch wheels. The same year, a little more than 22,000 cars were sold. This put

Hupmobile was a good, reliable car. They looked good and were not (much) more expensive than the competitors' cars. Nevertheless, demand or the make continued to decline. In 1932, the make still occupied thirteenth place in America, but that year production was only just above 10,000 and in 1935 only 9,346 buyers decided to plump for a Hupmobile. In 1936, all models had hydraulic brakes. An overdrive could even be delivered at extra cost. Buyers stayed away, however, and that year only 1,556 cars were delivered. In 1937, production ceased.

the make in seventeenth place in the list of American car manufacturers. In 1931, the Hupmobile dealer could offer a broad range of models. The cheapest version was the Century Six, which had a six-cylinder engine. The remaining four models were all powered by an eight-in-line engine.

These were called the Century Eight, Hupmobile C, Hupmobile H and Hupmobile U. The last delivered no less than 133 bhp and the limousine version cost $2,295. This was relatively expensive. A Century Six could have been yours for less than $1,000. The

In a 'death or glory' attempt to reverse the situation, completely new cars were developed for 1938. This measure failed to deliver the goods however. In 1938, sales slumped below 1,400. In the meantime, Hupmobile had acquired the presses and tools with which the Cord 812 had been produced. In 1939, the first Hupmobile Cord appeared with a new front. This model proved popular. Some 1,400 were sold that year. In the autumn of 1940, the last of the Skylark models left the factory. These were powered by a six-cylinder engine delivering 101 bhp.

This wonderfully restored Roadster was made in 1929.
Under the baggage cover was seating for two people, the
'rumble seat'.

The last Hupmobile rolled out of the factory in 1940.
The steering column gear change was very modern
for those days.

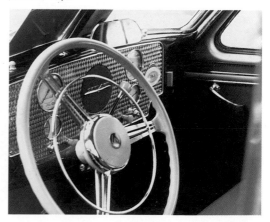

Invicta

Sir Noël Macklin constructed his first sports car in 1924. As is the case with most English sports cars of the time, it was a car without any form of comfort. The cars were produced in a shed behind his parents' house and it was here that the first Invicta saw the light of day – or rather the first rolling chassis, since Macklin actually sold all of his cars without bodywork. The open chassis was driven through the factory by a driver in a leather jacket, goggles and checked cap. After 1,000 miles (1600 km), each car's engine was dismantled, the components were checked and then the whole thing was rebuilt. An Invicta was guaranteed for no less than 5 years and this in a time when cars regularly broke down. The price was, of course, adapted accordingly. The six-cylinder

engines used in the Invicta were purchased from Coventry-Climax or Meadows. The most famous was a Meadows overhead valve engine with a capacity of 4467 cc and delivering 115 bhp. Purchasers of the first cars produced could choose between a chassis with a short or long wheel base. However, after 1929 only the short wheel base version was available. The capacity of the Meadows engines used in the last few cars to be made was increased to 140 bhp at 3600 rpm. Cars with these engines had a maximum speed of 100 mph (160 kph). In addition to this fast model, the range also included a 1.5 litre six-cylinder. This engine could also be fitted with a compressor upon request. Invicta twice tried to produce

In 1931, this Invicta with chassis number S 106 left the factory. The engine capacity was 4.5 litres.

The Invicta could easily attain a top speed of more than 100 miles/hr. Note the large brake drums behind the front wheels.

The bonnet accounted for more than half the car's length.

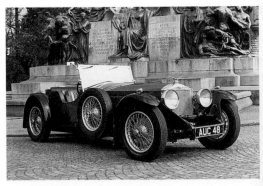

This Invicta 4.5 litre can still be admired at historical car
races. The question is whether the engines still use up so
much (Castrol) oil?

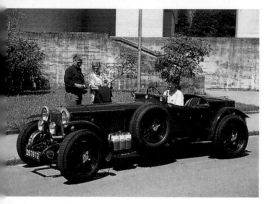

The 4.5 litre engine sucked in the petrol and air mixture
from four S.U. carburettors, delivering no less than
140 bhp.

cars which used engines with two overhead upper camshafts, but these models progressed no further than the prototype stage and a production series never materialised. During the Second World War, Invicta primarily constructed torpedo boats for the American navy. In 1946, the Black Prince was introduced, a streamlined family car with four doors, but similarly this model was never produced in series.Invicta chiefly became famous in England, but the make also made an impression elsewhere, for example when Donald Healey won the Austrian Alpine Rally in 1930 and the Monte Carlo Rally in 1931 in Invictas.

Isotta Fraschini

The last few years of the twentieth century were difficult times for Rolls-Royce. However, during the period before the war it was not always plain sailing for 'The best car in the world'. In that ethtime, there was a lot more competition. In Germany, everyone was g thdriving a Mercedes or a Maybach, in France the Hispano-Suiza was e bedominant, while in Italy the car people were driving was an Isotta petitFraschini. The story of this last make started in 1899 when , in Cesare Isotta and Oreste Fraschini decided to start producing cars peoin Milan. They made an excellent start with their first model mawhich had a 3.9 litre, six-cylinder engine which was introduced in ini Paris in 1905. The company almost exclusively built large cars. An exception was a series of small sports cars that were designed by Ettore Bugatti, who was eighteen at the time. The period of small model production did not last long however and soon the factory in Milan was once again producing only large and

This sports car body was constructed in 1927 by Cesare
Sala on the chassis of an Isotta Fraschini 8A-SS.

Like Rolls-Royce, Isotta Fraschini also sold his cars as rolling chassis. This structure was manufactured in America in 1928 by Le Baron.

expensive models. In 1910, Isotta Fraschini was the first producer to construct cars with brakes on all four wheels. In 1913, cars were on sale with four-cylinder engines with a capacity of no less than 10.5 litres. This four-cylinder engine had an upper overhead camshaft and delivered 100 bhp which was transmitted to the rear wheels by means of chains. During the First World War, the company specialised in the construction of V12 and V18 aircraft engines and after the war, the experience gained was applied to the production of cars. This therefore led to the production of, among other models, the Isotta Fraschini Tipo 8 with its 6 litre, eight-cylinder engine delivering 80 bhp at 2200 rpm. Isotta Fraschini was the first car manufacturer to build eight-cylinder engines in series and this engine was bored out to 7372 cc, thereby increasing the engine power to 160 bhp at 3000 rpm. These engines had an enormous torque which meant that the first and second gears were rarely used. Isotta Fraschini clients were predominantly kings, emperors and film stars, but even the pope and the Italian head of state Mussolini owned a couple. The Tipo 8B stayed in production until 1936. Then the company switched to producing engines for jet aircraft. After the war, they did produce the Monterosa, a large open car with a V8 engine at the front. A total of six prototypes of this model were constructed, but the car never went into production.

Carrozzeria Farina was responsible for the bodywork of this 1929 Tipo 8A. The model was sold under the name 'Imperial Landaulet'

In 1930, Carrozzeria Castagna constructed this Dual-Cowl Phaeton, based on a Tipo 8A SS with chassis number 1664.

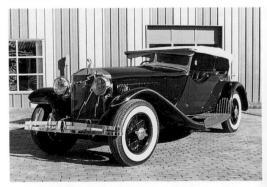

Jaguar

On 4 September 1922, William Walmsley and William Lyons laid the foundation stone of a company that would grow to become one of the most famous makes of car in the world. On the Bloomfield Road in Blackpool, the 'Swallow Sidecar Company' was established using a start-up capital of £1,000. The company had been set up to manufacture sidecars for motorbikes. The products were modern and of high quality and the company flourished during the first years of its existence. In 1922, Herbert Austin introduced his revolutionary Austin Seven. The car became a resounding success. The Swallow Sidecar Company shared in this success because in 1927 the company started selling a Seven with special bodywork. In contrast to the original, the Austin Swallow was a sports car that, despite its small 747 cc engine, was even successful in races and mountain stages. The success of the Seven resulted in Swallow producing, in addition to sidecars, more and more chassis with special bodywork. In 1928, the company moved to Coventry and it was here that the precursor of the modern Jaguar was created. In July 1931, the two Williams had allowed information to be leaked to the effect that they were going to present their own car. They placed advertisements bearing the text, 'Look out, the SS is coming'. The letters SS could stand for both 'Super Sport' and 'Swallow Sidecar'. The presentation was at last held in October 1932. The first cars were introduced at the London Motor Show. Next to the Wolseley Hornet-Swallow were two completely new models, the SS I and the SS II. And the SS I immediately stole the show. The two-person sports coupé had an incredibly long bonnet and a short, low driver's cab which offered enough space for two adults and two small children. The car had been constructed using parts from the Standard 16, but the 2 litre six-cylinder engine could, on request, be tuned up from 45 to 55 bhp. The car's finishing was particularly special.

William Lyons originally constructed sidecars for motorbikes.

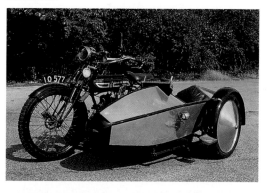

In 1933, the SS I was given a new chassis with a longer wheel base.

The roof of the SS I was covered in leather but could not be opened.

Despite its modest price the SS I was well appointed with opening windscreen.

The seat and the small rear seats were covered in leather and the dashboard was made of wood. However, the most striking feature was the price. For £310, the purchaser acquired more car than the competition could offer for double the price. And for an additional price of just £10, the car could even be fitted with a 2.5 litre engine.

At first, the SS II was received with much less enthusiasm. Most journalists did not even notice the small car. The S.S. II was constructed on the chassis of the Standard Little Nine. The model was driven by a four-cylinder engine with a capacity of 1006 cc. At its introduction, the SS II cost just £210, but not many were sold even at this price.

More and more improvements were made to the SS I. In 1933, the chassis was completely changed and the wheel base increased from 285 to 302 cm. The car's total length also increased from 447 to 460 cm. In the Spring of 1933, a special convertible model was introduced. In 1934, the SS II was also adapted with the wheel base being extended from 227 to 264 cm. The adapted model was driven by a four-cylinder engine with a capacity of 1343 cc, that delivered 32 bhp to the rear wheels. In 1935, William Walmsley left the company and William Lyons decided to discontinue the 'Swallow Coachbuilding Company Ltd.', as the company had been called since 1929.

The new company, 'SS Cars Ltd.' was established for the exclusive production of cars. Another important fact was that William Munger Heynes joined the company. He had previously been the chief constructor at Humber. Together with Harry Weslake, he designed a 'new' engine for the SS. The block, including the rotating parts, still came from the Standard factories. However, a new feature was the cylinder head with its drop valves. Heynes then started the construction of a new chassis for his overhead valve engine.

As of the Spring of 1933, the SS I could also be ordered as an open sports car.
The picture shows a car from 1936.

This led to the creation of the SS 2.5 litre Jaguar. It took just five months before the car was ready to be shown at the London Motor Show in 1936. The lines of the earlier SS I were still easily recognisable, but this time the factory had opted for a body with four doors. Wood was only used in the interior since the new models had a steel body. Different versions of the cars were available. The cheapest and smallest version was still driven by the 1.5 litre four-cylinder side-valve engine used in the SS II.

However, the other versions included the new overhead valve engine. The capacity of this six-cylinder engine was 2663, or after 1938 3485 cc and it delivered 102 bhp (125bhp) at 4600 rpm. The wheel base of these large cars was 302 cm and after 1938 even 305 cm. And once again, the cars' low prices

were what attracted clients to the showrooms. Before the war, only small details of the models were adapted. For example, the spare wheel disappeared from the front left-hand fender to a space under the floor of the boot. In 3 October 1936, the engineer R. Tijken tested an SS Jaguar with a 2663 cc six-cylinder engine for the Dutch magazine 'Autokampioen'.

He wrote about his findings as follows, "As soon as you take your seat at the wheel, you feel you are experiencing something special. A small push of the accelerator immediately releases a considerable number of bhp and the car reaches cruising speed in no time. The second and third gears and the transmission are synchronised. If you want to get a little more acceleration out of the car it is better to change gear in the old-fashioned way so as to save a couple of seconds. That is incidentally one of the attractive aspects of the Jaguar. You can drive it as a dignified six-cylinder car that does practically everything on the transmission input prise, fits calmly in with the traffic in town and hardly stands out alongside other cars with large engines, or you can make the most of the vehicle's sports car qualities so that by changing gear differently you get a car which satisfies the more sports car-oriented driver."

Tijken concluded his test with the sentence, "The experiences gained after having driven the Jaguar several hundred kilometres can be summarised by concluding that this car combines luxury and sports car qualities in a particularly pleasing manner, whereby an entirety is created that will satisfy both the seasoned motorist and the sportsman in numerous ways."

By creating the four-door Jaguar, William Lyons had made a giant step in the direction of the sports passenger car but this did not mean that he had forgotten how to make real sports cars. On the contrary. It was clear that a new

The SS 100 is, without doubt, one of the most beautiful pre-war sports cars.

The SS 100 was ideal for rallying on unpaved roads with mesh lamp guards as standard to protect against stones thrown up.

sports car had to be produced for William Heynes' engines. The stunning SS 90 really only had one disadvantage, namely that under the long bonnet was the rather old-fashioned six-cylinder side-valve engine. Even though the cylinder capacity was 2663 cc, it only delivered 72 bhp. The speedometer went no further than a disappointing 87 mph (140 kph). Between May and September 1935 only 23 SS 90s were sold. During the winter of 1935/ 1936, Weslake and Heynes developed a new overhead-valve engine. This engine was used in the new SS 100 which came into being in September 1936 and was the ultimate pre-war sports car with a 2663 cc six-cylinder engine delivering 102 bhp.

But once again, the top speed was under the promised 100 miles and hour. This only changed in 1937 when the SS 100 with a new 3.5 litre engine was introduced. For understandable reasons, William Lyons decided to drop the name SS in March 1945. After the Second World War, his cars were sold under the name Jaguar.

Jeep

Willys-Overland is generally acknowledged as being the inventor of the Jeep. The make Jeep-Eagle, which these days is part of Chrysler, will not deny this. However, the truth of the matter is that the American Bantam Company was the real inventor. In 1940, the American Ministry of War asked car manufacturers to draw up designs of a small, light-weight off-road vehicle. A number of conditions applied however. On 11 July 1940, 135 factories were approached. They had to submit their designs within eleven days. If the design was approved, the first prototype had to have been manufactured within 49 days. Only two manufacturers replied. Willys-Overland managed to get the deadlines extended. The Bantam factory was the only one to keep to the original assignment. The small factory, that constructed Austins under licence, was given an order to supply 70 complete vehicles on 25 July 1940. Eight of these vehicles had to be equipped with four-wheel drive. On 23 September, the first prototype left the factory and on

The Bantam prototypes had well-protected headlights.

The Ford prototype was practically identical to the Bantam one.

17 December, colonel (later general) Dwight D. Eisenhouwer had the other vehicles at his disposal. The first Bantam off-road vehicles were constructed from a variety of parts. The four-cylinder engine came from Continental, the three-way gearbox from Warner and the coupling from Spicer. Once the technicians at Willys had seen the Bantam, they designed a new model that looked a lot like the Bantam. Bantam accused Willys of plagiarism but the Ministry of War managed to avoid legal action being taken. Bantam was allowed to supply another 1,500 cars. The company gained in recognition during the war thanks to its Jeep trailers. On 23 November 1940, Ford also introduced a prototype of an off-road vehicle. However, this 'Pygmy'

The 'great-grandfather' of the Jeep, the Bantam. The Ministry of War had prescribed that the car had to have four-wheel drive, a wheel base of 203 cm and a maximum weight of 590 kg (1298 lb).

The Ford models had headlights behind the grill. The lights could be turned right round to provide light in the event of a breakdown.

And this is what the Jeep eventually looked like. The picture shows a Ford with a Bantam trailer.

368,000 vehicles meaning that in total more than 600,000 cars were produced. According to general George C. Marshall, the Jeep was "America's greatest contribution to modern warfare". The model has been used all over the world as a mobile machine gun post, a reconnaissance vehicle, ambulance or taxi. It was used during the Normandy landings, was driven through swamps in New-Guinea, the sand of the Sahara and the snow of Iceland. On 13 June 1950, the name Jeep was patented as a Willys-Overland trademark. Although modern Japanese off-road vehicles are often sold as Jeeps, there is only one real Jeep. The fact that the design was created originally at Bantam and not at Willys does not alter this fact.

Jeffery

also looked exactly the same as the Bantam. That is not surprising because Ford had been sent the original drawings from Bantam. Both Willys and Ford were allowed to produce 1,500 cars as well. Willys called their model the 'MA'.

The car was powered by a four-cylinder 'Go-Devils' engine. Ford called its off-road vehicle the 'GP'. Under the bonnet of this model was a 45 bhp tractor engine. The different models were continually being improved. Eventually, all the companies produced production models that would write history under the name of Jeep. Ford constructed 277,896 Jeeps. Willys and Bantam together produced more than

Thomas Jeffery was responsible for one of the best-selling American cars, the Rambler. From 1902 to his sudden death in 1910 he sold thousands of cars. When his son Charles Jeffery took over the factory, he changed the

The last Jeffery left the production line in 1917. The picture shows a Jeffery 472.

produced. During the First World War, the factory constructed more lorries than passenger cars. In 1916, Jeffery, who by now was forty years old, sold his factory to Charles Nash. Nash kept the name Jeffery on for just one year, after which the cars were sold under the name Nash.

brand's name from Rambler into Jeffery as a mark of respect for his father. In 1914, the first car bearing this name left the factory in Kenosha, Wisconsin. It was more than a Rambler with a facelift, since the vehicles could be supplied with four-cylinder or six-cylinder engines. In contrast to the Ramblers, the steering wheel was on the left-hand side of the car. In 1914, more than 10,000 passenger cars and slightly more than 4,000 lorries were

Jensen

Similarly to William Lyons (Jaguar), the brothers Alan and Richard Jensen started by constructing special bodies on existing chassis. However, whereas Lyons soon regarded the specials as a side issue, the Jensens always considered the construction of their own cars to be of secondary importance. In 1934, the first Jensen left the workshop in West Bromwich. The model

One of the first Jensen-Fords from 1934. The rear passengers entered the car via the third door on the left-hand side of the bodywork.

was based on the American Ford and was also driven by a Ford V8 engine with a capacity of 2227 or 3622 cc. However, in those days, Jensen also used the famous Nash eight-in-line engine. Jensen's speciality was a reverser gear for the differential whereby the original three-speed gearbox became a six-speed one. The convertible version was also remarkable since the rear passengers were seated behind two small windows. They were able to get into the car via a third door on the left-hand side of the bodywork. The Jensens were very popular predominantly in America. Film stars such as Clark Gable were among the company's regular clientele. Until 1938, Jensen was not permitted to present his models at the London Motor Show because his company was registered as a bodywork builder and not as a car manufacturer. It was only in 1938 that the wider public were introduced to the make. In 1939, Jensen built a couple of cars with a V12 Lincoln engine. One of these was also sold to Clark Gable. Incidentally, Clark Gable's producer also owned two Jensens, a coach with a Ford V8 engine and a smaller convertible with a Nash engine.

Jowett

Some car manufacturers stuck to certain principles no matter what it cost. In the case of Voisin, the only option was four-wheel drive, Frazer Nash remained faithful to his drive mechanism based on chains and William and Benjamin Jowett only constructed boxer engines. As early as in 1906, their first two-seater was driven by a two-cylinder boxer engine. The engine had a cylinder capacity of

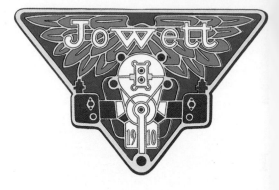

just 816 cc and after 1914, 907 cc, but produced sufficient hps to achieve a satisfactory top speed. In 1923, the factory in Bradford introduced its first model that was large enough for more than two adults. And this car also had a two-cylinder boxer engine. Jowett primarily constructed cars with small engines.

Only the J type from 1936 was an exception to this rule. This model was driven by a four-cylinder boxer engine with a capacity of 1166 cc. In 1937, the trusty twin with 907 cc was replaced by a heavier 946 cc version. The last pre-war models dating from 1940 even had a four-speed gearbox of which the highest three gears were synchronised.

Who would suspect that this high radiator concealed a two-cylinder engine? This Jowett HP7 dating from 1927 had a two-cylinder boxer engine with a capacity of 907.2 cc and a bore/stroke ratio of 75.4 x 101.5 mm.

Kissel

In 1905, George and Will Kissel built their first motorcar in Hartford, Wisconsin. It signalled the start of the 'Kissel Motor Company' that was officially set up in 1906. The cars sold well. Ten years after the company had been established, all the models on sale could be supplied with four, six or twelve-cylinder engines. Up to 1918, the company specialised in reliable and reasonably cheap passenger cars, but after 1918, the company entered the sports car market. In 1917, therefore, the Kissel brothers introduced the 'Kissel Kar Silver Special Speedster'. The model was named after its constructor, Conover T. Silver and in 1918 the 'Kissel Golden Bug' was on display at the New York Motor Show. The car was powered by a six-cylinder side-valve engine with a capacity of 4.3 litres. From 1928 onwards, clients could also opt for an eight-cylinder 4.9 litre engine. In the meantime, work was still being carried out on the passenger cars. In 1929, a new model, the White Eagle was introduced, but the approaching world-wide economic crisis made large, expensive cars difficult to sell. During that year, only 931 were sold. In 1930, sales dropped to just 93 cars. For this reason, the factory was forced to shut for good in November 1930.

The Golden Bug, which dates from 1929, was an excellent competitor of well-known makes such as Stutz or Mercer.

Knox

Harry A. Knox was the first car manufacturer to use air-cooled engines. In 1900, he set up the 'Knox Automobile Company'. In that same year he sold fifteen three-wheelers and in 1901, more than one hundred of these strange vehicles were produced. In 1902, Knox introduced a car with four wheels. In that year, more than 250 models of this car were sold. These cars were also fitted with air-cooled engines. As of 1907, the cars were driven by a cardan shaft instead of by chains. In 1908, the client could also opt, for the first time, for a water-cooled engine. Knox cars were relatively expensive and this was not conducive to sales. The company was regularly in financial difficulties.

In 1912, a petition for bankruptcy finally had to be filed. The new owner moved in 1914 to the construction of lorries, principally for the American army.

In 1900, Harry Knox constructed his first three-wheeler. The air-cooled two-cylinder engine was positioned at the rear. Note the steering rod and the giant flywheel under the vehicle.

Lagonda

At the end of the last century, Wilbur Gunnuit left his birthplace in Ohio to find his fortune in England. It was there, in 1900, that he constructed a number of motorbikes and sold them under the name 'Lagonda'. In 1904, the first Lagonda three-wheeler was constructed. The model was comparable to the old delivery bicycles with auxiliary motors.

The vehicle had two front wheels. The seat was mounted above the front axle while a second seat and the motor were located behind the rear wheel. In 1907, the first 'real' car left the factory in Stains. It was powered by a four-cylinder engine. Lagonda built both small and large cars whose high quality made then relatively expensive. Similarly to almost every make of the time, Lagonda also built sports cars. In 1910, Gunn and Bert Hammond won a race from Moscow to St. Petersburg.

In 1927, Lagonda introduced its first-passenger car with a six-cylinder engine. The engine originally had a capacity of 2692 cc, but was bored out to 3.0 litres in 1928. Moreover, it was equipped with overhead valves which was an innovation in those days. Lagonda no longer used four-cylinder engines after 1934. Motor racing became more and

The Lagonda 11 hp was a great success. The model was presented in 1913 and production continued until 1923.

The Three Litre was built between 1929 and 1934. The Maybach gearbox had eight gears.

more important for this make. Beautiful models were produced specifically for this purpose, for example the Rapier and the M45, that were introduced in 1933 at the London Motor Show. The first model had an engine with a cylinder capacity of 1104 cc and two overhead camshafts.

The M45 was powered by a 4.5 litre engine with overhead valves delivering 115 bhp, sufficient for a top speed of more than 94 mph (150 kph). Both cars won numerous races, including the 24 hour Le Mans race. Lagonda was

The six-cylinder engine with overhead valves dating from 1935 delivered 82 bhp at 3000 rpm. The top speed was around 81 mph (130 kph).

The Lagonda LG 45 was built in 1935 and 1936. The first owner of this car was the American film star Clark Gable.

This Lagonda V12 from 1938 was still with its first owner in 1996.

lucky to win the race. In the final hour, the Lagonda was overtaken by an Alfa Romeo. Over the loudspeakers, it was announced that the Alfa was now in first place, causing the driver to drive more slowly and carefully. One and a half minutes before the end came the announcement that a mistake had been made. The Alfa was a whole lap behind the Lagonda! If Louis Heldé had not slowed down he would certainly have won the race. After Walter O. Bentley

The V12 engine was designed by W.O. Bentley. The engine delivered 180 bhp at 5500 rpm.

An LG 6 Rapide from 1937. After the make Lagonda had been taken over by David Brown in 1947, he started using the same engine as in his Aston Martins.

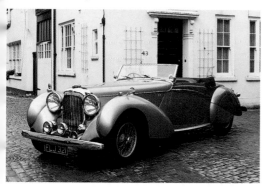

The Lagonda LG 45R did well on the various circuits.

was forced to sell his factory to Rolls-Royce he only worked at Rolls for a short time. Thereafter he became

An LG 45 during a mountain race for vintage cars.

technical director at Lagonda. He improved the existing engines and developed new models such as the LG6 and the Rapide. A new 4.5 litre V12 engine was designed specially for the Rapide. This engine was fitted with an overhead camshaft on each row of cylinders. The engine of the race version delivered, with a compression ratio of 8.8:1, around 225 bhp. At Le Mans in 1939, the Rapides finished in third and fourth place, behind a Bugatti and a Delage.

Lanchester

The English Daimler factory built the first (German) car in England but the brothers Frederick William and Fred Lanchester built the first true English car. The Lanchester had a worm wheel drive mechanism in the rear axle, a real accelerator pedal, wheels with brake drums, cantilever springs and a gearbox with a pre-select

The 1904 Lanchester was powered by a four-cylinder engine that was positioned between the front seats. There was, therefore, no real need for a bonnet.

The last real Lanchester was the 30 HP. The picture shows a car from 1929. The eight-in-line engine delivered 82 bhp at 2800 rpm.

This Lanchester dating from 1925 could be compared to a Rolls-Royce in every respect. The car had a six-cylinder engine with an overhead camshaft.

system. Moreover, the first model already looked like a real car rather than a small motorisedarriage. Production started in earnest in 1900. The car was powered by a two-cylinder engine that was positioned in the middle of the chassis. In 1904, a model with a four-cylinder engine was produced. This overhead valve engine was placed at the front of the car for the first time. The famous Forty dating from 1914 had a 6.2 litre six-cylinder engine with an overhead camshaft. The model could be compared with a Rolls-Royce in every respect, including price. Another Lanchester top model was the Thirty from 1929. The eight-cylinder engine with an overhead camshaft had a capacity of 4437 cc and delivered 82 bhp at 2800 rpm. The top speed was around 81 mph (130

kph). Due to the economic crisis, the very expensive car was difficult to sell during the '30s and the company ended up facing serious financial problems. The Lanchester brothers were eventually forced to sell their company in 1931 and the buyer was the German Daimler. The new owner tackled things in a radical way. The Lanchester factory was closed and all the parts that could not immediately be used were destroyed. The make Lanchester continued to exist but the cars were produced at Daimler from that moment on. The illustrious make of Lanchester was relegated to become a cheap version of the Daimler.

Lancia

Vincenzo Lancia liked to enjoy a good glass of wine in his favourite restaurant Gobato on the Via Superga in Turin. He loved to hold debates for hours with friends like Pinin Farina, Graaf Biscaretti or Mussolini. He

A Lancia Alfa Landaulette dating from 1908, the oldest Lancia in existence.

This Lancia Alfa Sport was built in 1908. The 2.5 litre engine delivered 28 bhp at 1500 rpm.

enjoyed listening to classical music and celebrities such as Ernest Hemingway, Erich Maria Remarque and Arturo Toscanini were some of his regular clients. However, despite his luxurious life, he also had a heart for his workers. Lancia was the first Italian entrepreneur to build rented houses and a large holiday home on the Mediterranean for his personnel. Vincenzo Lancia was born in Fobello on 24 August 1881. After he had finished attending technical school, he got a job as an accountant at Giovanni Ceirano's car factory in Turin. Shortly afterwards he moved to F.I.A.T. where he was employed as a test driver. He also raced on behalf of this company and with considerable success. In 1900, Lancia was already one of the best racing drivers in the world. In 1906, he established the 'Lancia & Co Fabbrica Automobili' together with his friend Cloudio Fogolin. In 1907, the company introduced its first prototype. Shortly after that, this model was succeeded by the famous Lancia Alfa. The car was powered by a 2.5 litre four-cylinder engine which delivered 28 bhp at 1800 rpm. The power was transmitted to the rear axle via a cardan shaft. The Lancia

The Lambda gave Lancia world-wide fame. Nine series of the model were built. The picture shows a Lambda from 1928 which was part of the eighth series.

Lambda, dating from 1922, represented the make's real breakthrough. The car had a self-supporting body which had been patented by Lancia and independent front wheel suspension with telescope springs. No fewer than 23,501 Lambdas were sold up to 1934. All the cars were powered by the revolutionary V4 engine with an overhead camshaft. The 2120 cc engines in the cars from the first series delivered 49 bhp at 3250 rpm. The engines used in the ninth and last series had a cylinder capacity of 2570 cc and delivered 69 bhp. Lancia built a lot of famous models.

The Lambda was powered by a V4 engine whose cylinders were positioned at an angle of just thirteen degrees.

The chassis of the Astura was the basis for some very beautiful creations. The car in the picture was fitted with a body by Pinin Farina in 1939.

The Dilambda had a V8 engine with a capacity of 3960 cc which delivered 100 bhp at 4000 rpm.

Lancia always built large and small cars simultaneously. The small Artena (1931-1936) had a wheel base of 295 cm and was powered by a 1924 cc four-cylinder engine.

The Lambda was the first model in which the cylinders were positioned in a V shape. All previous models had been fitted with four-cylinder engines. The Theta (1913-1918) and the Kappa (1919-1922) were even fitted with side-valve engines, but all subsequent models had engines with overhead valves. The Dikappa (1921-1922) was the only model not to have an overhead camshaft. The Trikappa (1922-1925) was powered by a V8 engine, as was the Dilamba (1929-1935) and the Astura (1931-1939). All other models were fitted with the famous V4 engine. Similarly to most Italian makes, Lancia also sold a lot of rolling chassis. Famous

The Lancia Augusta (1933-1936) had a top speed of around 62 mph (100 kph).

The Ardea was the last pre-war design. This adapted Aprilia was, incidentally, the smallest Lancia that has ever been built. It was just 364 cm long.
Even a modern Lancia Y is almost 10 centimetres longer!

bodywork builders like Pinin Farina, Zagato, Bertone and Touring were able to indulge themselves. The Aprilia was the last model developed under the management of Vincenzo Lancia. The famous Italian died from a heart attack on 15 February 1937 at the age of 56. The Aprilia and its little brother, the Ardea, were far ahead of their time. The most striking features were the doors without a central jamb. This made getting in and out a lot easier.

There was no central jamb between the doors of the Aprilia (1937-1949), making getting in and out a lot easier.

Some of the most beautiful bodies ever created were built on Aprilia chassis. The Aërodynamica by Pinin Farina was produced between 1937 and 1939.

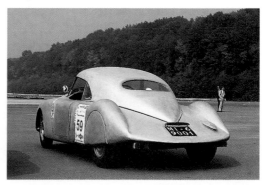

to the old engine being taken out of production. Later, cars were supplied with four-cylinder engines with capacities of between 1.7 and 2.7 litres.

La Ponette

From 1909 to 1925, the company 'S.A. des Autos La Ponette' was established on the Route de Versailles in Saint Rémy, Chevreuse. The owner and founder, Georges Granvaud, started with the production of so-called cycle cars. The two-seaters were powered by a 827 cc single-cylinder engine delivering 7 bhp. Power was transmitted by means of a cardan shaft instead of chains. In 1912, the cars could be supplied with a Ballot four-cylinder engine. These side-valve engines were a lot more reliable than the single-cylinder ones and this led, in 1913,

La Salle

The make La Salle was part of the Cadillac group and produced cars of the same excellent quality. The Cadillacs of the period still looked fairly conservative and that was exactly what clients wanted! The bodies of the cheaper and sportier La Salle were designed by the famous designer Harley Earl. The first La Salle was introduced on 5 March 1927. It was clear that Earl had been inspired by the attractive design of European motorcars like the Hispano-Suiza. The name La Salle was, incidentally, taken from René Robert de la Salle, the French explorer who had discovered the state of Louisiana. Various models were being supplied as early as in 1927. The most expensive version was the Imperial Sedan which costs $2,875, $120 less than the cheapest Cadillac. Most of the parts for La Salle came from Cadillac. The 5.0 litre engines were also completely

In 1931, clients could choose from a wide range of accessories. For example, a heater cost $41, two exterior mirrors cost $10 and fog lamps on the front bumper cost between $37 and $75.

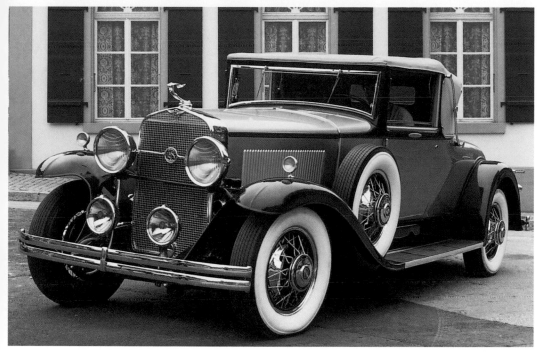

interchangeable. Along with all other car manufacturers, La Salle also suffered as a result of the world-wide economic crisis. In 1930, 14,986 cars were sold, but by 1931 that number had dropped to 10,098, in 1932 to 3,386 and in 1933 only 3,482 cars were sold. General Motors then wanted to discontinue the make. It is only thanks to Harley Earl that this did not happen. Earl designed new bodies and devised a way of producing the cars more cheaply. He replaced the Cadillac V8 engine with a cheaper eight-in-line Oldsmobile one. This meant that the sales price could be lowered in 1934. Nevertheless, despite this drop in price, only 7,195 cars were sold. In 1935, the

White-walled tyres were all the rage in the Twenties. The picture shows a La Salle from 1929 with a 5.0 litre V8 Cadillac engine.

In 1929, sidelights were for the first time mounted on the mudguards. At the time, this four-seater coupé cost $2,495.

Harley Earl designed a variety of modern and sporty bodies. The picture shows a La Salle from 1936.

In 1940, the last La Salle left the production line. The picture shows a Special Convertible Coupé from the same year.

prices were lowered once again. Sales rose to 8,851 cars. In 1937, La Salle cars were once again fitted with Cadillac V8 engines, but when only 10,382 cars were sold in 1940, Cadillac decided to discontinue the make altogether.

Laurin & Klement

Vaclav Klement and Vaclav Laurin started a bicycle repair workshop in 1896. It was only a short while later that they started to build their own two-wheelers which were sold under

the name Slavia. At the time there was a huge demand for bicycles. In 1898, a larger factory was built in Mlada Boleslav. A year later, the company started with the production of motor-cycles and in 1905 the first car was introduced under the name Laurin & Klement. The vehicles were powered by water-cooled, two-cylinder V engines with capacities of 1100 or 1400 cc. In 1907, the first cars with four-cylinder engines left the factory and in the same year, the first eight-cylinder version was introduced at the car show in Berlin. Only a few of the 'K models' were built, but the smaller models sold like hot cakes. In 1907, the company employed more than 500 people. The Laurin & Klement make also invested a great deal of money in racing and not

A Laurin & Klement 100 from 1925. The four-cylinder engine had a capacity of 1794 cc and delivered 20 bhp.

In 1911, Laurin & Klement produced cars with two-cylinder and four-cylinder engines.

The first Laurin & Klement was presented as the Type A in 1905. The two-cylinder engine had a capacity of 1100 cc.

Laurin & Klement
Voiturette Typ A
Baujahr 1905
Hubraum 1100 cm³
Zylinderzahl 2
2-sitzig / 680 kg

In 1925, cars like this Laurin & Klement 110 offered little comfort for the winter months.

without success. In 1908, an FC model broke the speed record of the time at the Brooklands circuit by averaging a speed of 74.2 mph (118.72 kph). But this was only the beginning. The cars won various long-distance races, such as the 'Prinz-Heinrich Fahrt' in 1909 and the race from Moscow to Riga in 1911. Between 1908 and 1911, the make won no less than 57 first prizes, 25 second prizes and 11 third prizes. In 1912, Laurin & Klement took over the RAF motorcar factory. This made them the largest car manufacturer in Austria. At the start of the First World War, export figures plummeted. The company had to switch to the production of army vehicles. After the war, the town of Mlada Boleslav was no longer in Austria but was part of the new republic of Czechoslovakia.

During the first few years, production was hardly affected, but there was new competition from the manufacturers Tatra and Praga. In order to strengthen the position on the internal market, the company merged with Skoda in 1925. Up until 1928, the cars were sold as Laurin & Klement-Skoda. Thereafter, the words Laurin & Klement were dropped. Once again, an illustrious make had disappeared from the market for ever.

Léon Bollée

Léon Bollée built his first horse-less vehicle in 1895. He called the vehicle a 'Voiturette'. The three-wheeler was powered by a 650 cc single-cylinder engine that drove the rear wheels. In 1898, Bollée developed his first motorcar with four wheels. He sold the production rights for this design to Alexandre Darracq for 250,000 francs.

A new Voiturette followed in 1901 but in the meantime the demand for small cars had fallen considerably. Because the customer is always right, Bollée built his first large car in 1902 and large really meant large to Bollée. The cars were powered by a four-cylinder engine with capacities ranging to no less than 8.0 litres. In 1907, a model was even introduced with an 11.9 litre six-cylinder engine. Bollée sold between 150 and 350 cars a year which ofcourse is nothing to get that excited about. In 1910, for example, De Dion-Bouton sold as many as 3,000 cars a year and Renault even sold more than 5,000. Bollée died in 1913 but was not forgotten. In his home town of Le Mans, a special monument was erected

After the take-over by Sir William Morris in 1924, the cars were sold under the name Morris Léon Bollée.

The Morris Léon Bollée from 1927 strongly resembled the English Morris. The model had been designed in France however.

to him and in Paris a street was named after him. In 1924, the company 'Automobiles Léon Bollée' was taken over by Sir William Morris. From that time onwards the company was known as 'Morris Motors Ltd., Usines Léon Bollée'. Of course, the French branch started to produce English models, such as the Cowley. However, the cars were fitted with French Hotchkiss engines. In 1928, a model with a 3.0 litre eight-in-line engine appeared and from 1929 onwards, English six-cylinder engines were included in the French cars. During the years of financial crisis, Morris sold his French company. A few more cars were produced under the name Léon Bollée up to 1933 but thereafter the make disappeared from the market altogether.

Leyat

During the First World War, Marcel Leyat worked as an engineer with the airforce. During this period, he designed the first prototype of the so-called 'Hélica'. The 'aircraft without wings' was built on the Quai de Grenelle in Paris. Between 1919 and 1925, he managed to sell 30 of the vehicles.The Hélica was made primarily of plywood.

The passengers sat behind each other, as in an aircraft. The vehicle was steered using the rear wheels. The propeller was powered by an 8 bhp Scorpion engine. The entire vehicle weighed just 250 kg (550 lb) and was therefore dangerously fast.

In 1927, a Hélica achieved a top speed of no less than 106 mph (170 kph) at the Monthéry circuit. Leyat continued to experiment with his Hélica. He tried using propellers with two and four blades and even produced a coupé version.

This Hélica was on display at the motorcar exhibition in Geneva in 1997. Whether the car still worked is not known.

The Hélica was steered using the rear wheels. Brakes were fitted to the front wheels. The picture shows a Hélica from 1922.

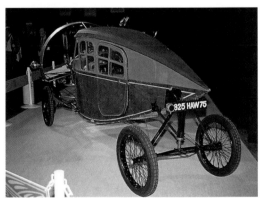

Engineer Leyat (at the front) during a demonstration drive in Paris.

Le Zèbre

Jules Salomon worked as an engineer at Unic. In his spare time he designed a small car with a single-cylinder engine. Unic was not interested in the project but did offer to assist with building a prototype. The car was financed by Jacques Bizet and Henri de Rothschild. They made sufficient funds

available for several dozen cars to be built. This led to the birth of the new make, 'Le Zèbre', in 1909. When Unic no longer had any space for the production of the small car, the partners decided to build a new factory in Puteaux. Only then did production really start in earnest. In 1912, more than 1,000 Zèbres were sold. Each car was fitted with a 600 cc single-cylinder engine. In 1912, two models with four-cylinder engines were introduced. However, these were still small and above all cheap cars. The cars sold so well that the factory soon became too small and the company moved to Suresnes in 1913. During the First World War, Jules Salomon left to join Citroën. There he developed the successful 5 CV. Meanwhile the Zèbre factory was becoming more and more susceptible to competition from cheaper makes such as Renault and Citroën. Before

the war, the Zèbre had been an authority in the field, but the situation changed radically after the war. Demand for cheap cars was so high that factories were mushrooming out of the ground all over the place. Companies such as Clément-Bayard, Peugeot, Sizaire and Naudin and Grégoire managed to acquire large numbers of clients. When Jacques Bizet committed suicide in 1922, things went from bad to worse for Le Zèbre. In 1925, the company introduced a large car with a 2.0 litre four-cylinder side-valve engine and brakes on all four wheels. This model continued to be available until 1931. However, in the same year, the factory was forced to close.

With more than 800 cars produced, Le Zèbre was one of the largest car manufacturers in France in 1912.

This Le Zèbre was built by Unic in 1909. A year later, cars were being built in a separate Le Zèbre factory.

In 1912, Le Zèbre presented a car with a four-cylinder engine.

Lincoln

Rolls-Royce and Daimler meant to England just as much as Lincoln and Cadillac to America. The fact that both these American makes had so much in common was no coincidence since they were both founded by Henry Leland. Henry Martyn Leland, known to his friends as 'Uncle Henry', was born on 16 February 1843 in Danville, Vermont. When he was nine years old he started his career as a shoeshine boy.

Ten years later he was working as a designer in a weapons factory. In 1890, Leland started a small machine factory in Detroit which built, among other things, engines for Oldsmobile. Next door, he set up a new company called 'Cadillac Motor Car Company'. In 1909, this company was taken over by General Motors. Leland and his son Wilfred continued to be employed by GM until 1917. In that same year they started their own factory for aircraft engines. The Ministry of War ordered no fewer than 6,000 engines and loaned the Lelands the tidy sum of 10 million dollars for the new company. Unfortunately for the Lelands, however, the war only lasted two years. The demand for engines plummeted and father and son found themselves in serious financial difficulties.

By now Leland was 77 years old and he and his son decided to develop a passenger car. Their business, the 'Lincoln Motor Company' introduced its first model on 20 September 1920. That same year around 834 cars were sold. The models were driven by a 5.4

A model L Lincoln from 1929. Under the long bonnet was a magnificently finished V8 engine. The car in the picture was fitted with a special Dual Phaeton body whereby the rear passengers sat in their own compartment and behind their own window.

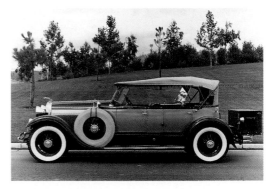

A car for heads of state. The Lincoln KB with its 7340 cc V12 engine offered space for seven passengers.

The bodywork of this Lincoln from 1931 was built by the famous bodywork builder Le Baron. The 'dickey seat' was large enough for two passengers.

litre V8 engine, the careful construction of which meant that it delivered no less than 81 bhp. When well over 3,000 had been sold, the Lelands found themselves once again in financial difficulties. Henry Ford took over the company for around 8 million dollars. In addition, he voluntarily gave his old friend and his son cheques for $635,000 and $325,000 respectively. Under Ford's management, the Lincolns were built with the same care

In 1938, the factory built another 416 K model cars. The car in the picture was driven by a V12 engine.

With his Zephyr, John Tjaarda saved the Lincoln make from disaster. The car was available with a variety of bodies. This picture shows the cheapest version from 1939, a six-person coupé.

This Lincoln Zephyr dating from 1939 was still as good as new in 1995. It had just 20,000 kilometres on the clock.

Raymond Loewy, the designer of the post-war Studebakers, the Coca-Cola bottle and the inside of NASA's Skylab, had this Continental built according to his own design.

as before. In 1922, Henry's son Edsel became company president. He managed to sell no less than 5,512 cars in that same year. The sales figures continued to rise despite the fact that the car was largely hand-made. In 1926, a record was broken with the production of 8,858 cars. The world-wide financial crisis also left its mark on the Lincoln company, however, and in 1933 only 2,002 cars were sold. Henry Leland died on 26 March 1932, the year in which the Lincoln KB was introduced.

Up to then, all the cars had been driven by V8 engines, but the new model had a V12 engine. With a cylinder capacity of 7.2 litres and delivering 150 bhp, the heavy car had a top speed of 100 mph (160 kph). The V8 engine was still being used in KA models.

In 1933, 13 different versions of the KA were available and there were no less than 23 versions of the KB. The cheapest Lincoln was a two-door KA type roadster. It cost $2,700. The most expensive car was a twelve-cylinder KN, costing $7,000. These were high prices in a time in which Ford was selling V8 sedans for just $500. In

1924, president Calvin Coolidge decided to purchase a Lincoln and from that time onwards Lincolns have been the White House's favoured cars. Despite such effective publicity, too few were sold. Ford was just about to close the factory when the Dutch designer John Tjaarda designed the small and inexpensive Lincoln Zephyr.

In actual fact, the model had nothing in common with the 'real' Lincoln. It was the first American production car with a self-supporting body, but it was attractive and modern. The Zephyr was driven by a V12 engine and cost just $1,275. The 4.4 litre V12

In 1940, Lincoln presented the Continental. The model was supposed to look European and that was why the spare wheel was located at the rear on the boot lid.

engine was based on the cheap Ford V8 engine. All the mechanical parts were taken from this engine which is why the V12 could be constructed relatively cheaply. During 1936, the first year of production, 14,994 Zephyrs were sold and in 1937 sales even rose to 29,997 cars. In 1939, the last Lincoln K series left the factory. The model was succeeded in 1940 by a new showpiece, namely the Continental. And this model also became an absolute hit. The Continental was designed by Eugene Gregorie.

It had a typical 'continental look', which included the spare wheel being mounted on the spacious boot. On 11 February 1942, Lincoln also switched to the production of army vehicles. A total of 145,000 Jeep bodies, 25,332 tank engines and 24,929 engine pods for B-24 bombers were produced.

Lohner-Porsche

When he was 23 years old, Ferdinand Porsche worked at the Bela Egger company which produced electric engines. In 1898, he was bought off by the famous bodywork builder Ludwig Lohner. Because the company had supplied carriages to the Austrian emperor, it was allowed to call itself 'K & K Royal Coach Company Jakob Lohner & Co.'.

Lohner had been interested in horse-less vehicles for a long time. He had even had a number of cars built with petrol engines imported from France. He nevertheless saw more advantages in the production of electric engines, which is why he had taken on Ferdinand Porsche.

A Lohner-Porsche dating from 1900.

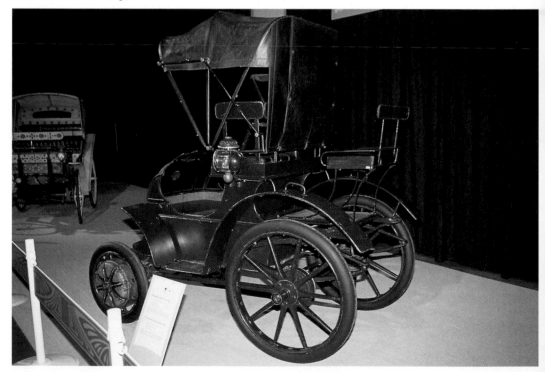

Porsche had developed engines for his previous employer which could be mounted in the wheel hub. This design made a cardan shaft or chains unnecessary.

The result of the partner-ship was the Lohner-Porsche. The car was driven by two 2.5 bhp electric engines in the front wheels. The model was the main attraction at the World Fair in 1900.

With its 90 volt batteries, the car had a top speed of 31 mph (50 kph). If you drove carefully, the batteries would provide power for around three hours. Porsche and Lohner also built the first so-called 'hybrid'. This was a car with batteries that were charged by a dyna-mo that was driven by a petrol engine. Porsche worked with Lohner until 1905. During that time they primarily produced large lorries and tractors with electric motors in one or two wheel hubs.

Lorraine-Dietrich

The company 'Dietrich and Cie' in Lunéville had a reputation as a manufacturer of railway materials. In 1896, however, the board of directors decided to start building cars. The first three-wheeler was designed by Amédée Bollée, the older brother of Léon Bollée. Shortly afterwards, the young Ettore Bugatti was commissioned to design a few models for the new make.

The small and large cars designed by Bugatti were driven by two, four and six-cylinder engines. In 1909, customers were able to choose from no less than nine different models. The Dietrich company invested a great deal in racing. The racing cars had enormous

A Lorraine-Dietrich from 1911 with wheels with wooden spokes and brakes on the rear wheels.

The Lorraine-Dietrich B-3-6 from 1929 was a spacious five-seater, without any luggage space. The can of spare petrol therefore had to be placed on the running-board.

It is unbelievable but true - this huge car dating from 1912 was driven by a two-cylinder engine.

A B-3-6 Lorraine-Dietrich from 1929 had a six-cylinder engine with a capacity of 3436 cc. The overhead-valve engine delivered approximately 50 hp.

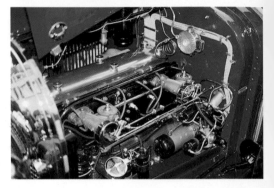

engines and were specially designed for the purpose. In 1905, a Dietrich appeared at the start of the Gordon-Bennet race. The car was driven by a four-cylinder engine with a capacity of no less than 17,012 cc. This capacity was still surpassed by the 17,657cc engine of the Locomobile. During the Gordon-Bennet race, the Dietrich achieved an average speed of almost 44 mph (70 kph) over a distance of 550 kilometres, but the car still only finished in sixth place. The race was won by a Bassier with a 22,259 cc engine. In 1923 the 24-hour Le Mans race was organised for the first time. The Dietrichs featured in this race too. In 1925, the duo of Gérard de Courcelles/André Rossignol won the race with an average speed of 58 mph (93.08 kph). In the following year, first prize again went to a Lorraine-Dietrich and for the first time the average speed barrier of 100 kph (62 mph) was broken. In 1905, the car's name was changed to Lorraine-Dietrich. From that time onwards the cross of Lotharingen was mounted on the massive radiator. The company never produced small cars. The model with the smallest engine was the A4 10/12 CV type dating from 1923. The A4 had a four-cylinder overhead valve engine with a capacity of 2296 cc and delivering 50 bhp. All the other models had six-cylinder engines with capacities of 3446 cc (model B3-6 15 CV, 1921-1932) or 6104 cc (D2-6 30 CV, 1919-1927). The factory also produced V12 engines, for the first time in 1919 and later again in 1931.

However, neither model progressed further than prototype stage. Like everyone else, during the crisis years Lorraine-Dietrich had to endure difficult times. It was very difficult to sell the expensive cars. In 1934, it was decided to halt production. The concern focused once again on the construction of railway materials and tank and aircraft engines.

Marmon

Indianapolis owes its fame to its annual 500-mile race, held for the first time in 1911. The winner Ray Harround drove a car built by Howard Marmon. Harround covered the 800 km in 6 hours, 42 minutes and 8 seconds, at an average speed of 74.59 mph (119.344 kph). He was given $10,000 for this victory and this provided a great deal of free publicity for Marmon.

Howard Marmon studied at Berkeley University in California. In 1902, the twenty-three year old engineer built his first car. The Marmon company was situated on Kentucky Avenue in Indianapolis. The cars were really something special. The first model had an air-cooled V2-engine with overhead valves and a cardan shaft. The second car was powered by a V4-engine. In 1905, this was followed by a V6-engine, and, in 1908, even a V8. In the early years, all the engines were air-cooled overhead-valve engines. The first cars were sold to friends and acquaintances, but the clientele soon grew.

Especially the models with V4-engines, such as the 1910 Marmon 32, sold well. The models had an aluminium body and a water-cooled, four-cylinder engine. The gearbox was installed close to the differential gear, resulting in better weight distribution. Not only was the bodywork made of aluminium,

The interior of the 75. Judging by its size, a hand brake was still very important in 1927.

This five-seater version of the Marmon 75 from 1927 was powered by a 5566 cc six-cylinder engine that delivered 84 bhp.

The Little Marmon was only built in 1927. The 3115 cc eight-in-line overhead-valve engine delivered 64 bhp at 3200 rpm.

Marmon was an expensive make and that also applied to the 74, such as this one, which was delivered in 1925. As a seven-seater tourer this car cost $3,165.

this modern material was also used for various engine parts, such as the engine block, cylinder head, crankcase, water pump and radiator. The Marmon Wasp was built on the chassis of the 32. This racing car that was sprayed yellow and won the 1911 Indianapolis race. In 1912, Marmon launched the

Howard Marmon used a great deal of aluminium. This was clearly visible when you opened up the Sixteen's bonnet.

Marmon 48, its first model with a water-cooled six-cylinder engine. It was a large car with a 368 cm wheel base. Most of these cars seated seven grownups. In 1914, the last Marmon with a four-cylinder engine was manufactured.

Meanwhile, the company had become well-known as a manufacturer of luxury motorcars and cars in this price-range were expected to have at least a six-cylinder engine. The model 34 was introduced in 1916. This car also had a six-cylinder engine.

The engine was continuously improved, increasing its power from 74 bhp in 1916 to 84 bhp in 1924. In 1925, the 34 was succeeded by the Marmon 74. The engine had not changed much, only the details of the model had been adjusted. Howard Marmon had always been content with low production figures.

The large Marmon Sixteen had a 368 cm wheel base. The model was available in eight different body versions. The picture shows a 1931 four-door convertible.

Not till 1926, were over 3,512 cars were sold in one year. The low sales figures were caused by the fact that the cars were relatively expensive. The cheapest model was the 74 Speedster which cost $3,295. The most expensive limousine cost no less than $3,900. Compare: in that year, a T-Ford only cost $260.

From 1917 onwards, Marmon only had one model, which was of course available in countless versions. The 1927 range only featured Little Marmon. The car cost between $1,795 and $1,895. This gave the customer a 64 bhp eight-cylinder engine and a chassis with a 332 cm wheel base.

The Little Marmon was a great success. In the first year, 10,095 were sold. In 1927, this number had increased to 14,770, and in 1928 even to 22,323. In 1928, the range consisted of three basic models, including the 68 which had a 42 bhp engine, and the 78 which had a 86 bhp eight-in-line engine. In 1931, Marmon launched a car with an 8.0

litre V16-engine at the New York motor show. Despite its price, which was over $5,000, the model was sold until 1933. But the depression was immanent. American industry suffered and sharp blows also fell at Marmon.

In 1930, only 12,369 cars were sold, and in 1932 this number fell to 1,365. When it could only manufacture 86 cars in 1933, the company was forced to close down.

Marquette

It is no disgrace to never have heard of this make, because despite the fact that it was a General Motors' product, the total number sold was a meagre 35,007. The car was introduced as model 1930 on 1 June 1929. In America, it was distributed via the Buick dealer network. For that matter, the Marquette

Although the Marquette was only manufactured in 1929, all the cars are from the 1930 range.

car. The timing for the launch of the Marquette make was all wrong. Due to the impending depression, business in Detroit was not what it used to be. After less than a year, the make was already discontinued.

General Motors was not satisfied with the sales figures and in January 1930 they put a stop to production. Which was an unfortunate step, because they were good cars for areasonable price.

Martini

The Martini logo depicts a gun which is convincing evidence that the company produced weapons. The decision to start manufacturing motorcars as well was not made until late last century. The first Martini left the Swiss factory in 1897.

Switzerland never played an important part in the manufacture of passenger cars, but this make became a household name in Switzerland. It started out small. Until 1900, only one car was built each year. In 1898, it was still a

was also manufactured at the Buick factory in Flint, Michigan, although cheaper parts were used. The six-cylinder engine, for instance, was a 3491 cc side-valve engine which delivered 67 bhp at 3000 rpm. The car's wheel base was 290 cm and it had 18 inch wheels.

The Marquette was available in six different versions. Prices ranged from $990 for a two-seater business coupe, up to $1,060 for a five-seater passenger

racing cars. In 1904, they were very successful in hill climbs in Switzerland, Italy and France. Anyone who has ever driven in the Alps in a modern car can imagine how difficult it must have been to drive over 3,000 km through the mountains in those days. Martini built a special Voiturette, the Sport Spéciale, for the 1913 Tour de France.

This model was powered by a four-cylinder engine with an overhead camshaft, and four valves for each cylinder. Still, this impressive car failed to win the 5,000 km race. In the same

'Vis-à-Vis', but the engine in the car that rolled off the assembly line of the factory in Frauenfeld in 1899 was already mounted in the front of the car. 'Mass production' started in 1902. In that year no less than thirty cars were built. The cars had a V4-engine that delivered 10 or 16 bhp. Just like most other factories, Martini also built

Before the First World War, Martini mainly built racing cars. The picture shows a 1908 Voiturette.

The FU had a 3.1 litre six-cylinder side-valve engine. The engine delivered 55 bhp in 1927, and as much as 70 bhp in 1932.

year, Martini sold a total of 276 motor-cars. They were available as a rolling chassis or as complete cars. At that time there were 265 employees on the payroll.In 1903, the company moved from Frauenfeld to Saint-Blaise. Beautiful and sturdy cars were built in this new factory and exported to many countries. After the First World War, Martini faced hard times.

American and German cars were sold at such low prices that Martini could not compete. In 1919, the Swiss built the TF model, with a 3.8 litre four-cylinder side-valve engine. This model was to remain in production until 1927. In that same year, Martini switched to using six-cylinder engines only. New

In 1932, the last Martini model the NF was sold as a rolling chassis for which Reinbold & Christie of Basle created bodywork.

Nowadays such an advertisement would have the opposite effect.

Due to its thorough finishing the price of a Martini was prohibitive and this made it completely unsuitable for export during the depression. The picture shows a 1932 FU.

models were launched, such as the FU (1927-1931), the KM (1930-1932), and the NF (1932-1934). The Swiss market for expensive, luxury motorcars was limited and due to the high cost price of these (fastidiously) thoroughly built cars, export was out of the question. Martini tried to acquire new clients with its KM model. The car had a cheap engine, a Wanderer developed under licence. It had a 2540 cc and according to the factory the overhead-valve engine delivered 50 bhp at 3000 rpm.

The KM model was a relatively small car, with a wheel base of only 300 cm. Because the demand for this car remained limited, the factory found itself in increasing financial trouble.

The NF was its final model and technically its best. The 4379 cc engine delivered 95 bhp. A synchronised four-speed gearbox, mounted behind the engine, drove the rear wheels. Its hydraulic brakes and suspension meant the car was ahead of its time.

Maserati

The Officina Alfieri Maserati was founded in Bologna on 14 December 1914 by the brothers Alfieri, Ettore, Bindo and Ernesto Maserati. The four brothers were licensed by Isotta Fraschini, and were soon renowned as specialists in tuning cars of this make. In 1926, Diatto ordered Maserati to design a Grand Prix car, but when this company went bankrupt before the car was delivered and paid for, the brothers decided to rename the model Maserati Tipo 26. The number 26 referred to the year in which it was built. The Tipo 26 had a beautiful eight-cylinder engine. On 25 April 1926, Alfieri Maserati won his class with a

In the twenties, the famous Italian racing driver Luigi Fagioli raced this Tipo 26.

Tipo at the Targa Florio in Sicily. As was common in those days, the car could be used both as a racing car and as a tourer. Before the Second World War, Maserati only built racing cars. The Tipo 26 was the only model that could seat two adults.

This sports/racing car was powered by a 1.5 litre eight-in-line engine. In 1927, the engine was bored out to 1980 cc, creating the Tipo 26B. Ten cars were built in the first series, and 9 in the second. An exception was the prototype of a four-seater car that was introduced in 1939. The model was

Evidence for the fact that a Tipo 26 had two seats. The car in the picture still regularly enters classic car races.

The dashboard of a Tipo 26. A mileometer was not needed yet.

The dashboard of a Tipo 26. A mileometer was not needed yet.

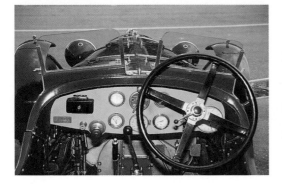

Maxwell

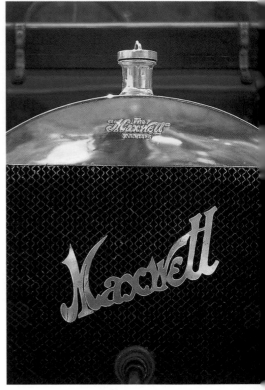

highly successful, and won the Indianapolis 500 in 1939 and 1940. Very few factories managed to subsist on nothing but racing cars. Maserati was no exception in this respect. When the brothers discovered that their hobby was not generating enough income, it was already too late.

In 1938, they were forced to sell their company. The new owner, Omar Orsi demanded that the brothers continue to work for him for ten years. Only in 1947 were they able to move to Bologna where they founded the make OSCA.

The superb engine of the Tipo 26: a 1493 cc, eight-in-line engine with two overhead camshafts, a compressor, which delivered 115 bhp at 5300 rpm and had a top speed of 100 mph (160 kph).

Benjamin Briscoe and Jonathan Maxwell owned a small car factory in Tarrytown or rather Maxwell built the cars and Briscoe financed them. The first Maxwell was introduced to the public in 1903. The model was not really special. The two-seater runabout was powered by a two-cylinder engine. The car was not particularly beautiful either, but it was fast. It was not surprising that a Maxwell won several races with it in New York state, where the company was located. In the early days, production was limited. In the first year, 632 cars rolled off the assembly line. In 1905, this number had risen to 3,000 and in 1909, it had even risen to 9,000. Along with Reo, Fort and Durant, Maxwell was one of the four largest American makes. In 1912, far too much money was invested in the

The Maxwell Runabout of 1911, an open two-seater, had a two-cylinder engine and a two-speed gearbox. The model, which was only available in red, cost $500.

This Maxwell also became available in 1911. The model Q Tourer was powered by a four-cylinder engine which delivered 25 bhp.

development of a new model. There was hardly any money left, whereupon Maxwell decided to withdraw from the company. Briscoe continued on his own. Walter Flanders, president of the Flanders Motor Car Company, took over the lead of the Maxwell factory. Cheap cars were manufactured under his management including the Mascotte and the Mercury. The cars were powered by four-cylinder engines. The manufacture of trucks proved more profitable. In 1917, the company manufactured over 100,000 vehicles in total. In 1923, the Maxwell make was sold to Walter P. Chrysler for 15 million dollars. No less than eight

different models were now available. But when, in 1925, Chrysler noticed that selling a Chrysler with a six-cylinder engine was a much simpler task than selling a Maxwell with a four-cylinder engine, he discontinued production. Chrysler subsequently developed its own four-cylinder engine, which was installed in the Plymouth as of 1928.

Maybach

After the Second World War, the Allies prohibited the Germans from building aircraft. Famous manufacturers, such as Ernst Heinkel, Willy Messerschmitt and Fritz Fend then decided to start manufacturing small cars. After the First World War, Karl Maybach had done the same thing. As the son of the famous Wilhelm Maybach the designer of the first Daimler-Benz cars, Karl Maybach also opted for a future in engineering. Before the First World War, he built engines for Count Zeppelin's airships. When the 1918 Versailles Treaty prohibited this, he switched to manufacturing engines for motorcars, locomotives and ships. One of his first customers was the Dutch car manufacturer Spyker. In 1920, this company purchased roughly 150 Maybach engines. The same year, a Spyker with a Maybach engine broke a record over a distance of 30,000 km.

Maybach sold most of its cars as a rolling chassis. Nearly all the cars were equipped with superstructures by bodywork builder Spohn. The picture shows a 1937 Maybach SW 38.

This SW 38 was sold to the Director of Hoechst AG in May 1938. The body was built by the Spohn firm. The car cost RM 20,285.

Most Zeppelins were provided with bodywork by Spohn. However, the car in the picture was finished by the firm Dörr und Schreck.

Despite this success the company failed to sell its engines to other customers, hence Maybach's decision to start manufacturing cars itself. In 1921, an initial prototype was introduced at the Berlin car show. The model was called the Maybach W3. The car had a 5.7 litre, six-cylinder engine, with 275 Nm/1000 rpm torque which delivered 70 bhp at 2200 rpm. The gearbox had only two speeds, the first of which was only used uphill. Up to 1928, some 700 rolling chassis of the W3 were sold. Its successors, the W5 and the W5 SG were powered by a 7.0 litre engine. The letters SG stood for Schnell-Gang,

This Maybach Zeppelin was built in 1939 by order of Prince Von Waldeck.

The Zeppelin had a comprehensive and beautifully finished dashboard.

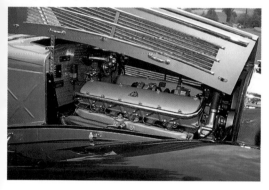

The powerful V12-engine of this Zeppelin delivered 200 bhp at 3000 rpm. Its top speed was approximately 109 mph (175 kph).

The Maybach even managed to have to appear on a Republic of Upper-Volta stamp in 1936.

which meant overdrive. Thanks to its extraordinarily high torque and the fact that it delivered 120 bhp, the indestructible six-cylinder engine was also highly suitable for trucks, buses and small ships. Between 1921 and 1941, Maybach only built 2,095 cars, 1,755 of which were equipped with a six-cylinder engine. The latter version of the Maybach was soon nicknamed the German Rolls-Royce. The cars were exceptionally expensive and very heavy (almost 3000 kg/6600 lb). Due to its weight the car could only be driven in Germany with a truck driving licence, but this did not bother the true Maybach-lover who usually had a driver anyway. In the mid-twenties, Maybach's mission to build engines for

airships was renewed. The legendary Graaf Zeppelin airship was created, powered by five Maybach V12- engines each delivering 550 bhp. The airship covered a distance of almost 1.7 million km between Europe and South-America. Maybach was now experienced enough to be able to make the engines suitable for cars too. This technical miracle was introduced in 1929 as the Maybach 12.

Because the engine largely consisted of aluminium, the powerful 7.0 litre engine only weighed 510 kg, (1122 lb), but delivered 150 bhp at 2800 rpm. In one year alone, 125 were sold. It was then followed by the Maybach Zeppelin DS 7 and DS 8, with their

turned eighty. Maybach died on 6 February 1960, the year in which Daimler-Benz took over the company.

Mercedes-Benz

seven and eight litre engines. These extremely expensive cars were primarily supplied as rolling chassis. This version of the Maybach cost 17,300 Reichsmark. For a complete Pullman-Limousine the customer had to pay RM 24,300. In comparison: an Opel Six with a 2.0 litre engine and Pullman body was already available for RM 5,000. In the mid-thirties, the popularity of this kind of expensive, luxury models came permanently to an end. Customers now mainly bought the smaller models which the owners drove themselves.

Maybach also followed this trend. The factory introduced a smaller model, the SW 35. The number referred to its cylinder capacity. The car was powered by a 3435 cc six-cylinder overhead-valve engine that delivered 140 bhp at 4500 rpm. The car weighed 1300 kg (2860 lb), and had a top speed of 87 mph (140 kph).

In 1936, it was succeeded by the SW 38 which had a 3817 cc engine and the last model of this series was introduced in 1939, the HL 42, with a 4197 cc six-cylinder engine that delivered 140 hp. Maybach celebrated its fiftieth anniversary in 1959 and Karl Maybach

It is a generally acknowledged fact that Mr. Daimler and Mr. Benz built the first usable cars, although the French still feel that their Delamare-Deboutteville was earlier, as do the Austrians, who claim that Siegried Marcus was the great pioneer. Gottlieb Daimler lived and worked in Cannstadt and Carl Benz in Mannheim. They did not know each other, but independently from one another, each developed his first motorcar in about the same period. Not until 1926, did the two companies merge into Daimler-Benz AG. The company produced small cars in the medium price-range, as well as luxury top-class models and fast racing cars. It makes little sense to attempt to describe all the different types and models, because there were far too many. The large cars with compressor engines were of course the most interesting ones, but we should certainly not forget the smaller models, such as the 130 and 170 H. Before the war, directors of car factories were of course content with different sales figures than today. In those days, a car was a luxury product which one could usually only afford at an advanced age. The Stuttgart, for instance, was the best selling model in the twenties. In autumn 1928, the car was sold with a 1988 cc six-cylinder engine. In 1929, it was followed by the Stuttgart 260,

which was powered by a 2581 cc engine that delivered 50 instead of 38 bhp. A total of 14,716 cars were built, including 1,507 that served as Kübelwagen for the Wehrmacht. Another model was the small Mercedes 170, which was introduced at the Paris Motor Show in 1931. Its body was very similar to that of an American car, but that did not bother the buyers. A total number of 13,775 170s were sold. 1935 saw the launch of the 170V. This new model's e engine was a four-cylinder instead of the familiar six-cylinder engine and its cylinder capacity had not diminished at all. On the contrary, because whereas the six-cylinder 1692 cc engine

Between 1931 and 1934, the 170 was also available as the Cabriolet C. It was not a beautiful car, but thanks to its six-cylinder engine it was extremely powerful.

One of the most attractive small Mercedes was the 170V A convertible.

4,298 130's were sold (see picture). The sales figures of the Mercedes 150 came to a grinding halt at a mere 25.

delivered 32 bhp, the 1697 cc side-valve engine delivered 38 bhp. Its body looked a bit more modern than that of its predecessor, because the 170 was much less angular and its radiator was no longer installed upright. The 170V was still in production after the war. In the thirties, the European car industry experimented with rear mounted engines. Tatra and Volkswagen had been doing this for some time and of course Mercedes could not afford to lag behind. The company launched the 130; its shape and price were comparable to that of a Volkswagen. The Mercedes 130 was powered by a four-cylinder rear mounted engine. The

Messrs Barretts from Scottsdale, Arizona, with their 1912 28/60 PS. Its 7195 cc, four-cylinder engine delivered 60 bhp at 1300 rpm.

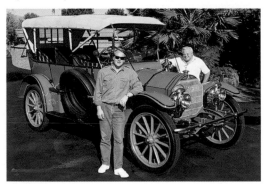

In 1928, a Mercedes 630 K cost 26,000 Reichsmarks. For this amount, the driver did get 2000 kg (4400 lb) of driving pleasure.

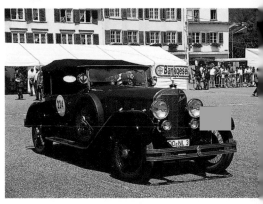

The SS was huge, even as a two-seater.
The model's wheel base was 340 cm and its length ranged from 470 to 520 cm depending on the bodywork.

The 1928 Nürberg was the first car to be powered by an eight-cylinder engine. The car in the picture left the factory in 1929.

side-valve engine had 1308 cc and delivered 26 bhp at 3400 rpm. There was also a larger version, the Mercedes 150, which had 1498 cc that delivered 55 bhp. The models were not very successful, which explains why they were only sold between 1934 and 1936. Incidentally, the 170V was also already available with a rear mounted engine.

This model was called the 170H. The car was built between 1936 and 1939 and was much better than its predecessors as far as its handling was concerned. Mercedes always built cars with heavy engines. Four-cylinder engines with cylinder capacities between 6.0 and 9.5 litres were no

The buyer of a Grosser Mercedes could choose from six different bodies or a rolling chassis. The picture depicts a 1930 four-door convertible.

Technically speaking the engine of the Mercedes 770 were very interesting. The overhead-valve engine delivered 150 bhp as a standard. With the compressor turned on this rose to 200 bhp.

The double carburettor was installed at the heart of the 540 K's huge engine, and the compressor was mounted on the right.

1930. The model had a six-cylinder 6240 cc engine and was available with or without a compressor. The engine delivered 110 or 160 bhp respectively. In 1928, Porsche developed the first eight-in-line engine for the Mercedes Nürberg.

This relatively small engine had a cylinder capacity of 4622 cc and delivered 80 bhp at 3400 rpm. In 1931, the engine was bored out from 80 to 82.5 mm, increasing its cylinder capacity to 4918 cc and it therefore deliverd 100 bhp. And then of course there were the racing cars, such as the Mercedes S, SS and SSK. It took immense strength to keep these brutes on the road.

The Mercedes-Benz S was launched in 1926 and remained in production until 1930. The 6800 cc six-cylinder overhead valve engine had an overhead camshaft with a Rootes-compressor and delivered 180 bhp at 3000 rpm. The engine used no less than 26 litres of petrol for every 100 km, but it did reach a top speed of 106 mph (170 kph). In 1928, the SS and SSK were equipped with a 7065 cc engine that delivered 200 bhp. The abbreviation SSK means Super Sport Kurz, and referred to the shorter chassis.

exception. Before the First World War, most cars were chain-driven. The 28/60 PS was available with a cardan shaft as well as with chains. The advantage of the chain-driven car was that the system was less sensitive. Besides, the chain could easily be replaced in the event of a breakdown.In 1922, technical director Paul Daimler was succeeded by Ferdinand Porsche.

Under his leadership, Mercedes in Untertürkheim produced its most beautiful cars. Porsche was not only responsible for the racing cars, but also for the massive tourers, such as the 630 K, which was sold between 1926 and

A 540 K Convertible A cost approximately 22,000 Reichsmark.

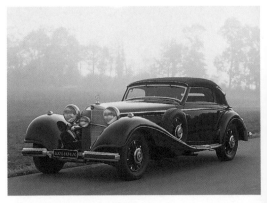

The engine of this version delivered 250 bhp at 3300 rpm. The highlight of this series was the 1929 Mercedes SSKL.

The letter 'L' stood for Leicht, because the model only weighed 1500 (3300) instead of 1700 kg (3740 lb). The 300 bhp engine enabled a top speed of 148 mph (235 kph). The Grosser Mercedes, which was launched as model 770 in Paris in 1930, was the top-of-the-line model. The 770 remained in production until 1938. Its 7655 cc eight-cylinder engine and delivered 150 bhp without or 200 bhp with a compressor.

The model's wheel base was 375 cm, its length 560, its breadth 184 and its height 183 cm. Its fuel tank could hold 120 litres. However, since the 770 used more than 30 litres of fuel for every 62 miles (100 km), this never got you very far. Its top speed was approximately 100 mph (160kph), which was not bad for a car that weighed 1950 kg (4290 lb). The series 500 K and 540 K were built for people who preferred a sporty car, but did not want to go without creature comforts. The K-series succeeded the S-series, but its models were much easier to handle and, furthermore they provided more convenience. They were only intended for use on public roads. Most were sold as rolling chassis, for which the German bodywork builders built the most magnificent superstructures. The stretched and armoured K model was very popular with the Nazi's. The first 1934 500 K was powered by a 5018 cc eight-in-

line compressor engine. In 1936 this model was succeeded by the 540 K with a 5401 cc engine. Until 1944, only an armoured version of this model was available.

354 500 K's were built and even 459 540 K's. The last twelve cars had a 5800 cc engine.

In 1916, Mercer equipped its cars with a four-cylinder engine that delivered 70 hp. The runabouts were built on a short, 292 cm chassis. The tourers had a 335 cm wheel base.

Mercer

Stutz and Mercer, the American car makes of the early twentieth century can be compared to modern makes such as Ferrari, Lamborghini or Aston Martin. The runabouts were every sporty driver's dream, even though the model only consisted of a chassis with an engine that was too powerful, two bucket seats and a large, round fuel tank. Mercer was already building such sports cars in 1908 and they made the make world famous. The Mercers blew the competition away.

In 1912, one of the make's founders, A. Roebling, died in the Titanic disaster. From then on, the company went downhill. The new owners manufactured new models, but with normal bodies. From 1923 onwards, Mercer only manufactured cars with a six-cylinder engine, they were however expensive.

The cheapest Mercer was a four-seater tourer and cost $3,750. A seven-seater limousine cost $5,000 in those days. These cars were no longer genuine Mercers really. When the customers abandoned the make, the management was forced to close down the company in 1925.

Mercury

In the mid-thirties many Ford customers switched to the competition, because the most expensive Ford cost $947 and the cheapest Lincoln Zephyr $1,399. The make could not deliver a model in the medium price-range. That is why many people bought a Dodge, a Pontiac or a Studebaker Commander. In order to solve this problem, Edsel Ford introduced the Mercury make.

The first 1939 Mercurys rolled off the assembly line in October 1938. The American Ford dealers could be satisfied. The beautiful, modern cars were designed by Bob Gregorie. They were also technically up to date. The cars had finally been provided with hydraulic instead of mechanical brakes.

This Mercury rolled off the assembly line in 1939. Yes, the hub caps are by Ford and therefore no longer original!

The Mercury's engine delivered 95 hp, 10 hp more than the Ford V8 engine.

for the car. This 3917 cc V8, delivered 95 bhp at 3600 rpm. The engine's quality was also much better than that of the Ford competitor. Its crankshaft was heavier, and it had reinforced connecting rods and wider bearings.

The new make became a hit. In the first year, Ford was already able to sell about 70,835 cars and in 1940 the company even sold over 86,000. However, not much had been altered in this last model. The car's doors now had ventilation windows and the model was called the Mercury Eight instead of the Ford Mercury.

Chevrolet had already switched to this type of brakes three years earlier, and Plymouth had made the change some eleven years earlier. The new Mercury's wheel base was 10 cm longer than the Ford's. This way, the model offered passengers considerably more space. A special engine had been developed

In 1941, the Mercury's body was completely renewed which was somewhat higher and wider than that of its predecessors. When a station wagon and a coupe were added to the range, sales rose to 98,412 cars. On 2 February 1942, the US government confiscated all passenger cars in stock.

The 1939 cars can be recognised by their grill. In 1940, they were given more horizontal bars.

M.G.

In 1921, a meeting took place between Messrs Cecil Kimber and William Richard Morris. Morris offered Kimber a job as salesperson at his Morris garage in Oxford. A year later, Kimber had already become works manager, but he had his sights on even greater goals. In a corner of the garage, he built a special on the chassis of a Morris Cowley, with which he won the 'London-Lands End trial' in 1923.

A week later, the production of passenger cars was prohibited in the United States.

Orders for the specials flooded in. In the meantime, other new models were emerging from the Morris garage on Alfred Lane in Oxford. The 14/28 was supplied as an open two-seater, as a closed four-seater and as a small saloon. Until 1927, the models were clearly recognisable from their rounded

The first MG by Kimber dating from 1923.

Morris Cowley radiator, after which date they were fitted with flat versions. In 1927, an improved version became available, namely the 14/40. The fast Morris Oxford engine delivered 35 bhp at 4000 rpm. In the Autumn of 1927, Morris introduced the Morris Six with a six-cylinder engine with an overhead camshaft, a cylinder capacity of 2468 cc delivering 52 bhp.

Specially for this six-cylinder car, Kimber designed a new chassis, the MG 18/80. The engine was fitted with two S.U. carburettors and delivered no less than 80 bhp. Approximately 750 of these cars were sold. In 1930, a special race version was produced, the 18/100

The MG M from 1930 was a mini-sports car. The four-cylinder engine had a cylinder capacity of 847 cc and an overhead camshaft and delivered 20 pk/4000 rpm.

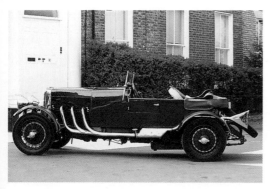

In 1997, a 18/100 Tigress was auctioned for £111,500. That amount would have bought the entire MG factory in 1930.

The K3 symbolised the international breakthrough of the MG make. Racing drivers Johnny Lurani and George Eyston won their class in the Mille Miglia in this model of car.

Mark 3 Tigress. Only five of these cars were built. In comparison with the heavy Tigress, the M-Type Midget was a real dwarf. The mini sports car was based on the Morris Minor of 1929. The four-cylinder engine, with an overhead camshaft, had a capacity of just 847 cc and delivered 20 bhp at 4000 rpm. The car could carry two people and could be supplied either as a convertible or as a coupé. The first Midgets had a plywood body covered in imitation leather, but soon afterwards clients also had the option of a steel body.

This MG M-Type Midget was a great success. 3,235 were sold up until 1932. The M-Type was also successful in various races, but because of its cylinder capacity of 847 cc, the car had to start in the class 750 to 1100cc. This was the reason for the presentation, in 1931, of the C-Type Monthéry Midget. The 746 cc engine delivered 44 bhp at 6400 rpm.

If more power was required, a compressor could also be added. All C-Types (44 cars) had an open two-person body. At the London Motor Show of 1931, Kimber introduced two

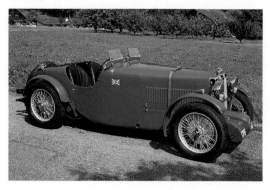

The MG 'N' was launched in 1934. Charles Dodson won the Tourist Trophy in it in 1934 at an average speed of 75 mph (120 kph).

The MG 'P' was an improved version of the 'J'. The 'PB' shown, recognisable by its eye-catching grille, went on sale in 1935 with 939 cc 43 bhp engine.

new models, namely the D-Type, a four-person version of the M-Type, that could be supplied as either an open-topped or closed model, and the interesting F-Type Magna with a six-cylinder engine. This last model could be supplied as an open-topped two or four-seater model or as a four-person coupé.

Within a two year period, 1,250 F-Type cars were sold. In the summer of 1932, M.G introduced a body that was produced until the Fifties. The car, that was sold as the J-Type Midget, was immediately recognisable due to its low-cut doors and the spare tyre attached to the petrol tank by straps. The J-Type was powered by an improved

The engine of the MG L was actually designed for the Wolseley. The 1087 cc six-cylinder engine delivered 47 hp.

version of the 847 cc M-Type engine, that now delivered 36 bhp at 5500 rpm. Customers could choose from four versions. The J-1 had four seats with an open or closed body. The J-2 was built exclusively as an open two-seater. The J-3 was identical to the J-2 but was powered by a compressor engine. The J-4 was intended specially for racing. Its compressor engine delivered 72 bhp at 6000 rpm. In the spring of 1933, simultaneously with the J-4, another new model was introduced, namely the race version of the K-Type Magnette. This Magnette could be supplied with a variety of chassis.

The convertible version had a short chassis. The model with a long wheel base was sold as a four-person saloon or four-person tourer. The six-cylinder engine was available with three different capacities, ranging from 1087 to 1286 cc. The K-3 had been specially designed for races. It was powered by a 1087 cc engine with a compressor that delivered 120 bhp at 6500 rpm.

In 1933, the models referred to above were complemented by the arrival of the successor to the F-Type Magna, namely the L-Type. Once again, the reliable six-cylinder engine was used

Most cars left the factory as rolling chassis to be given bodies by a bodywork builder. The cars were not fast. The six-cylinder engine with a capacity of 2288 cc and later 2322 cc had in fact everyday overhead valves without an overhead camshaft. They were genuine passenger cars with accessories intended to make driving a more pleasurable experience. For example, the brakes were hydraulic and the later models had synchronised third and fourth gears. Around 700 SAs were sold up to the Second World War.

and although the cylinder capacity had been reduced (1087 cc instead of 1171 cc), the engine delivered 41 bhp at 5500 rpm. Incidentally, the same engine was also used in the K-Type Magnette. The open sports car version of this model sold best. There was considerably less interest in the Saloon and Contintental Coupé versions. Of the latter MG, only 100 were sold. In 1934, the L-Type Magnette was succeeded by the N-Type and the J-Type was replaced by the P-Type. The latter model became an absolute best-seller. In a two year period no less than 2,500 were sold.

The car boasted a great many improvements. The chassis had been built more solidly and the brakes worked better, however the little 847 cc engine in the PA still delivered just 36 bhp. So in 1935, the PB model was introduced. It had a more powerful 939 cc engine delivering 43 bhp. In July 1935, Lord Nuffield, as William Morris had been entitled to call himself since 1934, sold the 'M.G. Car Company' and 'Wolseley Motor Ltd.' to 'Morris Company Ltd.'. By order of the director at the time, Leonard Lord, the SA-Type was introduced in 1936. This large car could be supplied as a saloon or a tourer.

In July 1936, a new Midget, the TA, went on sale and this model was also fitted with hydraulic brakes. The four-cylinder engine had a capacity of 1292 cc and delivered 50 bhp. In May 1939, the TA was succeeded by the TB, with only the engine being different. This now had a capacity of 1250 cc and delivered 54 bhp at 5200 rpm. The TB was the predecessor of the post-war TC. The TA and the TB were available in the usual bodywork styles. In 1937, a smaller version of the SA, the TA was introduced. This model had a wheel base of 275 instead of 312 cm. The capacity of the four-cylinder engine was still only 1548 cc delivering 55

Production focused on saloons like this SA of 1936 after MG was taken over in 1935.

hp. In total, 2,407 were produced Incidentally, a smaller and a larger version of the SA were also produced. These models were called the VA and WA respectively. The WA was powered by a 2562 cc six-cylinder engine delivering 100 bhp at 4400 rpm. In 1939, the production lines at MG were halted. The company switched to the production of war materials.

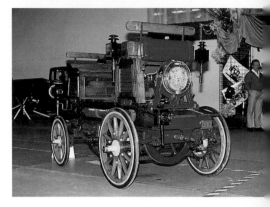

The Millot's radiator was placed at the rear of the vehicle. Note the heavy flywheel, visible between the rear wheels.

Millot

The Millot brothers built their first car in 1896 in the French town of Gray, although it must be said that their carriages have never really resembled cars. It was difficult to tell the front from the back. The radiator was actually at the rear of the car and the steering column, with a proper round steering wheel, was closer to the rear seats than the front ones. The one or two-cylinder engine was situated under the rear seat and drove the wheels via a heavy chain. Another striking feature was the enormous flywheel.

In this car from 1889, the passengers sat with their backs towards the direction of travel.

This Millot was powered by a one-cylinder engine with a capacity of 1500 cc. The car was not exactly speedy and the rear wheels could be braked using small blocks.

This pretty neglected Minerva AK was supplied in 1928 as a Cabriolet de Ville. The car was powered by a six-cylinder engine.

In 1901, the 'Via-à-vis' body was replaced by a modern 2+2. The brothers also built cars with four-cylinder engines. The exact number produced is not known, but there can't have been many. The company was in fact closed in 1902.

Minerva

The most important Belgian make of car, Minerva, was set up by a Dutchman. Sylvain de Jong, from Amsterdam, was just twenty

when he established himself in Antwerp as a bicycle repairer. De Jong not only repaired but also constructed bicycles. He experimented with a bicycle with a De Dion-Bouton engine and eventually even started producing motorbikes. The two-wheelers were sold under the name Minerva, the goddess of craftsmen and artists. In 1900, Sylvain and his brother Jacques built their first motorcar.

An image of the same goddess Minerva adorned the radiator cap. During the early years, only a small number of prototypes were built. The bicycles and motorbikes still constituted the greatest source of income. After 1904, the factory started to produce more and more cars. Two or four-cylinder engines were fitted into the wooden chassis. The bodies were huge, but a small voiturette was also produced, named the Minervette. This car had a steel tube chassis and a 5 bhp two-cylinder engine. The wooden chassis were soon replaced by steel ones and after 1905, the rear wheels were no longer chain-driven, but driven by a solid cardan shaft instead. In addition to the successful Minervette, De Jong mainly produced large cars. Engines with capacities of more than six litres were no exception. The cars were of such good quality that they could easily compete with a Rolls-Royce or an expensive Mercedes. Similarly to all other manufacturers, the Minerva factory also produced sports cars. The cars took part in races such as the one from Paris to Bordeaux in 1905.

In 1907, four Minervas started the Ardennenrace. The cars were driven by famous racing drivers such as Lord Brabazon, Frits Koolhoven and Lee Guiness and finished in first, second, third and sixth places. In 1908, De Jong introduced the sleeve valve engine that had been developed by the American Charles Y. Knight. These engines were practically noiseless but did consume a lot of oil. The dark clouds of smoke

The radiator was adorned with the head of Minerva, the goddess of craftsmen and artists. The picture shows a 4.0 litre four-cylinder from 1925.

The small, lightning-quick Minervettes were extremely successful.

emitted from the exhaust pipes were typical, but despite this disadvantage, this type of engine was used until 1937. Small four-cylinder models were also produced, for example the model AG from 1922 (1980 cc) as well as cars with six-cylinder 5954 cc engines such as the prestigious AK from 1928. And the manufacturers were not even afraid of using eight-in-line sleeve valve engines in, for example, the models AL (1930-1938 with 6615 cc) and AP (1929-1938 with 3958 cc). In 1928, Sylvain de Jong died after a lengthy illness. His brother Jacques assumed control of the factory. At that time, the factory employed some seven thousand people. At around the same time, Europe was flooded with cheap American cars. The consequence

This dignified Minerva 26 CV was built in 1913. The car was powered by a four-cylinder engine with a capacity of 4250 cc.

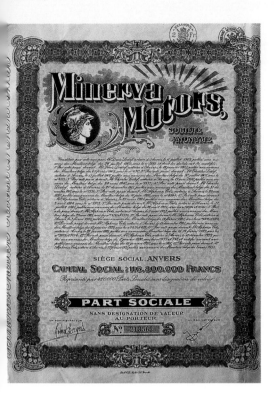

Mitchell

Most pioneering car manufacturers started out by building carriages. This was also the case with regard to Messrs Henry Mitchell and William T. Lewis who built their first motorcar in 1903. They first introduced a number of two-person runabouts with air-cooled two-cylinder engines. In 1906, a few models with four-cylinder engines followed and in 1910 the model S was produced which had a six-cylinder side-valve engine delivering 50 bhp. Mitchell and Lewis never managed to sell many cars.

In 1912, for example, around 6,000 were sold. After 1916, the company in Racine, Wisconsin stopped producing cars with four-cylinder engines. An experiment with an eight-cylinder engine did not really turn out to be successful so after that they focused exclusively on six-cylinder cars. In the '20s, competition between the various car manufacturers was cut-throat. Mitchell rode the storm bravely. In 1919, he even sold slightly more than 10,000 cars. However, he still ended up worse off. In 1923, the company was sold to Charles Nash.

In 1914 the client could choose from different standard models, with 29 hp four-cylinder or 44 hp six-cylinder engines. The 'Big Six' (picture) had a wheel base of 366 cm.

for Minerva was not only a decline in exports but also in sales in Belgium. Minerva tried to stem the tide with cheaper models such as the AR 3000, introduced in 1932, that had a 2970 cc six-cylinder sleeve valve engine. In 1935, this model was followed by the M4. This car also had a 1980 cc four-cylinder sleeve valve engine. The engine had already been developed in 1922 and could therefore be produced very cheaply. The four-cylinder engine was terribly old-fashioned and the model was not successful. On the contrary, it contributed to the company going bankrupt. The director at the time of the Belgian Imperia factory, Mathieu van Roggen, took over the bankrupt's assets. He limited activities, with some success, to the production of lorries. After the Second World War, a few more prototypes were developed, but shortly after that, the make disappeared definitively from the market.

Morgan

H.F.S. Morgan built his first motorcars even before the First World War. The design was quite modern for the times but who could have imagined that the practically unchanged model would still be in production today? The cars have always been completely hand-built.

H.F.S. Morgan was succeeded by his son Peter who in turn transferred the company to his son Charles. Currently, around 450 Morgans are built per year and there is a client waiting list of at least a year. Up until 1952, the company primarily produced three-wheelers. These vehicles had two front wheels, in between which an enormous V-twin engine was positioned. The three-wheelers had a lot of advantages. For example, the driver only had to have a

motorbike driving licence. In addition, the car tax was cheap and they were easy to maintain. The first models had air-cooled two-cylinder engines with capacities of approximately 1000 cc but after 1932 the vehicles could be supplied with water-cooled Ford side valve engines. A variety of versions of the three-wheelers were available, ranging from a two-person racing car to

The Morgan was not a car for people with a lot of luggage.

From 1936 onwards, Morgan was also able to supply 'normal' sports cars. The first model was christened 'Flat Rads' because of its flat radiator.

You cannot just get into a Morgan and drive off. You first have to study the handbook.

a four-person family car. All the models were fitted with independent front wheel suspension which was a guarantee for the car holding the road well. The drive consisted of a chain to the rear wheel. In 1936, the Morgan range

The V-twin engine by J.A.P. To the right above the number plate is the magnet for the ignition.

included a car with four wheels. This so-called Morgan 4/4 had a four-cylinder Coventry Climax overhead-valve engine with a capacity of 1122 cc, delivering 34 bhp. The last pre-war models could also be supplied with a 1267 cc Standard overhead-valve engine.

Morris

In 1912, William Morris, later Lord Nuffield, sold the first cars under his name. The Nuffield group became one of the largest and most important car companies in England. During the '40s, the company was responsible for manufacturing more than half of all the cars produced in England. The first model was called the Morris Oxford and, due to its rounded nose, was soon nicknamed the 'Bullnose'. During the early years, the cars were driven by White & Poppe engines, but after the First World War, an American Continental engine was used, first of all in the Morris Cowley. From 1920 onwards, Morris produced its own engines based on a drawing by Hotchkiss. In the autumn of 1927, the Morris Six was introduced in London.

One of the first of William Morris's cars, an Oxford from 1913.

*The first Morris Oxford was powered by a White &
Poppe engine. The last models of the 'Bullnose
Series' had a four-cylinder engine designed by
Hotchkiss.*

*The Bullnose was succeeded in 1927 by the 'Flatnose'.
The picture shows a Cowley from the early Thirties. Gol
instead of chrome? It's all a question of taste.*

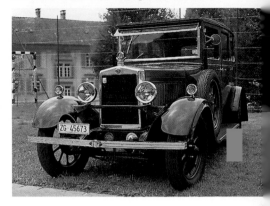

The car had a 2468 cc six-cylinder
engine with an overhead camshaft.
Between 1929 and 1935 the same
model was sold as the Morris Oxford or
Isis. In addition to these large and
expensive cars, the Morris range also
included smaller models, such as the
Morris Minor. This model was available
between 1929 and 1934 with an 847 cc
four-cylinder engine. The client could
choose from a range of bodies. In 1931,
a cheap version of the Minor with a
side-valve engine went on sale. The
Minor did not have bumpers and
parking lights and the chrome had
been replaced by paint, but at not even

This Isis-Six was presented in July 1929. The 2.5 litre six-cylinder engine had an overhead camshaft.

Although the factory did not build any racing cars, a lot of cars were specially converted for this purpose. The picture shows a sports Oxford from 1926.

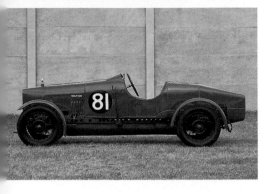

A very great number of Morris Eights were sold. The picture shows a four-person convertible from 1935.

among other items, electrical equipment was made. In 1880, his sons Louis and Emile joined the company. In 1887, one of the employees, the twenty-two-year-old Henri Brasier, built a three-wheeler that was powered by a steam engine. In 1892, Louis Mors bought a Panhard & Levassor in which, in 1895, the brothers took part in the race Paris-Bordeaux-Paris. From that moment onwards they were in love with cars. In 1896, Brasier designed a car very similar to the Benz and a year later a model V4 engine followed with battery ignition and a dynamo. In 1898, the 'Société de l'Electricité et des Automobiles Mors' was established using a capital of two million francs.

In the same year, the two hundred or so employees built ten cars a month. Racing cars, with engines of capacities of more than 10 litres were also created on Brasier's drawing board. These models made the make world-famous. The company also produced cars for a wider public. In the peak years of 1902 and 1903, the company's annual

£100 it was a fast-selling model. Morris also built a lot of other, less well-known models. For example the Morris Major, that was built from 1931onwards and the Fifteen-Six dating from 1935. The Morris Eight, Ten and Twelve from 1933, 1934 and 1935 respectively, were all still being produced after the Second World War.

Mors

In 1874, Louis Mors bought a small factory in which,

The Mors saloon cars were nothing very special. The picture shows a four-person saloon car from the Twenties.

turnover was around 4 million francs. The models sold were still being developed by Brasier, even though the talented engineer had already left the company in 1901. From 1902 onwards, the engines were fitted with water-cooling systems and in 1903 clients could choose from engines with capacities ranging from 8 to 30 bhp. In the same year, Mors employed around 1,000 people and a total of 325 cars were sold. The management opened branches in New York and London, which nevertheless had to be closed due to disappointing sales results in 1904. From that time onwards things went downhill. The financial year 1905 was the first one in which a loss was recorded. Mors tried to save the company with a number of new models. When André Citroën was named director in 1907, production increased again to 319 cars in 1908 and 647 in 1910. This brought Mors out of the red for the first time. Once Brasier had left

the company, no more racing successes were achieved and in 1905 the special racing department was disbanded. In 1908, a last attempt at success was nevertheless made. The racing cars with 12.8 litre engines took part in the French Grand Prix. The result was however disappointing. The Grand Prix was won by Dario Resta in an Austin with a 9635 cc six-cylinder engine. Camille Jenatzy ended in his Mors in fourteenth place and the other driver Landon had to give up after only four rounds. For the Mors factory this was enough. The make that together with Panhard & Levassor had built the best racing cars in France no longer saw a future in racing. The First World War was a successful period for Mors. Citroën had entered into a contract with the government for the produc-tion of grenades. In 1922, the company was sold to Citroën. The last Mors saloon car left the factory in 1925.

NAG

The German Emil Tathenau was the founder and managing director of the well-known company AEG. Initially he manufactured electrical appliances, but in 1901 Rathenau also plunged into the motorcar manufacture. In order to avoid the costs of developing his own model, Rathenau purchased the existing car factory of professor Klingenberg, the Allgemeinen Automobil Gesellschaft. Klingenberg had already built its first motorcar in 1899. Rathenau was to sell the same model under the name NAG (Neue Automobil Gesellschaft) until 1902. In 1902, the company launched its first own model, in which the engine was mounted in the front of the car instead of over the rear axle. NAG built beautiful cars in various price-ranges. The most expensive

NAG was the first German manufacturer of V8-engines. This 1931 car was also powered by a V8-engine with 4508 cc, that delivered 100 bhp at 3200 rpm.

models were offered as cars '...für die mondäne Frau und den verwöhnten Herrenfahrer' [for chic women and men who have everything]. The factory in Berlin also manufactured racing cars, which successfully competed with makes such as Alfa Romeo, Mercedes and Opel. In 1924, a four-seater NAG won the Monza 24 hour race. The car covered 2,583 km at an average speed of 75 mph (120 kph). In that year, over 5,000 people were employed by what had become one of the most modern car factories in Germany. However, the company's management made some strategic mistakes.

Models were introduced that could hardly be sold, and car factories that were operating at a loss were taken over, such as Protos, Presto, Voran, and Dux. Despite their take-over these factories still went bankrupt, which did not contribute to NAG's reputation. The management decided to stop manufacturing passenger cars in 1934, when its production ground to a halt during the depression.

Napier

The Napier firm had already existed for almost one hundred years when Montague Napier decided to also start manufacturing motorcars in 1899. The models were powered by 4.5 up to over 17.0 litre, four-cylinder engines that delivered over 100 bhp. In 1902, Napiers partner, Selwyn F. Edge won the international Gordon-Bennett race from Paris to Innsbruck. The car was powered by a 6.5 litre engine. Edge covered the 566 km distance in 11 hours, 52 minutes and 52 seconds at an average speed of 32.05 mph (51.295 kph). Napier established many records. For instance, in 1905, it broke the one-kilometre record on Blackpool promenade. Clifford Earp drove the 1,000 metres in 21.4 seconds at an average speed of 104.53 mph (167.248 kph). In 1907, Selwyn Edge drove non-stop on the Brookland track for 24 hours at an average speed of 65.90 mph (105.448

Napier only sold a total of 4,258 cars, including this 12 HP from 1904.

The Napier 60 HP was the best selling model. Its six-cylinder engine's capacity was 7.7 litres, and delivered 85hp.

kph). No less than 24 tyres were worn out during this drive.The Napier make introduced many novelties. In 1904, it was the first company to manufacture mass-produce a six-cylinder engine. The engine was used in fast racing cars, but also in beautiful passenger cars, which compared well with famous makes, such as Rolls-Royce. After the First World War, the company introduced a passenger car with a 6.2 litre six-cylinder engine and an overhead camshaft and from 1924 onwards, the cars could be fitted with brakes on all four wheels. But even this novelty could not tempt enough people to visit the showroom. In that year, only 187 cars were sold, as a result of which the management decided to close down the factory.

Nash

Charles Warren Nash (1864-1948) was born on a farm in Illinois. When Charles was six years old, his parents decided to divorce. Neither wanted the child, so the court assigned him to a family of farmers. Nash had to work for them until he reached the age of 21

In 1929, this Nash 441 cost $1,345. The car was powered by a six-cylinder overhead-valve engine.

The dickey seat was especially popular with children.

and only then was he free to do as he pleased. Nash escaped when he was only twelve. He was given a job in a car factory, where he filled upholstery for a dollar a day. By 1906, he had made it to vice-president of the same company. In 1910, Nash was charged with the management of the Buick car factory.

At that time, the company was still suffering losses, but as early as 1911 profits had risen to $800,000 and even rose to over $12 million in 1914. In 1912, Nash switched to General Motors, but the country boy's ambition to found his own car make remained. In 1916, he purchased the Jeffrey Company, where the first Nash was manufactured in 1918. Nash was already selling 31,008 trucks and passenger cars a year by 1919. Business went so well that Nash was able to take over several companies including the Seaman Body Corporation, the Lafayette Motors

Corporation, and the Mitchell Motorcar Corporation. In 1928, the number of sold cars was 138,137, a record that would not be broken until after the war. What kind of cars did Nash build? The first Nash from 1918 had a six-cylinder overhead-valve engine. In

The dashboard of a 1929 Nash shows that imitation wood was already very much in demand in those days.

1922, it was followed by a model with a four-cylinder overhead-valve engine which cost $985. In 1930, the first model with an eight-in-line engine

A 1930 Dual Cowl Phaeton could seat seven. The four in the back sat behind their own windscreen.

In 1932, this was one of the cheapest models at $995. The car could seat five grownups.

Nash produced a total of 14,315 motorcars in 1934. The car in the picture was also built in that year.

rolled off the assembly line. In that year, there were three basic models in the range: the series 450 SingleSix, the series 480 Twin-Ignition Six and the series 490 Twin-Ignition Eight. The addition twin ignition meant that the engine had double ignition with two spark plugs for each cylinder. The three series were available in no less than 31 body versions, from a two-door coupe to a seven-seater limousine.

NSU

The make NSU is as old as the car itself, because this company constructed the rolling chassis for the Daimler Motorwagen in Neckarsulm, before Daimler and Maybach. NSU built a total of twenty Daimlers and also the majority of the subsequent models of that make were manufactured by NSU. In addition, the NSU company specialised in building bicycles and motorcycles. It was soon the largest company in this field in Europe. In 1905, the company acquired the licensing rights of the Belgian car make Pipe and a year later it introduced its own design. Until the First World War, it mainly manufactured cars with small, four-cylinder engines. The NSU 8/24 PS remained the basic model for about fifteen years. After the war, the sports and racing cars became particularly

The NSU 8/24 PS, here a 1912 Pheaton, was the basic model for fifteen years. The 2110 cc four-cylinder engine delivered 30 bhp at 2100 rpm.

From 1934 onwards, the NSU/Fiat 50 was built in Heilbronn. The picture shows a 1937 convertible by Weinberg.

This 1926 NSU with a compressor engine can still be admired regularly at classic car rallies.

1000 was launched, which was sold from 1934 to 1938. Later on the 1100 and the 1500 followed, which hardly differed from their Italian originals. The NSU/Fiat 500 became almost as successful in Germany as the Fiat 500 in Italy. Karrosserie Weinsberg built a beautiful roadster on the 500's chassis.

Countless advertising posters depicted the impressive cars.

well-known, including the famous NSU 5/25/40 PS. This car was powered by a 1232 cc four-cylinder side-valve engine, which with the compressor on, delivered some 40 bhp. As the car only weighed 510 kg (1122 lb), its top speed was about 78 mph (125 kph).

The two-seater racing car, the NSU 6/60 from 1926 was also interesting. This model had a six-cylinder compressor engine, 1476 cc and delivered 60 bhp at 4000 rpm. The 6/60 reached a top speed of 109 mph (175 kph) and won several races. In 1929, NSU relocated to a new factory in Heilbronn, but the company was in such financial trouble that it had to be sold to Fiat. First the NSU/Fiat

Oakland

After Alanson Brush designed the first Cadillac, he started an engineering firm in Detroit. There, he designed a new two-cylinder engine for Edward Murphy. This resulted in the Oakland, a passenger car that was introduced in 1907. The Oakland Motorcar Company was on Oakland Avenue in Pontiac, Michigan. The number of cars the company sold was so small that Murphy decided to sell the make to General Motors. Subsequently, a new and better engine was developed with the money from the new owner. This four-cylinder was introduced in 1910, and in that same year, no less than 3,000 Oaklands were sold. In 1915, this number even rose to 12,000 cars. In that year, the range included several models in different price-ranges. The 37 was powered by a four-cylinder engine, a six-cylinder engine was installed in the Oakland 49, and the 50 even had an eight-in-line engine. In 1926, General Motors founded Pontiac.

The price of a Pontiac was lower than that of the Oakland. The car sold so well that even Oakland's turnover was affected. In 1930, General Motors tried to save the make by presenting a new model, the Oakland 101. The 101 had an inexpensive V8-engine. But the model was a disaster: in 1926, 56,909 cars were sold and in 1931 this number fell to 8,672 cars. Subsequently, General Motors decided to withdraw the make from the market.

A beautifully restored 1928 Oakland. Its wooden wheels with spokes were very popular in those days.

This five-seater tourer was sold in 1929, when Oakland only sold 22,866 motorcars.

Oldsmobile

Oldsmobile is the oldest American car make. On 21 August 1987, the company celebrated its 100th anniversary. Oldsmobile was founded by Ransom Eli Olds. His Oldsmobile Curved Dash Runabout was one of the most popular cars in the United States between 1900 and 1904. Despite the fact that the entire factory was destroyed by fire in 1901, 2,100 cars were sold in 1902, and 5,000 in 1904. Olds left his company in the same year.

He started a new factory under the name Reo. Until 1905, Oldsmobile only installed single-cylinder engines. The B model that was used later on, was powered by a twin, whilst in 1906 a four-cylinder engine was added to the range. The four-cylinder was, among others, installed in the S model, a car the factory announced as "The Best Thing On Wheels" The model became a resounding success. In the first year, 1,400 of these cars were sold. The Oldsmobile S was available as a two or three-seater roadster or as a six-seater tourer. In 1905, the company started developing a six-cylinder engine, but it was only marketed in 1908 in the Oldsmobile Z. The Z was an large, expensive car. The model had a 330 cm

The Oldsmobile Curved Dash was a resounding success. The R model, as it was officially known, was the best selling car in the early 20th century.

Every Oldsmobile lover's dream: a two-door convertible with a dickey seat. In 1935, the model cost under $800.

wheel base and cost no less than $4,500 in America. Smaller and cheaper types were also manufactured, such as the model X that had a 269 cm wheel base and cost $2,000. The top-of-the-line model was the 1910 Mighty Limited. This gigantic car was powered by a 11.5 litre, six-cylinder engine that delivered over 60 bhp. This model was available as a roadster, as a seven-seater tourer or as a limousine. Priced between $4,600 and $5,400, not many were sold. In 1908, William Crapo Durant founded the General Motors Company. One of Durant's best deals was the take-over of Oldsmobile. The make was not cheap, however. General Motors paid $17,000 in cash

In 1937, a car with an eight-cylinder engine had a distinctive checkerboard grill. The bars of the grill of the six-cylinder were small and horizontal.

An Oldsmobile from just after the First World War. Room and fun for four!

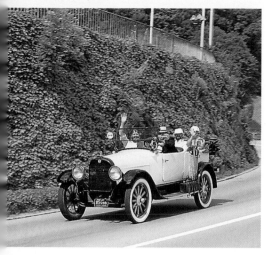

Oldsmobile introduced many novelties. The most striking was the introduction of the automatic Hydramatic gearbox in 1940.

One year later, in 1941, half of all of the Oldsmobiles supplied were fitted with such a gearbox.

and $3 million in shares. Not until after the Second World War did the sales of Oldsmobile pick up again and over 10,000 cars were sold on an annual basis. Demand varied wildly, however. In 1919, 39,042 cars were sold and in 1921 the number fell to 19,157.

The year 1929, became a peak year with a sales figure of 103,973 Oldsmobiles, but the following year not even half that number left the showrooms. In 1941, the last full pre-war production

year, another 230,703 Oldsmobiles were sold. That year also saw the two millionth Oldsmobile roll off the assembly line.

O.M.

The 'SA Officine Mechaniche', which after 1928 was called 'O.M. Fabbrica Bresciana di Automobili' was founded in Milan in 1899, but the first car only left the factory in 1918 and it was not even designed by the company. O.M. bought the company from Roberto Züst, who built the Brixia-Züst in Brescia. They were reliable, fast cars with 4.7 litre, four-

'The devil of the Alps...'

Although there is a long waiting list for participants in the annual Mille Miglia for classic cars, O.M. drivers always have one up on the competition - for after all, it was an O.M. that won the first Mille Miglia in 1927. The picture shows a Superba at the 1997 Mille Miglia.

cylinder side-valve engines. The first cars designed by O.M. were powered by a small 1496 cc four-cylinder engine and a 1991 cc six-cylinder engine. The six-cylinder became the standard engine for the O.M. Superba. As of 1923, all O.M.'s were fitted with brakes on all four wheels. The make

built many sports and racing cars, which were available with a Roots compressor on request. The factory even had its own racing team, which finished fourth in the 1925 Le Mans. At the first Mille Miglia in 1927, the competition were made to look like complete fools. The Minoja/Morandi team won the long race in an O.M. 665S, with a 2.0 litre six-cylinder engine.

The 1,000 mile distance was covered in just over 21 hours. The average speed was 48.27 mph (77.238 kph). O.M.'s also finished in second and third place. As of 1928, Alfa Romeo took over the lead. In 1928 and 1929, O.M. had to settle for second place. The factory built a special Grand Prix car, fitted with a 1477 cc eight-in-line engine with two overhead camshafts for the 1927 racing season. Despite a top speed of no less than 122 mph (195 kph), the model never won a race.O.M. not only built sports and racing cars. Passenger

An O.M. at the start of the 1991 Mille Miglia. In spite of the rain, the English drivers did not even think about using the cover.

car buyers could choose from the models 465 (= four cylinders and a 65 mm cylinder bore), 467 and 469. In 1921, the latter model was powered by a 1496 cc side-valve engine. The cars were available in countless body versions, which were usually manufactured at O.M. itself. The 665 model or Superba remained available until 1930.

In the second half of the twenties, O.M. increasingly focused on manufacturing trucks. Eventually, in 1930, the last passenger car rolled off the assembly line. In 1933, the company became part of the Fiat corporation.

The first car from the Opel brothers was their 'Opel-Patent-Motorwagen System Lutzmann'. At first these had single cylinder motors but some were later driven by twins.

Opel also built Grand Prix cars. This car was driven by Carl Joerns in the 1913 French GP.
It has a 3970 cc engine with overhead camshaft.

Opel

It is remarkable how many brothers built motorcars. For example, there are the Maserati brothers, the Studebaker brothers, the Duesenbergs, Chevrolets, Renaults, Packards, Peugeots, Jensens and ....the Opel brothers. At Opel no less than five brothers were concerned, who started out building bicycles and sewing machines and, later on, in 1898, their first motorcar. The model was called Opel-Patent-Motorcar System Lutzmann, because it was built under licence and based on the designs of Friedrich Lutzmann. The Opel was fitted with a single-cylinder engine which was rear mounted. However this was soon replaced by a twin. With this engine, the car reached a speed of 28 mph (45 kph). That turned out to be fast enough for a victory in a hill climb at Heidelberg in 1899. Still, the brothers were not content with the car. That is why in 1901, they switched to a Darracq rolling chassis. Subsequently, the chassis was given a superstructure in the factory in Rüdelsheim. By 1902, the brothers had gained enough experience to be able to build their own car, the Opel 10/12 PS. The Opel 10/12

was powered by a front-mounted twin that drove the rear wheels by means of a cardan shaft. Because the Opel-Darraq was also still in production, Opel's range was considerable and an increasing number of models were added to it. In 1905, the first model with a four-cylinder engine was introduced, the 35/40. The engine's cylinder capacity was 6880 cc and it delivered some 40 bhp at 1300 rpm. Its top speed was about 44 mph (70 kph). Opel did not just manufacture expensive cars. On the contrary, most models were quite affordable. In 1908, the one-thousandth car rolled off the assembly line. The factory had its own racing team, because the Opel management

The Opel Laubfrosch was very successful. The three-seater car was marketed in 1924 and soon became Germany's best selling car.

The Opel Super 6 had a six-cylinder, 2473 cc overhead-valve engine that delivered 55 bhp at 3600 rpm. The car had a top speed of 72 mph (115 kph).

The Kapitän was one of the top models of the German car industry. In 1938, the model cost almost twice the price of an Opel Olympia. The Kapitän had a 2473 cc six-cylinder engine and a three-speed gearbox.

The Admiral was the top-of-the-line model. This car was available with different bodies or as a rolling chassis. The 3626 cc six-cylinder overhead-valve engine delivered 75 bhp at 3200 rpm.

was also aware that a victory at a race or hill climb could generate a lot of free publicity. Special models were developed for the racing team, such as a racing car built in 1910, with a 7.3 litre four-cylinder overhead-valve engine. The engine delivered no less than 100 bhp. During the First World War the production of passenger cars stagnated completely. The assembly lines were now used for the production of trucks and aircraft engines for the army. As early as 1919, the first post-war Opel left the factory and in 1923 production was increased to 25 cars a day. In 1924, the Opel 4 PS Laubfrosch

was presented. The model owed its name to the only colour it was available in: frog green. Production sky-rocketed even further. In 1927, over 7,500 people worked at the factory and over 100 cars a day were manufactured there. In the winter of 1928, the brothers sold their company to General Motors. The American influence on the models was clearly noticeable. In 1921, for instance, Opel was the first German factory to manufacture a car with an eight-cylinder engine. But when, in 1929, it tried to penetrate the luxury market with the Regent, General Motors foiled that plan. If anyone wanted such a car they would have to buy a Cadillac.

Opel's advertisements were almost more beautiful than its cars.

In 1931, a six-cylinder engine was developed in Detroit, that was specifically designed for the 1.8 litre Opel. The engine was also installed in the 1935 P4. The P4 soon became the best selling German car. More such successful models followed, such as the Kadett and the Olympia, the first European car with a self-supporting body. Expensive models, such as the Kapitän and the Admiral also rolled off the assembly line. The latter model was presented in 1938.

Packard

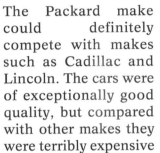

The Packard make could definitely compete with makes such as Cadillac and Lincoln. The cars were of exceptionally good quality, but compared with other makes they were terribly expensive and the factory never sold any inexpensive models. In most cases the models were ahead of their time.

The make was also very successful in racing and record-breaking.
A selection:

1903: Tom Fetch is the first motorist to drive from the West to the East coast of the United States. It took him 61 days to accomplish this.

1904: The Packard racing car called Grey Wolf broke the single as well as the five mile record.

1912: Packard presented the 48 model with a six-cylinder engine, the first luxury passenger car.

1915: On 1 June, the first mass produced V12-engine, the Twin Six, was presented.

1917: Packard supplied the first V12 aircraft engine to the American government.

1924: The first Packard with an eight-in-line engine. From then on, all the cars were fitted with brakes on all four wheels.

The customer could choose from different bodies. The picture shows a large passenger car from 1931 with an eight-in-line engine. Priced at $5,950, this model was the most expensive Packard of that year.

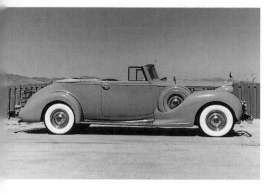

This five-person Convertible Victoria was introduced in 1938. The model was powered by a V12-engine.

In 1924, this two-seater Packard with an eight-cylinder engine was introduced. The model was called the Single Eight. Note the small step up to the dickey seat.

In 1921, Packard sold a total of 8,800 cars. The picture shows a Single Six built in that year.

After the Second World War, Packard soon ran into trouble because the company had taken over Studebaker which was making losses. In 1956, production stopped in its own factory, and the Studebaker assembly lines were used, but not for long. On 13 July 1958, the assembly lines also closed down in this factory signalling the demise of another famous car.

The adventure started in 1899. In that year, the brothers James Ward and William Doud Packard built their first motorcar. They called the small open cart, which was powered by a single-cylinder engine, the model A. In 1902, it was followed by the model G which had a two-cylinder engine and in 1903

their company the Ohio Automobile Co was renamed Packard Motorcar Co. Business was booming. The cars sold quite easily and new models were presented on a regular basis. In 1912, they introduced their first model with a six-cylinder engine. In that year, customers could choose from the Eighteen with a four-cylinder engine, the Thirty, also with a four-cylinder engine and the 48 with the new six-cylinder engine.

The latter model was available with no less than nine different bodies. The sales figures were evidence of the customers' confidence in the new model of which 1,329 were sold, all

In order to survive the depression Packard was forced to manufacture cheaper cars, such as this 1932 Light Eight as a two-seater convertible. The model was called the Shovel Nose because of its distinctive grill.

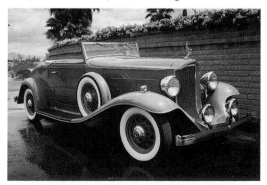

The 1939 Rollston Town Car was powered by a V12-engine. The rear passengers sat behind their own windscreen.

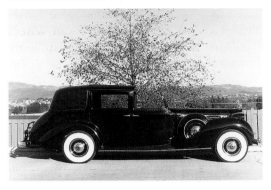

The side windows of this 1941 Super One Eighty with a seven-seater body opened and closed hydraulically.

fitted with electrical lights and a starter motor. The Twin Six, America's first production car with a V12-engine made a huge impression in 1916. For some years it was the only car Packard could sell. And why would the factory build inexpensive cars when the demand for the exorbitantly high-priced V12 remained?

Only in 1921 was another Packard with a six-cylinder engine introduced the Single Six. The company also built eight-cylinder engines and in 1924 that was still a remarkable feat. In the first year, over 3,500 cars were sold immediately. As did any other car manufacturer, Packard suffered severely

from the depression. In 1934, production fell to 6,552 cars. But as soon as the war was over, demand immediately rose again.

In 1935, 37,653 cars rolled off the assembly line and in the record year 1937, no less than 95,455 cars were sold, a figure that was not to be matched until 1949.

Paige

Were IFA and DKW the first makes to have a three-cylinder two-stroke engine? No, because Fred O. Paige and Andrew Bachle built such an engine as early as 1909. And nobody even noticed that the engine smelled even worse than a four-stroke did in those days. The engine also ran excellently.

That is why Harry M. Jewett showed interest in the project. Subsequently, Jewett founded the Paige-Detroit Motor-car Company. Fred O. Paige became its first managing director, but it did not take long before Jewett discarded the two-stroke engine. Paige was fired and Jewett appointed himself managing

In 1923, Paige was still doing fine. In that year the company sold over 4,000 cars.

At a sales price of $2,195, this Paige Touring 6-70 was the cheapest model in 1923.

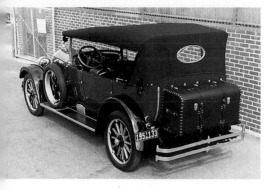

At a sales price of $2,195, this Paige Touring 6-70 was the cheapest model in 1923.

director. His next model was powered by an ordinary four-cylinder engine, with less defects. In 1914, 4,631 cars were sold and in 1916 this number had risen to over 12,000. In 1915, the Paige Motorcar Co, as the company was now called, presented its first model with a six-cylinder engine.

From then on, four-cylinder engines were no longer installed. Paige built beautiful cars of very goodquality. Sports cars were presented, but also stately limousines, that the company advertised as 'The Most Beautiful Cars in America'. Paige cars also broke records. In 1921, a Paige Daytona Speedster broke all the records for passenger cars across 5 to 100 mile distances. The same car broke the one-

In 1923, the six-cylinder side-valve engine delivered some 70 bhp.

mile record at a speed of 103 mph (164.4 kph) on Daytona beach in Florida. In1927, the company launched a car with an eight-cylinder engine. This Paige 8-85 had a 334 cm wheel base and was therefore very suitable for luxury bodies.

The top-of-the-line model was the seven-seater limousine, which cost $2,905. In the same year, a Paige with a six-cylinder engine cost $1,360. However, the number of motorcars the company sold decreased. In 1927, the car make Paige was sold to the Graham brothers. Until 1928, the models were sold as Graham-Paige.

Panhard & Levassor

René Panhard (1841-1908) and Emile Levassor (1843-1897) met at university. Together they took over an engineering factory after graduating. In 1887, they obtained a licence to construct Gottlieb Daimler engines and two years later the first Panhard & Levassor was launched at the Paris car show. In 1900, the two friends developed their own engine and in 1901 they presented a model with a front mounted engine, instead of the more traditional rear mounted engine.

Panhard & Levassor invested a lot of time and money in racing. The frequent victories were invaluable for the make, but racing did not only bring fortune. In 1897, Levassor took part in a race from Paris to Marseille. Near Avignon he hit a dog crossing the road. His car overturned and Levassor died from his

In 1913, this car was available with a conventional or a sleeve-valve engine. Prices ranged from 16,000 to 18,000 French francs.

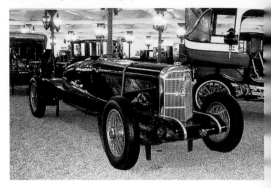

One of the flagships of the Collection Schlumpf in Mulhouse: the 1929 35 CV. The car reached a top speed of 133.79 mph (214.064 kph).

A sporty 1914 2+1. The third passenger sat on top of rather than inside the car.

the American Charles Y. Knight presented his sleeve-valve engine. Panhard & Levassor was particularly interested in this 'valve-less' engine. Just like the engineers at Daimler, they were very impressed by the virtually silent engine.

In 1909, they fitted a model with a 4-cylinder sleeve-valve engine for the first time. The engine delivered 42 bhp, sufficient for a top speed of 62 mph (100 kph). From then on, all the larger models were equipped with such an engine. The smaller, inexpensive cars still had engines with valves until the First World War. In 1919, the first

injuries. Production continued as normal. New models with large and small engines were unveiled, intended for racing or everyday use. In 1904, the factory manufactured cars with a 15.435 cc four-cylinder engine, which delivered slightly over 100 bhp at 1050 rpm.

Even larger engines were manufactured in the factory on Avenue d'Ivry in Paris, such as a 18.279 cc four-cylinder engine, which was installed in a racing car in 1906. Increasingly powerful engines were also used in the passenger cars, such as a 11.0 litre six-cylinder engine from 1905. In the early twenties,

The letters SS mean: Sans Soupapes i.e. without valves. This X57 rolled off the assembly line in 1929.

The striking body of the 1938 Dynamic.

Up to the sixties, it was not possible to bend a windscreen. Here is the French solution for the Dynamic.

Panhards with a 2280, 3178 or 4849 cc sleeve-valve engine were presented. The models were to remain in production until 1930. The small models, such as the 10CV, built between 1921 and 1925, had 1188 cc engines. An eight-cylinder engine with a cylinder capacity of no less than 6355 cc throbbed in the larger cars, such as the 35CV. These almost silent engines delivered 80 bhp at 2200 rpm. The sleeve-valve engines consumed a large amount of oil and could therefore be immediately recognised by the blue exhaust smoke.

In the thirties, the company stopped racing and focused on breaking records instead. For instance in 1929, the English Captain George Eyston broke the world speed record with a top speed of 133.79 mph (214.064 kph). This car's engine delivered 235 bhp at 3200 rpm. Today, the car can be seen at the Musée National de l'Automobile, Collection Schlumpf, in Mulhouse, France. In 1938, one of the most interesting European cars was presented, the Dynamic.

With its aerodynamic body, it was far ahead of its time and also technically the car was very remarkable. The Dynamic seated six grownups. The driver sat in the centre of the front seat.

The Dynamic was available with different bodies, including a six-seater saloon. The driver sat in the middle on the front seat.

The front wheels had independent suspension and the windscreen was panoramic. The Dynamic was available with three different engines. Of course they were six-cylinder sleeve-valve engines which had either 2516, 2861 or 3832 cc. The most powerful engine delivered 100 bhp at 3500 rpm. They turned out to be the last pre-war models.

After the war, completely different models were presented, with small, air-cooled two-cylinder engines. The days of the luxury models were over once and for all.

Peugeot

The Peugeot family already owned a foundry in the 18th century. The company expanded fast. The products they manufactured included pepper mills and tools. In the late 19th century, the company's bicycles, the Les Fils de Peugeot Frères were very famous. When engineer Armand Peugeot heard that the company had manufactured its first motorcar, he was immediately interested.

In 1888, he concluded an agreement with Léon Serpollet, granting him a licence to build the three-wheeler Serpollet designed, which was powered by a steam engine. This led to the Peugeot Type 1. On the advice of Mr Panhard and Mr Levassor, Peugeot soon switched to a petrol engine, which resulted in the Peugeot Type 2 and 3. The Type 4 was a Vis-à-Vis with a two-cylinder V-engine mounted under the rear seat. The car was steered by means of chains to the front wheels. In 1896, Armand Peugeot founded

In 1892, Peugeot built the Type 4. The Vis-à-Vis was powered by a two-cylinder Daimler engine.

In 1905, Armand Peugeot's brothers manufactured motorcars under the name Lion Peugeot. Despite their sometimes large dimensions, they were powered by small single-cylinder engines.

After the brothers were reunited, Lion Peugeot remained in production until 1915. The picture shows a 1913 Phaeton with a four-cylinder engine.

the company Société des Automobile Peugeot. He built a new factory, which built an engine developed by Peugeot himself that same year. In the 19th century, motorcars were also used for racing. Peugeot built special racing cars for this purpose. For instance, the first Paris-Bordeaux-Paris race was won by a Type 3 Peugeot, driving at an average speed of 13.62 mph (21.8 kph).

The Michelin brothers also took part in this race and they also drove a Peugeot which was fitted with pneumatic tyres. As of 1897, al Peugeots were provided with this novelty. Peugeots sold well and therefore the factory soon became too small. A new factory was built in Lille, where 156 cars were manufactured in 1898. In 1900, this number had already risen to over 500 cars. Armand Peugeot's brothers founded their own company in 1905. They manufactured motorcars under the name Lion.

They were cars with light engines, because they left the manufacture of the more powerful engines to their brother Armand. In 1910, the two companies merged and became the Société des Automobiles et des Cycles Peugeot. The company had branches in various parts of France.

IIn 1922, Peugeot introduced the Quadrilette. In the first cars of this model, the passengers still sat one behind the other. The car was 315 cm long and 120 cm wide.

Ettore Bugatti was responsible for the design of the Peugeot Bébé. Between 1913 and 1916, 3,095 were sold.

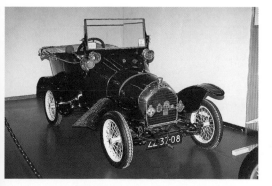

This picture proves that Peugeot did not only build large cars. The car is a Type 184 with a 3770 cc six-cylinder sleeve-valve engine and a Gangloff body.

The range was further expanded with a small car, the Bébé Peugeot after a design by Ettore Bugatti which had an 855 cc 4-cylinder engine, and the larger models 144, 145, 146, 148. Before the First World War Peugeot was actively involved in racing. Beautiful cars with 7.6 litre engines and two overhead camshafts and four valves for each cylinder were built for this purpose.

The cars won various Grand-Prix races, but in 1913 they also won the Indianapolis 500. At the Brookland race track, a Peugeot broke the world record with a top speed of 106.56 mph (170.5 kph). After the First World War, the European car industry faced hard

The steel roof of the 1934 601 convertible could be folded into the boot using an electrically driven mechanism. In the fifties, Ford introduced a similar system as a novelty.

times. Peugeot presented a mini car to succeed the Bébé. The model was called the Quadrilette. In the first cars of this very small and narrow model, the two passengers sat one behind the other. With a top speed of 37 mph (60 kph), this vehicle was not very fast, but that was not yet really important in those days.Larger models were also presented, such as the Type 156, a limousine with a six-cylinder sleeve-valve engine, that was sold to the French upper ten between 1921 and 1925. In 1921, Peugeot manufactured 6,327 cars and in 1927, almost 24,000.

In 1929, the Peugeot 201 was presented. In 1932, the model was available in eight different basic versions. In 1935, the range consisted of the 201, 301, 401 and 601. The first three models were powered by 1122, 1465 and 1720 cc four-cylinder engines. A 2148 cc six-cylinder engine was installed in the 601. The 1932, 202 was the start of a new era for Peugeot. With its striking nose and the side-by-side headlights this model was the basis for a series of new models.

In 1936, the Parisian Peugeot dealer, Emile Darl'Mat manufactured a sports car on the chassis of a 302. The car was powered by a tuned 2.0 litre engine

taken from the 402. The car was lightning fast and achieved an average speed of almost 87 mph (140 kph) for a period of 24 hours at the Montlhéry race track. In 1937, three Darl'Mat's appeared at the start of the Le Mans 24-hour race. The race was won by Jean-Pierre Wimille, driving a Bugatti and thePeugeots finished a well-deserved seventh, eighth and tenth. In 1938, the duo Cortanze/Coutet took part in the Le Mans race. They finished fifth with their Darl'Mat overall and had an average speed of 75 mph (120.33 kph).

They won their own 2.0 litre class. Immediately after the Second World War, the 202 was once again taken into production. It was to remain one of the best selling French cars until 1949.

Pic Pic

In 1906, Swiss Paul Piccard and Lucien Pictet founded the S.A. des Ateliers Piccard et Pictet et Cie company, which became known under the name 'Pic Pic'. Although they were specialised in designing and building-

turbines, they accepted an order from SAG (Société d'Automobiles a Genève) to build a motorcar. The small car was designed by Marc Birkigt, who later became famous for his work with Hispano-Suiza. The first cars rolled off the assembly line in the Autumn of 1906. They were powered by four-cylinder engines that delivered 20 or 35 bhp. In 1907, the range was expanded with a 5500 cc six-cylinder engine. Between 1907 and 1910, 165 rolling chassis were manufactured for SAG. When this company withdrew from the car market, they were henceforth sold under the name Pic Pic. The models

The cars built in 1912 already had a cardan shaft instead of chains and for the first time, a differential.
That year the range consisted of two models, the 14/18 and the 18/22 PS.

were modernised and the range was expanded. Some models were even fitted with a sleeve-valve engine. Within a short space of time, the company became known as the builder of the 'Swiss Rolls-Royce'.
When the First World War broke out, Pic Pic had built a total of 353 cars, of which 21 were exported. During the war, the factory mainly built trucks for the Swiss army. When the war was over, the company failed to restart production. As a consequence, the company was declared bankrupt in 1920.The estate was taken over by Ateliers des Charmilles. Subsequently, a few more cars were built from the parts still in stock.

This 1919 Pic Pic Torpedo had a 2.9 litre four-cylinder sleeve-valve engine. The Rudge spoke wheels and four Houdaille shock absorbers were still something special in those days.

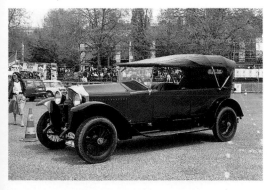

Pierce-Arrow

In America the cars of this make, that unfortunately has now become obscure, could easily compete with makes such as Lincoln, Cadillac and Packard. The expensive, deluxe models were assembled with the greatest possible care. In 1900, George Norman Pierce built his first two motorcars with financial help from Charles Clifton. One of them, which remained a proto-type, was powered by a steam engine. A whole range of motorcars were manufactured on the basis of the other model that had a petrol engine. The car was sold as the Pierce Motorette. The small car was powered by a single-cylinder engine that was suspiciously similar to that of De Dion-Bouton. The following models were also fitted with this type of engine. In 1903, Pierce

Pierce-Arrow also built sports cars.
This 1919 tourer broke 14 world and 66
national records.

Additional luggage space could be found behind the
small square door in the rear mud guard. The car in the
picture is a 1928 Convertible Coupé.

presented a car with a two-cylinder engine that delivered 15 bhp. Some 50 of these were sold. The model was called Pierce-Arrow. The later version with a four-cylinder engine was called the Great Arrow. Business went well. When a new factory was built in Buffalo, New York in 1900, it was the most modern car factory in America. Almost 900 cars were sold that year. In 1907, a model with a six-cylinder engine was presented, the Great Arrow Sixty-Five.The car was so beautifully and meticulously finished that it was soon considered one of the best cars of America. George Pierce started his career manufacturing bicycles and for a long time this activity remained an

IIn 1932, Pierce-Arrow exclusively delivered cars with an
eight-in-line or a V12-engine.

important source of income. In 1909, he split up his company. The Pierce Arrow Motorcar Company was situated at Hannover Street 18, in Buffalo, New

In 1929, the factory manufactured its first model with an
eight-cylinder engine. The 5988 cc side-valve engine
delivered 125 bhp.

The interior of a 1932 tourer. The three-speed gearbox
was operated by means of the huge gear handle. The
windscreen wipers used vacuum technology.

The Silver Arrow, here one from 1933, was to save the make from its downfall. Unfortunately, it failed.

York. Beautiful cars were built in this factory, which even featured partly aluminium bodywork. This material was used for mechanical parts as well. For instance, the crankcase, gear box and differential were made of the light alloy. In the early cars, the steering wheel was fitted on the right. Pierce-Arrow continued to do this until 1921.

This type 840A saloon was built in 1934. It had an 6309 cc eight-cylinder engine that delivered 135 bhp.

Its headlights were another remarkable feature, as they were placed in, instead of on the mud guards. This was very unusual in those days. In 1913, engineer Herbert Dawley even obtained a patent for this construction. In 1918, the company presented the Dual Valve Six model. It owed this strange name to the fact that the six-cylinder engine had four valves for each cylinder; two inlet and two outlet valves. The engine had a cylinder capacity of 8.6 litres. In the twenties, Pierce-Arrow had increasing difficulties competing with makes such as Cadillac and Packard. Its sales figures fell dramatically.

The company presented a new model, the Type 80, with a smaller 4727 cc six-cylinder side-valve engine that delivered 70 bhp at 2600 rpm. The car cost under $3,000. Over 16,000 were sold. In 1928, the Type 80 was replaced by the Type 81, but this model was less popular. Neither were people queuing up to buy the expensive Dual Valve Six.

When Studebaker offered $2 million for Pierce-Arrow in 1928, the offer was immediately accepted. Pierce-Arrow continued to build its own cars, but was now financially supported by its new owners. In 1929, the first Pierce-Arrow with a 6309 cc eight-in-line engine that delivered 115 bhp was unveiled.

In 1932, the Type 52 and Type 53 followed, with V12-engines that ad capacities of 7030 and 6525 cc and delivered 150 and 140 bhp. Pierce-Arrow recovered, but, unfortunately, at the expense of Studebaker. This company had to file for bankruptcy in 1933. Pierce-Arrow was more or less saved, but it did get a new owner. The profits of this company fell as well. The Silver Arrow was developed as a last ditch attempt to save the company.

It was a huge car with a V-12 engine and all the technical novelties available at that time. But even this model was unable to save the company from its downfall. In 1934, 1,740 cars were sold, but in 1936 this number fell to 787. When in 1937, only 167 cars were sold, the company was permanently closed down.

Pipe

The Compagnie Belge de Construction Automobiles was founded by the brothers Alfred and Victor Goldschmidt. They presented their first motorcar in 1900 in Brussels, under the name Pipe. The small car was quite similar to the car made by Panhard & Levassor. The first car was powered by a two-cylinder engine. In 1901, a sporty model – the

Once, Pipe was one of the main Belgian car manufacturers.

15 CV -followed with a four-cylinder engine. This model was a very good racing car. The prototype was immediately used to participate in a Paris to Berlin race.

Like many other makes in those days, Pipe also built cars with powerful engines, such as the 90 CV from 1903 and the 60 CV from 1904. The latter model had a 13.5 litre four-cylinder engine.

In 1907, over 300 cars of the types 28, 50 and 80 CV were sold. Because of this, Pipe became one of the largest Belgian car manufacturers. The Pipes were not only sold in Belgium, but they were also exported to countries such as Russia.

During the First World War, the Pipe factory was partly destroyed. Only in 1921 was it able to resume manufacturing passenger cars. In that year, the company presented two new models with 3.0 and 9.0 litre badly. The management therefore decided to switch to the manufacture of trucks and buses.

Plymouth

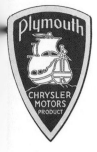

In 1918, Walter Chrysler was one of the main American car manufacturers. The company mainly built cars for the higher price-ranges, such as the makes Imperial, Chrysler and Dodge. Chevrolet and Ford were the manufacturers of cheaper cars. This changed in 1928. In that year, the Chrysler Corporation launched some new models with six-cylinder engines, which caused Walter Chrysler to found a new make for the familiar four-cylinder engines. He called the make Plymouth, after the English town the founders of the state of Massachusetts had come from in the 17th century. The sailing ship of these pilgrims, the Mayflower, was chosen as the company's logo. The founding of the Plymouth make hit the mark.

In 1928, its first year of production, 53,427 cars were sold. In comparison: Chevrolet sold 888,050 cars and Ford sold 633,594 cars in that year, but it was a start. In 1930, the whole world was suffering at the hands of the depression and the car industry was particularly hard hit. Expensive cars

In 1931, Plymouth sold over 100,000 cars for the first time.
This placed the make third on the list of American car manufacturers, behind Chevrolet and Ford.

This 1934 Plymouth PE had a 3.8 litre six-cylinder engine.
The car was exported as a rolling chassis and Tüscher in Switzerland provided the bodywork.

In 1933, customers could choose from the PC or the PD models. The PC had a distinctive chrome-plated radiator.

A 1937 Plymouth four-door saloon. Fresh air came in by means of the small inlet flap in front of the windscreen.

253

could not be sold at all in those days. As a Plymouth was relatively cheap, this make was least affected by the depression. Although it is true that in 1929, the company managed to sell 93,592 cars and this number fell to 67,658 in 1930, as early as 1930 sales figures rose again to 100,000 cars. In 1933, the Plymouth was also fitted with a six-cylinder engine, in response to Ford presenting an inexpensive V8-engine. The new Plymouth was sold as the PC type, but the model was less successful than its predecessor, the PB.

The PC was only 4 cm shorter than the PB, but seemed much smaller. The audience did not feel that this suited a car with a six-cylinder engine. Therefore, a new and larger model was launched in April 1933, the Plymouth Six or PD. The car was almost identical to the Dodge PD, but that did not seem to bother the customers. In 1934, the 1,000,000th Plymouth rolled off the assembly line. In that year, customers could choose from the following models: the Plymouth DeLuxe, the PE, PF, PFXX and the Standard Six and PG. All models were available in different body versions. In 1936, all sales records were broken once again. In that year, Plymouth manufactured

no less than 527,177 cars. Because the models were lowered by 3 cm, they looked a lot more sporty. In that year, only two basic models were available, the Plymouth Business and the more expensive DeLuxe. All the models had six-cylinder engines, which now delivered 82 bhp. In 1938, Plymouth celebrated its tenth anniversary. On this occasion, the Plymouth Business was renamed the Plymouth Roadking. The car had a new, distinctive wind-screen, which in contrast to previous years could no longer be opened. In 1939, the cars were given an entirely new body. This body was to remain the same until the Second World War. On 9 February 1942 the last pre-war Plymouth rolled off the assembly line.

Pontiac

In contrast to Buick, Chevrolet or Oldsmobile, the make Pontiac was not named after its founder, but after a famous Indian. The Pontiac was constructed in the Oakland factory. The latter had become part of the General Motors group company as early as 1909. When in January 1926, the cheaper Pontiac was presented, Oakland was still one of General Motors' top makes, but the consumers opted massively for the new make. Oakland's turnover collapsed, causing its termination in 1931. The first Pontiac was powered by a six-cylinder side-valve engine. Its closed body was available with two or four doors. In 1927, already over 135,000 cars were sold and in 1928 over 200,000 cars were sold; the first time that this number was achieved. The cars built in 1928 were given an entirely new and more modern body, but the wheels still had wooden spokes. In 1932, the Pontiac Series 302 was presented. Actually, this model was the same as the 1931 Oakland, but the new model was powered by a V8-engine in contrast to its predecessor. The model was not a great success. Only 6,281 of the total number of 36,352 cars sold were Series 302 cars. In 1933, all Pontiacs were fitted with an eight-cylinder engine. But this time it was an eight-in-line engine and not a V8. The most striking feature of the models was their pointed radiator. They had a 292 cm wheel base. The engine delivered 77 bhp at 3600 rpm, which was sufficient for a top speed of 78 mph (125 kph). The cheapest version was the Sport Roadster, which cost $585 and the most expensive one was the five-seater Touring Saloon, at $710. In 1934, the Pontiacs were provided with a larger and heavier body.

The engine,however, now delivered 84 bhp, increasing the top speed to 84 mph (135 kph), despite the additional weight. The brakes were still operated mechanically but, on the other hand, the cars were equipped with independent front wheel suspension. In 1935,

The first and cheapest Pontiac, a 1926 coach. In those days the car cost $825. The model was powered by a 3.0 litre six-cylinder side-valve engine that delivered 40 bhp at 2400 rpm.

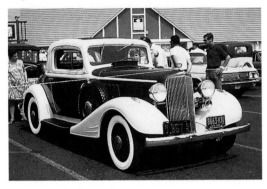

In 1933, Pontiac only sold cars of the Economy Eight type with an eight-cylinder in-line engine, although customers could choose from seven different body shapes.

Sixty-Two. In the same year, two new models additional were marketed with a six-cylinder engine, as well as two models with an eight-cylinder engine.

The engines for the 1941 cars were tuned even more. The 3.9 litre six-cylinder engines now delivered 90 bhp at 3200 rpm and the 4.1 litre eight-cylinder engines delivered 103 bhp at 3500 rpm. In 1942, the assembly lines were adapted to the production of army equipment. That is why, in that year, only 15,404 motorcars were manufactured.

customers could once again choose between a six or an eight-cylinder engine. The six-cylinder delivered 80 bhp and was installed in a chassis with a 284 cm wheel base. The wheel base of the cars with an 84 bhp eight-cylinder engine was 297 cm. Finally both models were equipped with the much better hydraulic brake system. In 1937, the models were given another face lift and the range was further expanded.

The Standard Six was available in three different versions and no less than nine different body versions were planned for the DeLuxe Six. The Standard Six looked somewhat dingy. The model had only one taillight, one windscreen wiper, one sun flap and only the driver's door had an arm rest. With regard to its mechanics, it was identical to the more expensive DeLuxe, which for many taxi-drivers and representatives was a reason to buy the cheaper version.

In 1940, almost 250,000 Pontiacs were sold, but 1941 with a sales figure of 282,087 was an even better year. In 1940, Pontiac presented a new model, the Torpedo Eight. The car was a cross between the Oldsmobile Ninety, the Buick roadmaster and the Cadillac

The 1939 range consisted of three basic models: the inexpensive Quality Six, the DeLuxe Six and the Eight. On request, the cars could be equipped with footboards and steering column gear change for an additional fee.

In 1939, the convertible was the most expensive version. Fitted with a six-cylinder engine, the model cost $993 and an eight-cylinder cost $1,046.

Railton

When in 1933, Invicta moved to London, the factory in Cobham was taken over by Reid Railton. One of Railton's principal clients was John Cobb who was completely obsessed by speed. There was nothing he liked better than breaking world records. Especially for Cobb, Railton built cars including the Napier-Railton, a car with an aircraft engine with which Cobb reached a speed of 143.44 mph (229.504 kph) at the Brooklands race-

track. Railton had already gained a great deal of experience with the E.R.A. sports and racing cars. When he decided to start manufacturing cars under his own name he definitely knew what he was letting himself in for. The first models, with a four-seater body, were built on a reinforced Terraplane or Hudson chassis. Railton replaced the weak suspension by real sports car suspension. In 1933, the eight-in-line engine had 4010 cc and delivered 95 bhp at 3600 rpm.

The cars had a top speed of 94 mph (150 kph). When the original models were improved in America, Railton immediately adapted his cars. For example, in 1934 the cylinder capacity was increased to 4168 cc which delivered 113 bhp at 3800 rpm. In 1937, Hudson presented a six-cylinder model. This model then constituted the basis for the Railton Light Sports. The

Reid Railton built the very first European sports car on an American rolling chassis.

model was powered by a six-cylinder, 2723 cc, 76 bhp at 3800 rpm engine. In 1938, customers could also opt for a 3475 cc cylinder capacity which delivered 114 bhp. In 1939, Railton presented the Baby Railton with a 10 bhp Standard engine, but no one was interested in the model. In total, Railton built just over 1,400 cars. Just before the war he sold his company to an American Hudson dealer in London.

Rally used to be one of the most well-known French sports car manufacturers. The make classed alongside the likes of Amilcar or Salmson. The picture shows a 1923 car with a SCAP engine.

Rally

The cars which were manufactured under this name between 1921 and 1933 in Colombes, France were of exceptionally good quality. This is why the company lasted a lot longer than most of its competitors. The first Rally was a 'cycle car' powered by a Harley Davidson motorcycle engine. In 1922, the model could also be supplied with a SCAP, Chapuis or CIME four-cylinder engine. The small overhead valve engines had cylinder capacities of 989, 1098 or 1170 cc. Rally also built several models which never outgrew the prototype stage, such as a car with a 1492 cc eight-in-line engine by SCAP and a sports car with a four-cylinder Rally engine with two overhead camshafts which delivered 40 bhp at 3800 rpm.

This Rally was very similar to the Bugatti as far as appearance was concerned. The car in the picture has to have been built at the end of the twenties.

Rambler

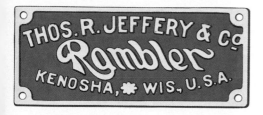

Thomas B. Jeffery also manufactured bicycles before he took the gamble and started manufacturing motorcars. Jeffery, who emigrated from England, first built a motorcar in 1897 in Chicago. The model had a single-cylinder engine which powered the rear wheels via chains. At the end of the nineteenth century, Jeffery and his son Charles moved to Kenosha, where he specialised in the manufacture of motorcars. In 1902, the company already sold over 1,500 runabouts.

Rambler became one of America's most popular cars. 1905 saw the unveiling of the first model with a two-cylinder engine. In 1909, the last Rambler with such a two-cylinder engine rolled off the production lines. In 1910, the

In Europe, the Rambler is a rare sight. This car belongs
to the automobile museum in Aalholm, Denmark.
The model is from the first year of production (1902)
and was therefore powered by a single-cylinder
engine.

customer had a choice of two different four-cylinder engines, with either 34 or 45 bhp. The cars were definitely not cheap. One of the owners in that time was the American president William Howard Taft. Guarantees were unheard of in that era, but Jeffery had so much faith in his cars that he gave his customers full warranty for the first 10,000 miles. Thomas Jeffery died of a heart attack on 2 April 1910 during a holiday in Italy.

His son Charles then took over the business. Out of respect for his father he called the make Jeffery instead of Rambler from 1914 onwards.

Renault

Luis Renault was the black sheep of the family. His brothers Marcel and Fernand went to university while Louis struggled to finish primary school. He was more interested in technology than in schoolbooks. Louis got a job as an apprentice mechanic at companies

The first Renault from 1898. This replica was built in
1998 to mark the one hundredth anniversary of the
factory.

In 1907, Renault also built stately cars such as this XB limousine with a 3.0 litre four-cylinder, 14 bhp engine.

including De Dion and Serpollet. But because his father was rather rich he could afford a car in spite of it all. In 1898, Louis disassembled his De Dion three-wheeler. He built a new chassis with separate suspension for all four the wheels, mounted the engine in the

Racing cars also appeared, such as this two-seater which could be supplied with engine capacities varying between 12.0 and 18.0 litres which delivered up to 90 bhp.

front instead of the back of the chassis and replaced the chain drive by a cardan shaft. He then had the construction patented. In 1899, he founded his own company with his brother's financial support. The first Renault was already unveiled in Paris after a few months. The orders flooded in. A short while later, a closed version of the model came onto the market.

In 1900, Louis Renault already sold more than 200 cars. Due to the success, Louis' brothers also became increasingly interested in cars. They took part in the long distance races that were so popular in France in those days. That had a sad ending when in 1903 Marcel Renault died during a race from Paris to Madrid. That year, France was the biggest motorcar manufacturing country in the world with a production

This Renault NN as a four-seater Torpedo version was 335 cm in length, weighed 1100 kg (2420 lb) and had a top speed of 37 mph (60 kph).

This four-seater convertible was unveiled in 1921. It was the first Renault which could be supplied with left-hand drive.

of 30,000 cars. 780 of these cars were built at Renault. Some 600 people worked in the factory. Ten years later in 1913, the number of employees had risen to 15,200 and for the first time over 10,000 cars were built. Renault built both large and small models. In 1904, the company supplied 1,500 cheap taxis to the Compagnie des Fiacres. Besides these taxis, Renault also built buses. In 1908, Fernand Renault died and Louis became the company's sole owner. During the First World War, Renault built small tanks, aircraft engines and hand grenades. The taxis also made the headlines

A sports car from 1903, photographed during a historic car rally in 1982. This car did not have a great deal of luggage space.

From 1928 onwards, the models were given the most beautiful names such as this Monastella. The six-cylinder engine had 1476 cc and the car had a top speed of 56 mph (90 kph).

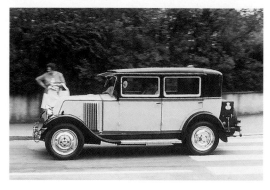

The Juvaquatre of 1939, was ahead of its time. It was the first Renault with a self-supporting body.

cars which could compete with makes like Mercedes and Hispano-Suiza were also launched. The models were given beautiful names like Monastella, Reinastella, Nervastella or Vivaquartre. The cars were also extremely interesting from a technical point of view.

As early as 1939, the Juvaquatre already had a self-supporting body and independent suspension. In 1940, the Renault company employed more than 40,000 people and besides cars they also built aeroplanes. During the Second World War, Renault could not think of any other way to survive than to work for the Germans. Naturally, people did not take kindly to this after the war. Renault was jailed in 1944 and died there under mysterious circumstances.

Advertisement for one of the Renault brothers' first cars.

again. On 25 September 1914, German troops had come to within 25 kilometres of Paris. To enable a counter attack, 12,000 French soldiers were taken to the battlefield near the Marne under the cover of darkness. Half travelled by train, the remaining soldiers were taken to Paris in 600 Renault taxis.

After the war Renault bought a number of its subcontractors, including an entire blast furnace. In 1922, the company was re-christened the Société Anonyme des Usines Renault. Louis Renault owned 98% of the shares.

Once more Renault built cars in all price categories. Extremely expensive

The Renault company was expropriated on 16 January 1945 by General de Gaulle.Four years later Louis Renault was rehabilitated and his wife and children received a small allowance.

This Reo was sold as a two-seater runabout in 1912. It cost $1,000 then and had 30 or 35 bhp engines.

Reo

In 1904, Ransom Eli Olds had a conflict with his financiers. They had had enough of the Curved Dash and wanted to develop a much more luxurious model. Olds did not agree and left his own company. He then started all over again with the Reo Motor Car Company. In contrast to the small Curved Dash, the Reo was equipped with a five-seater body. The cars sold well.

In 1907, three years after the company was founded, Reo was already the third largest car manufacturer in America. Right behind Ford and Buick. When Ford brought out the Model T, Olds countered in 1909 with a new model with a four-cylinder engine, differential axle drive and a left-hand drive.

In 1908, Reo had already built its first truck. During the First World War the company bloomed thanks to the production of army trucks. 1916, saw the unveiling of the first model with a six-cylinder engine. This Reo M delivered 45 bhp.

The Reo's were quite conservative as far as appearance was concerned, but all that changed with the launch of the Flying Cloud in 1927. This car had modern lines and a powerful six-cylinder engine delivering 73 bhp. The model was available in five different body versions, all equipped with hydraulic brakes. A cheap version of the Flying Cloud was the Wolverine.

1931 saw the launch of the top of the line model, the Reo Royale. The long bonnet hid an eight-cylinder, 125 bhp engine. The wheel bases varied between 332 and 386 cm. From 1933 onwards, this model could be supplied with an automatic gearbox. Naturally, in

the year of the great depression, the demand for such luxury cars was very limited. Total production dropped to 3,623 cars. In 1936, the Board decided to stop manufacturing passenger cars. From then on, the company would specialise solely in the manufacture of trucks. Olds did not agree with this decision and once more left this own company. Ransom Eli Olds died in 1950.

Riley

Perhaps it is starting to get rather tedious, but William Riley started out manufacturing bicycles in Coventry in 1888. When his sons Victor, Stanley, Allan, Percy and Cecil were old enough to help out in the factory, father decided to start manufacturing cars too. Percy Riley primarily drew three-

The TT Riley was the last real racing car. As of 1935, the company only manufactured sports cars.

The Sprites dashboard features a handle for the pre-selector gear box to the right of the steering wheel.

wheelers with two front wheels and an extra seat over the front axle. The first car was driven by a 517 cc single-cylinder engine. In the later models the V2 engine was mounted over the rear wheel. Before the First World War Riley only manufactured light Voiturettes, but after the war the Coventry factory primarily manufactured large, sporty-looking cars. During the thirties the fast roadsters were particularly popular. Famous racing drivers like Malcolm Campbell, George Eyston, Sammy Davis and Raymond Mays booked many victories in Riley's like thi one.

Riley also built four-cylinder sleeve valve engines or six-cylinder overhead valve engines such as the MPH 1.5 litre from 1934 and the Sprite from 1935. One of the most popular models was the 1935 Riley IMP. The car had a 1087 cc, four-cylinder engine with two overhead camshafts which delivered 35 bhp.

In 1937, the company experienced financial difficulties after which the make was sold to William Morris in 1938. Victor and Percy Riley stayed on as directors for a while, but Percy

The 1937 Riley Sprite had a 1496 cc, four-cylinder overhead valve engine with two camshafts.

already died in 1941, aged 58. His 93 year-old father died three years later. Riley would definitely have celebrated the make's one hundredth anniversary if British-Leyland had not discontinued the make in 1969.

Roamer

The Roamer make was founded in 1916 by Albert Barley. The company from Kalamazoo was named after the famous racehorse Roamer, which was winning regularly around that time. The first Roamer was unveiled in 1916 in Chicago. It was a comparatively cheap car, even though it looked the same as a Rolls-Royce. The car's windscreen was already angled and the wheels had steel spokes. This model sold well.

In the initial years more than 2,000 Roamers were sold annually. One of which was exhibited at the 1917 car show in New York. The car had a polished aluminium roadster body.

All four, six and eight-cylinder engines were made by Continental or Rochester-Duesenberg. The most popular model was a 5.0 litre, six-cylinder car. Between

This five-seater Roamer from 1924 was powered by a 3.8 litre Rochester-Duesenberg engine.

1927 and 1930 all the models were equipped with a Continental eight-in-line engine.

Röhr

Hans Gustav Röhr's cars were conspicuous because of their techno-logical innovations. The chassis was made of welded steel plates, the cars featured axle half shafts, the rear seat was located in front of, instead of on top of the rear axle and an eight-cylinder in-line engine was installed under the bonnet. Only three different models were manufactured under Hans Röhr's management. Between 1927

In 1933, the Autenrieth company built this convertible body on a Röhr F type chassis.

A total of 1,700 Röhr Juniors were sold.

and 1928 he sold approximately 100 R 8/40 cars. In 1928, this model was equipped with a more powerful 2246 cc engine. Until 1939, approximately 1,000 units of this model were built. Approximately 350 RA's were built (the final model, which featured a 2496 cc eight-in-line engine). The company was hardly realising a profit and in 1930, Röhr was forced to sell his company. He got a job at Adler and later at Mercedes. The new owners presented a new model with a 3.2 litre engine, the Röhr F in 1933. From 1934 onwards, the FK version of the car was also available with a compressor. In total, approximately 270 of these F models were sold. The company was more successful with the Junior, a Tatra 30 built under licence. The car was powered by the small Czech 1485 cc, four-cylinder boxer engine. This model no longer looked anything like the original Röhr luxury motorcars.

Rolls-Royce

Actually, Charles Stewart Rolls (1877-1910) and Henry Royce (1863-1933) had little in common. Rolls was a playboy, the son of rich, aristocratic parents. He was a Panhard dealer in London, but spent more time flying,

balloning and car racing than selling cars. Royce, on the other hand, had worked for his living his whole life. He was the fifth child of a working class family and had to go out and sell newspapers at age ten to make ends meet. In the evenings he went to school, learned languages and algebra and eventually rose to become a manufacturer of electric cranes in Manchester.

Royce was dissatisfied with his second-hand Décauville and decided to build his own car. In the Spring of 1904, this car – powered by a two-cylinder engine – drove out of his small factory. Rolls and Royce met for the first time in London that same year. Rolls convinced car dealer Royce to start mass producing cars. The first cars brought onto the market under the name Rolls-Royce had a 2.0 litre, two-cylinder engine. Only 19 of this model were sold between 1904 and 1906. The more powerful 3.0 litre, three-cylinder, 15 HP was also not a resounding success. In 1905 and 1906, only six

To save on import duties, the Silver Ghost was also manufactured in the American town of Springfield between 1920 and 1926. The picture depicts a Piccadilly Roadster.

In 1911, the customer had a choice of three different engines, with two, three or four cylinders.

were sold. However, there was more demand for the most powerful model, the 30 HP (1905-1906). 45 of these were built, all powered by a 6.0 litre, six-cylinder engine. Royce also manufactured a model with a 3.5 litre, V8 engine, the Legalimit. Only three of these were built. In 1907, Rolls-Royce unveiled its first best-seller.

The model came to be known as the 40/50 HP Silver Ghost. The car was named after the proto-type, that was equipped with polished aluminium bodywork. Not only had the Silver Ghost won a 3,000 km reliability run up to Scotland, but it had also travelled well over 23,000 km without technical

A Rolls-Royce Twenty as a Doctors Coupé from 1927.

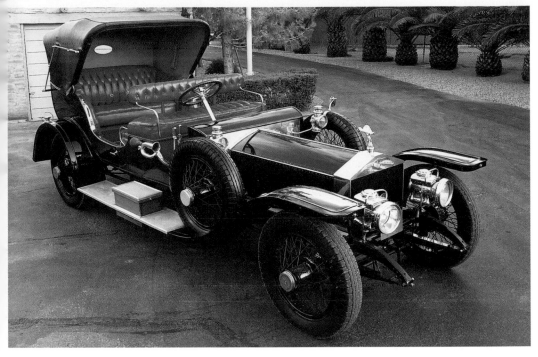

problems after that. The factory called the car 'The Best Car in the World'. The 40/50 HP was manufactured until 1925. All-in-all, some 6,220 were sold. The Silver Ghost was originally powered by a 7036 cc, six-cylinder engine, but as early as 1910 this was replaced by a 7428 cc engine. There was also a Rolls-Royce for Joe Public. Between 1922 and 1929 this car was sold as the Rolls-Royce Twenty.

The Twenty was equipped with a six-cylinder, 3127 cc engine. A total of

The bodywork of this Phantom II Continental Allweather Torpedo from 1933 was made by Barker.

Rolls-Royce only sold rolling chassis before the war. The customer could then select the bodywork builder of his choice. Barker equipped this Phantom I with a body in 1928.

The Phantom II's six-cylinder engine capacity is 7668 cc with unknown power output.

The Phantom II's six-cylinder engine capacity is 7668 cc with unknown power output.

The last pre-war model was the Wraith. The picture depicts a Sedanca Coupé with bodywork by Gurney Nutting.

2,890 of these small cars were built.The Silver Ghost was followed by the New Phantom, which would later be called the Phantom I.

This car had an even more powerful engine than the Silver Ghost. The cylinder capacity amounted to 7668 cc. The model was only manufactured for four years.

After 2,250 had been sold, the model was succeeded by the Phantom II. The Phantom II had an entirely new chassis. Only 1,767 cars of this model were manufactured until 1935. The last

The V12 engine of the Phantom III was not entirely problem free. The picture shows a car from 1936 with bodywork by Gurney Nutting.

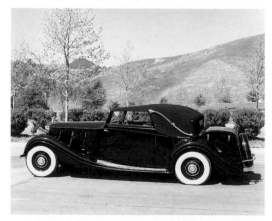

pre-war Phantom was the Phantom III (1936-1939).

The car was powered by a rather unreliable 7340 cc, V12 engine and was also really expensive which led to only 715 being sold. Rolls-Royce always had a 'cheap' model in its range.

In 1929, the Twenty was succeeded by the 20/25. This car was powered by a 3,669 cc engine. The engines became increasingly powerful. The 25/30 from 1936 had a six-cylinder, 4,257 cc engine.

This model was only manufactured for two years. In total 1,200 were built. The last pre-war model was the Wraith. The car housed the same engine as the 25/30, but the bodywork had been entirely modernised.

Rosengart

Jules Salomon drew the first cars for André Citroën, but decided to start for himself in 1928. He signed a cooperation agreement with Lucien Rosengart (1881-1976). Rosengart owned

This Rosengart LR 539 Supertraction from 1939 was still modern after the war. In 1947, the car was equipped with an American Mercury engine.

a company with 4,500employees which manufactured car parts. The first model by both partners was the Rosengart LR 2, an Austin Seven built under licence.

The LR 2 was a resounding success so the small car was soon followed by more. The Rosengart LR 4 was unveiled in 1931. The car was powered by an engine bored out to 1097 cc. The longer chassis could be supplied as a sedan, coupe or delivery van. In 1932 Rosengart signed a licensing contract

The Rosengart LR 2 was an exact copy of the Austin Seven. Even the 747 cc, four-cylinder engine was adopted unaltered.

with Adler. From that moment on, the German Adler Trumpf was built as the Rosengart LR 500. This car had a 1650 cc, four-cylinder engine which delivered 38 bhp.

Another model, the LR 130 was derived from the Adler Primus. Lucien Rosengart and Jules Salomon never invested much money in the development of their own products. They preferred to buy the rights. This why, just before the war besides 'Austins'

Just like the Austin seven, the small Rosengart was also available as a sports car. The picture shows such a two-seater during the 1993 Klausen hill climb.

and 'Adlers' the Rosengart factory also manufactured 'Citroëns'. However, the bodywork of the LR 539 Supertraction looked nothing like the French original. The car looked a great deal more sporty.

The LR 4 was an LR 2 with bigger bodywork. The model was primarily used as a taxi in spite of its small 747 cc engine.

The Rosengart LR 4 could be ordered right up to the outbreak of the Second World War. The picture depicts a four-seater convertible from 1939.

The dashboard of the LR 4.

The engine, gearbox and front axle originated from the Citroën 11. The rear axle was by Adler.

Rover

James and John Starley owned the Rover Cycle Company. The company manufactured agricultural machinery and bicycles. In 1888, the duo built their first motorised tricycle. The vehicles with two rear wheels and a single front wheel sold very well. In 1904, they built their first real car. The two-seater was powered by a 1327 cc, water-cooled, single-cylinder engine. The Rover cost £200, but lights cost extra. In 1905, it was followed by a cheaper model, the 6 HP.

The company name was changed to the Rover Company when, in 1906, a further two models were added to the range, the 16/20 HP and the 10/12 HP. 1912 saw the unveiling of the Rover 12. The car which was powered by a 2.3

In 1904, Rover built its first real cars. The range consisted of small two-seaters and large passenger cars. They were powered by a single-cylinder engine.

A Rover 14 from 1934 during the 1991 Alpine Rally.

In 1937, all the Rovers – except the Ten – were provided with new bodywork. The Ten (see picture) was only modernised in 1939.

litre, four-cylinder engine was designed by Eenheid Glegg. The model was very successful. After the First World War, small, cheap cars were built including the Rover Eight. The Eight was powered by an air-cooled 1.0 litre, two-cylinder, boxer engine. This car was also a resounding success. By the time the model was taken out of production in 1925, over 17,000 had been sold.

In 1924, it was succeeded by the Rover 14/15 which was awarded a prize by the RAC (Royal Automobile Club) for its 'exceptional characteristics'. Besides passenger cars, the company also manufactured various sports cars. In 1907, a Rover 20 PS won the

International Tourist Trophy on the Isle of Man. The Rover beat famous makes like Mercedes, Alfa and Audi. Racing always provided plenty of free publicity. For example in 1930, when a Rover Light Six won a 1,200 km race across France against the famous Train Blue which in those days was the fastest train in Europe. The distance was covered at an average speed of 38 mph (60.8 kph). The Rover in Calais arrived 20 minutes before the train did. In the thirties the Rover make also suffered from the depression. Turnover decreased so much that new management was appointed in 1933 led by the brothers Spencer and Maurice Wilks. First of all the brothers cut the size of the range.

In 1934, only the following models were on sale: the four-cylinder Ten (1389 cc) and Twelve (1495 cc) and the six-cylinder Fourteen, Speed Fourteen (1577 cc), Speed Sixteen (2023 cc) and Speed Twenty (2565 cc). The prices varied from £238 to £505. In 1937, all the models were modernised. Besides technical improvements, the bodywork was also changed. The cars were now so modern that they remained unchanged after the Second World War.

The 1939 Twelve was powered by a 1496 cc, four-cylinder engine. In England the four-door version of the car with a steel sliding roof cost £300.

Salmson

During the First World War, Salmson had earned a great deal of money manufacturing products including aircraft engines. The company gained so much experience in this way that after the war it was small step for it to switch from aircraft engines to motorcars. The cars were very reliable. At first the company manufactured small Voiturettes. The factory on the Rue du Point du Jour in Billancourt initially manufactured licensed products by the English GN factory. They had an air-cooled, two-cylinder V engine with chain drive. In 1921, after approximately 1600 cars had been sold, a new model by Henri Petit was launched. The model was equipped with a 1987 cc, four-cylinder engine with overhead valves and had a top speed of approximately 44 mph (70 kph). The car sold well. To gain publicity for the make, Petit designed a racing car with a four-cylinder engine and two overhead camshafts. A large number of races were won with this model, including the 24 hour Le Mans race in 1923 and the Targa Florio of 1926. The model with a compressor engine was called the San Sebastian. When Amilcar launched a six-cylinder compressor engine in 1925, Salmson unveiled a 1085 cc, eight-cylinder engine with two overhead camshafts

This S4 took part in the Rally Neige Glace in January 1987. There was no shortage of snow and ice.

The first Salmsons, here a car from 1921, were small and light. Front wheel brakes really were necessary.

The bodywork of the 1924 GS (Grand Sport) was made entirely of aluminium. The car was built near Wenger in Basle.

The S4-61 had a 1730 cc, four-cylinder engine which delivered 50 bhp at 4200 rpm, enough to get the convertible up to its top speed of 75 mph (120 kph).

and two compressors. The engine delivered almost 100 bhp and had a top speed of almost 125 mph (200 kph). Unfortunately the very fast car was never taken into production as it was just too expensive. In 1927, Salmson stopped racing which was expensive. From then on, the company concentrated on manufacturing small, two-seater sports cars, but also built more deluxe models such as the 1932 Salmson S4. The S4 with its 1296 cc engine had a top speed of 56 mph (90 kph) and a fuel consumption of 1:12. In 1934, the cylinder capacity was increased to 1420 cc. It now delivered 30 bhp. The model became more and more expensive and bigger. In 1935, the S4 was powered by a 1596 cc

engine with two overhead camshafts and an electro-magnetic Cotal gearbox. The car cost 32,000 French Francs, the same as two Renault Deltas. In 1937, the S4 was succeeded by the S4-D4 which had a 1730 cc engine which delivered 48 bhp. There was a no less than two year factory guarantee on the chassis and bodywork and the engine was also guaranteed. The valves had to last at least 32,000 km and the pistons had to last at least 64,000 km. The company failed to restart after the war. The demand for expensive cars was still too low. In 1955, the Salmson make was sold to Renault. Once again a famous make had disappeared from the market.

S.C.A.P.

In many countries the car industry was concentrated in a particular town or area. In America the town of Detroit became inextricably bound up with cars, in England and France the towns concerned were Coventry and Billancourt respectively. The latter housed the Renault, Salmson and S.C.A.P. (Société de Constructeur Automobiles Paris). S.C.A.P. primarily

David and Goliath during the 1983 Lausanne GP as a 1922 S.C.A.P. is overtaken by a Bugatti.

manufactured car engines, small four-cylinders with cylinder capacities of 894 cc and up, but also large 3.0 litre eight-cylinder engines. The engine factory also built entire motorcars. Particularly sporty two-seaters and racing cars. The racing cars were powered by a 1100 cc engine with over-head valves which could be equipped with a Cozette compressor at the customer's request. The larger models had either 1614 or 1704 cc, four-cylinder engines. In 1929, the company unveiled a 2.0 litre, eight-cylinder engine with overhead valves. The S.C.A.P. also suffered from the great depression and in 1929 it closed its gates for good.

Schacht

The American coach builder Gustav A. Schacht built his first car in 1904. It was a high-wheeler; the high wheels were very functional at that time because there were almost no roads in rural areas. At least such a car did not sink

into the mud up to its axles. The first cars were powered by a water-cooled, two-cylinder engine which delivered 10 bhp, but larger models soon followed. In 1910, the first car with normal wheels was built. In 1913, the factory switched to the production of trucks. Up to that point in time, the factory had sold approximately 8,000 passenger cars.

Scheibler

Fritz Scheibler was one of the many German car pioneers, but in contrast to his colleagues who copied French designs and built in Daimler or Benz engines, Scheibler manufactured everything himself. The first Scheibler left the factory in Aken in 1900 and the model immediately won various prizes. The Scheibler won a gold medal at the Frankfurt car exhibition. The two-cylinder engine in the front of the car powered the rear wheels via chains. In 1903, several new models were launched, small Voiturettes with 5 and

The two-cylinder engine of the 1909 Schacht High-wheeler had a 2.4 litre cylinder capacity.

The four-cylinder engine of the 1904 Scheibler was still mounted under the front seats. The rear wheels were chain driven.

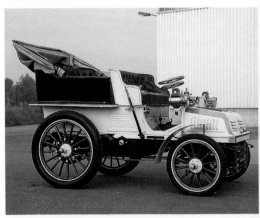

12 bhp twins. A year later, the first larger models were launched with 24 and 35 bhp four-cylinder engines. These engines were not just used for the passenger cars, but also for the Scheibler trucks.

The last passenger car rolled off the assembly line in 1907. In those days, truck building was much more profitable.

Scott

The Englishman Alfred Scott owned two companies. Scott Engineering Co. Ltd. built motorcycles with water-cooled engines and Scott Autocar Co. Ltd. manufactured three-wheelers, the Scott Sociables. Technically speaking, these three-wheelers were ahead of their time. 54 elements of the design

were patented in 1915. The car had a single front wheel and two rear wheels, whereby the front wheel was situated in front of the right rear wheel. The rear wheels were linked by a fixed axle. The two-seater had a 578 cc, water-cooled, two-cylinder, two-stroke engine. In the early years the British army was the principal client.

The Sociable was used both for transporting personnel and for transporting army equipment. The three-wheeler also sold well after the First World War. Production of the model only ceased in 1926.

Sears

The car factory Sears Motor Buggy was situated in Chicago in the United

The prices for the Sears varied between $370 and $485

After Chenard & Walcker took over Robert Sénéchal's company, the cars were no longer equipped with Ruby engines. The picture shows a four-seater convertible from 1926.

States. Between 1908 and 1911 the factory manufactured cheap cars for the famous Sears, Roebuck & Co. mail-order company. The large wooden wheels made the model especially popular in rural areas. The cars were marketed using thick catalogues.

The Sears was powered by a 14 bhp, two-cylinder engine. In spite of the wooden wheels and solid rubber tyres, the car had a top speed of approximately 25 mph (40 kph). In total some 3,500 cars were sold.

Sénéchal

When Robert Sénéchal built his first sports car in Courbevoie he was already a world-famous racing car driver. The first Sénéchal from 1921, the B4, was a sporty two-seater with a 900 cc, four-cylinder engine. The engines came from the Ruby company, a specialist in the field. Quite soon several larger models followed the small two-seater.

In 1922, a Grand Sport with a 975 cc engine with overhead valves was unveiled and in 1923 a model was launched with a 1100 cc engine. The cars

were perfect for racing. A Sénéchal won the Boulogne Grand Prix in 1923 and 1924 and the famous Bol d'Or in 1923, 1924 and 1925. In 1926, the company was taken over by Chenard & Walcker.

In that same year, there were three basic models in the range: the small Voiturette, the Sport and the Grand Sport. All the cars were powered by a 972 cc engine made by Chenard & Walcker. The Voiturette had a side-valve engine, both the other engines had overhead valves. Sénéchals were manufactured until 1929. From that moment on the company limited itself to its own products.

S.H.W.

Only three cars were built under the name S.H.W. (Schwäbische Hütten Werke AG). The company was located in Boblingen near Stuttgart. In those days, Wunibald Kamm, who was later to become famous as a pioneer in the field of aerodynamics, worked at Mercedes as a designer. His dream was a cheap car which almost everyone

Nunnibald Kamm's 'volkswagen'. The car had
a cheap, self-supporting body and seated
five.

The storage spaces between the mudguards were
primarily intended to strengthen the bodywork.

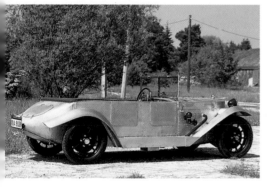

could afford. Mercedes was not interested in the idea so Kamm had to find another manufacturer. S.H.W. was up for the challenge and built three prototypes. The self-supporting bodywork was made entirely from aluminium. An air-cooled, two-cylinder boxer engine powered the front wheels which had independent suspension. The rubber silent blocks between the engine and the body, and the structure of the storage space between the front and rear mudguards were new. This space was primarily intended to strengthen the bodywork. Only one of the prototypes survived the war. The beautifully restored example can be seen in the Deutsche Museum in Munich.

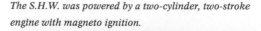

The S.H.W. was powered by a two-cylinder, two-stroke engine with magneto ignition.

Siata

Giorgio Ambrosini (1890-1974) spent a large part of his life surrounded by motorcars. Ambrosini was born in Fano in Italy on the Adriatic. As a small boy he moved to Turin where he founded the Siata company in 1926. The Società Italiana Auto-Transformazioni-Accessori on the Via Leonardo da Vinci in Turin specialised in tuning up Fiat engines, but the engines were also used in the small sports cars which were

Siata sports cars based on the Fiat 508 performed particularly well in long distance races such as the Mille Miglia.

sold under the name Siata. The company's speciality was the Fiat 508 Balilla whose 995 cc engine was bored out to 1057 cc. The Fiat 500 Topolino engine delivered 30 instead of 13 bhp after a 'Siata treatment'. In this version the two-seater had a top speed of 75 mph (120 kph).

The company also sold tuning sets, which included aluminium inlet manifolds for a double carburettor. Siata also sold moulded cylinder heads with overhead valves for Fiat engines which were originally equipped with side valves. Basically, Ambrosini would build anything. He mounted Rootes compressors and built a fourth gear

into a three-speed gearbox. Ambrosini proved the quality of his products himself. He took part in various races including the Mille Miglia of 1935. During this race, the famous bodywork manufacturer Nuccio Bertone was his co-driver.

Sima-Violet

The Sima-Violet is prominent on the list of ugly cars. French cycle cars were never very beautiful to look at, but the cars by Sima-Violet are downright ugly. The factory on the Rue Lazare in Paris manufactured the small racing cars between 1924 and 1929. The model was powered by an air-cooled, two-cylinder, two-stroke engine. The small racing cars were very fast though.

The relatively light car actually did not consist of much more than a chassis with an engine and a seat and the 496 cc engine delivered sufficient horsepower. In 1927, Sima-Violet finished in third place in the Boulogne Grand Prix. The make was justifiably proud as first and second place were taken by Bugatti. The Sima-Violet was

The women's team in a 1933 Siata: cutting corners and the first dent in the mudguard.

The 1922 Sima-Violet was not a beauty, but it was very fast. Note the petrol tank behind the seat.

Violet was a proponent of two-stroke engines. The picture depicts a two-cylinder engine with double ignition.

Simca started with the licensed construction of the Fiat Balilla. Here an example from 1936.

powered by a 1484 cc, four-cylinder, two-stroke, boxer engine equipped with a Cozette compressor.

Simca

At Simca the client could choose from more bodies than at Fiat. The picture shows a 1936 Simca 5 coupé.

Teodoro Enrico Bartolomeo Pigozzi founded the Société Industrielle Mécanique et de Carrosserie Automobile company in 1935. Fiat Director Giovanni Agnelli – who wanted to have the Fiat 508 Balilla built in France under licence – provided Pigozzi with financial support. The company was located in Suresnes on the outskirts of Paris. After the Balila with its 995 cc engine, the Ardita 518 followed with a 2.0 litre engine. Production only went into full swing with the Fiat 500 Topolino. In France this model was sold as the Simca Cinq. In 1936, 7,282 were built and in 1937 this number had risen to 12,925. The Cinq was succeeded by the Simca Huit in 1937 a model that was based on the Fiat 1100. Oddly enough, production continued

The Simca Cinq could also be ordered as Topolino. No Simcas were imported into the Netherlands before the war.

during the Second World War even though numbers were limited:

	Simca 5	Simca 8
1936	7.282	
1937	12.925	318
1938	1.419	46.739
1939	1.215	17.680
1940	3.604	1.911
1941	3.328	3.766
1942	632	2.217
1943	19	122
1944	23	180
1945	47	65
1946	3.411	4.832

In 1993, this 1925 Simson-Supra took part in the Klausen hill climb. The car had a 2.0 litre engine, two overhead camshafts and 16 valves.

After the war there was an enormous demand for means of transport. Simca was one of the first factories which could immediately start supplying cars again. In contrast to Fiat, the Simcas 5 and 8 could be supplied with various bodies. There was even a racing car version. The latter was designed by Amédée Gordini. To prove how fast and reliable such a Simca Gordini was, a Huit drove round the Montlhéry race track, non-stop for 24 hours. The car had an average speed of 56.74 mph (90.79 kph). In 1937, 1938 and 1939 a Simca Gordini won its class at the 24-hour Le Mans race.

Simson

The Simson & Co arms factory in Suhl in the Thüringerwald built its first motorcar in 1911, but it was only after the demand for arms decreased after the First World War that car production could be stepped up. The pre-war models were the company's own design. The engine and the gear box were also made by Simson. The car was powered by a four-cylinder engine with a cylinder capacity of 1559, 2595 or 3538 cc. The same engines were also manufactured after the war. In 1924, the name Simson was changed into Simson-Supra. The first car sold under this name was a sports car with a 1970 cc, four-cylinder engine with an overhead camshaft and four valves per cylinder. The engine delivered 50 bhp at 4000 rpm in the standard version and up to 80 bhp in the racing cars.

The touring car had a 300 cm wheel base and a top speed of 75 mph (120 kph). The racing car had a shorter chassis and had a top speed of 87 mph (140 kph). In 1925, Simson-Supra unveiled a model with a 3120 cc, six-cylinder engine with an overhead camshaft. The engine now delivered 60 bhp at 2800 rpm which gave it a top speed of approximately 62 mph (100 kph).

Between 1931 and 1934 the customer could also choose a model with a 4673 cc, eight-in-line engine. This Simson-supra was definitely a match for makes such as Mercedes or Horch. In spite of its weight it had a top speed of 75 mph

(120 kph). When Adolf Hitler came to power this signalled trouble for the Jewish company Simson-Supra. In 1934, Simson was expropriated by the Nazi party. From then on, the factory was once again used to manufacture arms.

Singer

Like so many, George Singer also started manufacturing bicycles and motorcycles. In 1905, he presented his first two motorcars. The first model, a two-seater called the 8 HP, featured a water-cooled, two-cylinder engine with a 10 cm bore and stroke and 80 cm rods. The cylinders lay horizontally in the car's driving direction. The cylinder head had an overhead camshaft. The Singer 12 HP had a more powerful engine and more spacious bodywork. Before the First World War, Singer built a staggering thirteen different models. The most popular of which was the Ten from 1912. This Ten was built specifically for the army during the war. The car saw active service in France,

The Singer Nine was renamed the Singer Le Mans after the car did well at Le Mans.

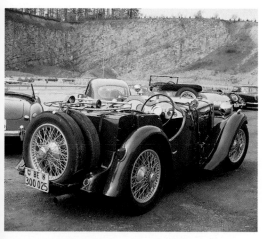

Before the war, the Ten was the most popular model. The model was still sold after the war.

The mudguards of the Le Mans were easy to take off. This turned the car into a real racing car.

Egypt and Italy. In 1919, it was followed by a sports car on the Ten's chassis, which could also be ordered as a racing car with a 33 bhp engine from 1921 on. In 1923, the Ten was provided with an engine with overhead instead of side valve. In 1922, the Ten had a 2.0 litre, six-cylinder engine. The model was available in various versions both with open and closed bodywork. In 1927, a small Singer was unveiled with an 848 cc engine with an overhead camshaft.

Singer called the model Junior. The Ten, with its 1.3 litre engine, was referred to as the Senior from then on.In 1932, the customer could choose from eight different models with four different four-cylinder engines and four different six-cylinder engines. One of the most famous models was the Nine from 1933. This sports car was a good match for the feared MG After a Nine finished thirteenth at Le Mans, the model was renamed the Singer Le Mans. Although in 1935 all the Singers were equipped with overhead camshafts they were however passenger cars as opposed to sports cars.

Sizaire-Naudin

Muarice Sizaire designed his first Voiturette in 1905. This small one or two-seater was very popular in France around that time. Although Sizaire had designed the model he depended on his friend Louis Nuadin to build it. The Voiturette was powered by a one, two or four-cylinder engine.

The simple structure of the cars made them an eye-catcher. For example, the first cars consisted of a mere 420 parts, not including the wooden spokes in the wheels. In 1903, Renault already needed 413 parts for just one of its

A 1908 Sizaire-Naudin, a sporty two-seater with a
1.5 litre, single-cylinder engine.

experimental, telescopically suspended wheels. The first Sizaires were already equipped with independent front wheel suspension. In contrast to most manufacturers, Sizaire and Naudin produced almost all their own parts. This included not only the engine and the bodywork, but also the carburettor and the radiator.

The company invested a great deal of money in racing, because this generated plenty of free advertising. In 1906, the Paris factory already employed a workforce of 50. In that same year, over 100 cars were built. In 1913, Sizaire left the company.

He went on to found the make Sizaire-Berwick. In the meantime, Sizaire-Naudin was starting to manufacture more passenger instead of sports cars. The four-cylinder engines were purchased from Ballot. After the First World War, the Sizaire-Naudin make sold poorly and in 1921 the board of directors decided to close down the factory.

Skoda

After the First World War, Czechoslovakia became independent. Skoda was this new state's largest machine works. The company was comparable to, for example, Krupp in Germany. Heavy weapons and locomotives were principal source of income for both companies. Motorcar production started in 1923. Skoda acquired Hispano-Suiza's licensing rights. The result was a Hispano with a Czechoslovakian body. The model had a large 6.6 litre, six-cylinder engine. The first car to roll off the assembly line at Pilsen

went to the then president Thomas G. Masaryk. After fifty of these cars had been sold, Skoda took over the Laurin & Klement factory in 1925. Cars had been built at this Eastern European company, which was located in Mlada Boleslav since 1906. After the take-over by Skoda, cars were sold under the name Laurin-Klement-Skoda. But in reality they were nothing but Laurin & Klement 110's. Real Skodas were only launched again in 1928, such as the 860 which had a 3880 cc, eight-cylinder engine which delivered 70 bhp or the Skoda 645 which had a 2490 cc, six-cylinder engine which delivered 45 bhp and hydraulic brakes.

1933 saw the launch of the Skoda 420. The car was powered by a small 20 bhp, 995 cc, four-cylinder engine. The car's chassis consisted of a single central

After in 1925, the Laurin & Klement car make had been taken-over, Laurin-Klement-Skoda was formed.

tube, just like the Hans Ledwinka's Tatra. The rear wheels were mounted on axle-half shafts. The Skoda Popular came into existence in 1934 when the engine had been bored out to 1100 cc which delivered 30 bhp. Other cars included the Rapid with a 1380 cc, four-cylinder engine and the mighty Superb with its 2480 cc, six-cylinder engine.

Just before the war, Skoda launched the Favorit. This model with a 1.8 litre engine was unveiled at the Monte Carlo Rally.

Production of the Favorit was halted prematurely by the impending war. During the war the company was forced to work for the Germans. On the last day of the war, the company was flattened by German bombers, but in spite of this setback production could soon be re-started.

Slaby-Beringer

During the First World War, Dr. Rudolf Slaby worked as an engineer in the German aircraft industry. After the

Dr. Rudolf Slaby was the son of the founders of the Telefunken corporation. He primarily attempted to sell his electro-car to handicapped war veterans.

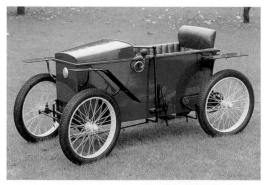

war, Slaby had to look for other work. He was convinced he had found his niche in the market with a small, single-seater car powered by an electro-motor. The model had a self-supporting, plywood body and was primarily intended for handicapped veterans.

However, the car was far too expensive. In 1921, Slaby met an engineer by the name of Beringer. He managed to convince Slaby to at least build the car as a two-seater. The result was the Slaby-Beringer powered by a single-cylinder DKW engine. This car also sold really poorly. In 1921, the partners had to file for bankruptcy. The company was taken over by Jörgen Skafte Rasmussen. The branch in Berlin became part of his DKW factory.

S.L.M.

In 1871, Charles Brown founded the Schweizerischen Lokomotiv und Maschinenfabrik (S.L.M.) in the Swiss town Winterthur. Brown already had a great deal of experience with steam engines when he built his first steam-powered, three-wheeler in 1886. The

The S.L.M. only weighed 550 kg. (1210 lb). The car seated two grownups.

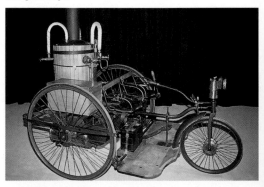

The S.P.A. 25-40 HP's body was provided by the young Nuccio Bertone. It was the first and largest commission the young bodywork manufacturer had received.

The S.P.A. 25-40 HP's body was provided by the young Nuccio Bertone. It was the first and largest commission the young bodywork manufacturer had received.

steam engine had a total of six burners, but it still took half an hour before sufficient pressure had built up to move the vehicle. Once it got going, it reached a top speed of 6 mph (10 kph). S.L.M. built just one passenger car. From then on they specialised in trucks.

S.P.A.

In 1906, the Italian Società Ligure Piemontese Automobili (S.P.A.) built its first motorcar. The model had been designed by the company's owner Matteo Ceirano. The S.P.A. was powered by a large four-cylinder, side-valve engine. Although the make primarily became famous for its expensive, luxury cars, it also manufactured sports cars. These did particularly well during long distances races which were popular at the time. In 1908, an S.P.A. finished third in the Targa Florio and in 1909 racing driver Ciuppo even

managed to win this race. Good racing results led to good sales figures. In 1912, the customer had a choice of cars with either four or six-cylinder engines. Over 500 cars were sold that year. Passenger car production stopped during the First World War, but in 1919 the first S.P.A.'s rolled off the assembly line again. The car had a 2.7 litre, four-cylinder, side-valve engine or a 4.4 litre, six-cylinder engine. One of the most successful models was the S.P.A. 25-40 HP launched in 1922. The car had a 4398 cc, six-cylinder engine with two overhead camshafts which operated four valves per cylinder which delivered 40 bhp. The pistons were aluminium and the engine had two carburettors and double ignition. The S.P.A. 25-40 HP was the first car that Nuccio Bertone's new company provided with a body. In 1927, the S.P.A. make became part of the Fiat corporation. Production ceased that same year.

Spag

Car manufacturers A. Simille and G. Péquinot were not all that successful really. In 1927, their first prototype left their factory in Asnières on the Seine and the final car rolled off the assembly line in 1928.

The company did not manufacture its own engines. The customer could choose from existing 1100 or 1500 cc, four-cylinder engines.

The Spag make offered a comprehensive range from a small sports car to more luxury passenger cars. It is not known how many cars the make sold, but it cannot have been all that many.

This SPAG from 1927 took part in a hill climb for classic cars in Switzerland in 1996.

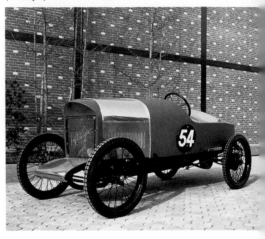

The racing car was powered by a 2.0 litre, two-cylinder engine manufactured by Müller & Vogel. 737 cc gave the car a top speed of 140 mph (225 kph).

In the first model, the driver and passenger still sat side-by-side, but in the second model from 1916 the seats stood one behind the other. In 1920, the company had approximately ten employees who built no more than a dozen cars all-in-all. In 1922, Speidel appeared at the start of the Swiss grand prix with his own racing car. However, the car never made it to the finish as it caught fire after only a few laps. Despite all this, the model was saved and can be seen in the Verkehrshaus der Schweiz in Luzern.

Speidel

Paul Speidel was also an enthusiastic, though not very successful car manufacturer. In 1915, he unveiled his first Voiturette in Geneva. The two-seater had a four-cylinder Chapuis-Dornier engine which delivered 8 bhp.

Spijker

The Spijker brothers became famous for building a royal coach but also built coaches for commoners.

A 1898 doctor's coupé is shown beside a 30/40 HP 1922 Spyker C-4.

The four-cylinder engine of the 1906 Spyker 14/18 HP Double Phaeton, had 2543 cc.

In April 1998, the Nationaal Automobiel Museum in Raamsdonksveer in the Netherlands presented a unique collection of Spijkers or Spykers as they were known from 1900 onwards.

Ten had been brought together, which is quite a feat as they are very rare. The Dutch 'Golden coach' (Dutch State Landau) is world famous, but few people know that it was built in 1898 by Hendrik-Jan and Jacobus Spijker. In 1900, the brothers built their first car in their new factory in Amsterdam. Although production got off to a slow start, the make became increasingly well known.

One of its most famous models was the racing car unveiled in Paris in 1903. It was the first car with a six-cylinder engine and four-wheel drive. The Trom-

The 1903 Spyker 60 HP was the first six-cylinder four-wheel-drive car. The 60 HP had a top speed of around 60 mph (almost 100 kph).

The 1922 30/40 Landaulette was the most expensive car Spyker ever built.
Only three were sold.

The 1922 30/40 Landaulette was the most expensive car Spyker ever built. Only three were sold.

The Standard Stratford was named after the company that manufactured the open bodywork. This car left the factory in 1926.

penburg, as the factory was known, did not only produce cars, but also manufactured 110 aeroplanes and over 200 aircraft engines.

After approximately 1,500 cars had been built, the company was forced to file for bankruptcy on 26 May 1926. It would take years before the next Dutch car, the DAF, was launched.

Standard

Tower Bridge's architect, Sir John Wolfe Barry borrowed £3,000 from his friend Reginald Walter Maudslay to build his first car. This money was used to lay the basis for the Standard Motor Company Ltd. The first car had a two-cylinder, 6 bhp engine; a three-speed gearbox and rear-wheel drive. In 1905, Standard unveiled the 18/20 HP. It was the first (affordable) English car with a six-cylinder, side-valve

engine. The famous racing driver Maudslay finished eleventh in the Tourist Trophy that year driving an 18/20 HP. It was the first and the last time the company entered an international race. In 1906, Standard already had 101 employees. The company manufactured various models with water-cooled, four and six-cylinder engines. The company experimented with air-cooled engines, but such a system was never applied. In 1913, Standard presented a cheap model, the S with a 1087 cc, four-cylinder engine. The board of directors

The 1926 Sportsman Coupé on the Standard Nine's chassis.

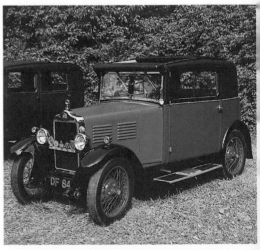

had so much confidence in the two-seater that there was a three-year guarantee on the car. Customers obviously appreciated this. Some 1,295 were still sold before the outbreak of the First World War. During the war, the assembly lines were converted for the production of aeroplanes, but in 1919 the first S type car left the factory once again. This model's engine had been bored out to 1328 cc. In 1921, the SLS could also be supplied with four-seater bodywork. In this version it was called the SLO. Entirely new models were also launched, such as the 6V. This car was available with a six, or a cheaper four-cylinder engine. The model was a resounding success.

In 1928, the cylinder capacity was increased from 1159 to 1287 cc. Some 9,000 of these Standard Teignmouth's were sold. In the company's best year 1932, the entire year's production had sold out by June. People who wanted to buy a Standard were put on a waiting list. In that year, the range consisted of four models: Little Nine, Big Nine, Sixteen and Twenty. Demand increased even further when Prince Philip purchased a Standard Nine in 1909.

Before the war, the make's popularity increased even further due to the unveiling of a new range of models at the London Motor Show, the Flying Standards. These cars had a modern aerodynamic body. They were available with a 1608 cc, four-cylinder or a 2143 or 2663 cc, six-cylinder engine. An eight-in-line engine was even built into 200 models. Three of these vehicles remain today. When the assembly lines were closed in 1940, over 50,000 cars had been sold that year.

Stellite

Wolseley's subsidiary, the Electric & Ordnance Accessories Co. Ltd., on Ward End in Birmingham, built a cheap car called the Stellite in 1913. The model was manufactured between 1913 and 1919, except for a brief interlude during the First World War. The Stellite was cheap to buy, but was finished cheaply. The chassis was made of wood and the gearbox only had two speeds. The engine was an 1100 cc, four-cylinder. After the war the company presented an improved model with a three-speed gearbox, but it was not a success and production was halted in 1919.

The Stellite, here a 1914 model, was only available as a two-seater.

Stephens

The Moline Plow Company manufactured agricultural tools and coaches in Freeport, Illinois, but business was slumping. The demand for coaches was decreasing, but at the same time the demand for motorcars was growing. Because the company had a large permanent clientele,

presented its own six-cylinder, over-head-valve engine, the Salient Six. For the first few years, everything went according to plan, but at the start of the twenties the turnover decreased dramatically. In spite of the fact that the prices were lowered, the company did not manage to stimulate sales. In 1924, the last Stephen rolled off the assembly line. In total some 35,000 Stephens had been sold.

Steyr

The Steyr-Werke in the town of Steyr in eastern Austria was a weapons and bicycle manufacturer. During the First World War the company had some 14,000 employees. Per day the factory manufactured approximately 4,000 (machine) guns and several aircraft engines. When the war was over the

Stephens Motor branch was founded especially for the production of motorcars in 1915. The company was named after the first managing director Mr Stephens. In early 1916, a few early prototypes were built and at the end of that year the first car was delivered. The first Stephens was powered by four-cylinder engines made by Continental. In 1917, the company

The Stephens Salient Six was definitely not cheap. This two-seater roadster cost $1975 in 1920.

Steyr also built a large number of sports cars such as the type V. The car had a 4014 cc, six-cylinder engine and a top speed of 87 mph (140 kph).

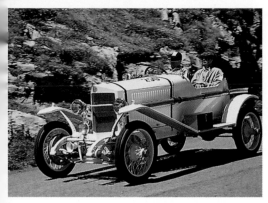

The Steyr 220 was the last pre-war model.

The 220 had a 2260 cc, four-cylinder, overhead valve engine which delivered 55 bhp at 3800 rpm. This was enough to give the car a top speed of 75 mph (120 kph).

company had produced a total of 3,00,325 rifles, 234,919 pistols and 40,524 machine guns. In 1918, the demand for weapons went into sharp decline. Steyr's board of managing directors decided to try their luck with cars. In 1920, the famous designer Hans Ledwinka designed and built the first Steyr, the Waffenauto. The model was powered by a 3325 cc, six-cylinder engine. Ledwinka left the company again in 1921, but by then he had already drawn so many cars that Steyr had years of designs to work with. The second model was the Steyr IV which featured a 1814 cc, four-cylinder, side-valve engine. The car was manufactured between 1924 and 1925. It was the first four-cylinder and there would not be another until 1932. All the other cars had six-cylinder or eight-cylinder engines, with valves powered by overhead camshafts. A number of beautiful models were developed under the leadership of Ferdinand Porsche such as the 1929 Austria. The long bonnet concealed a 5300 cc eight-in-line engine. In total, Steyr built 28 different models before the Second World War. One of the most popular models was the Steyr 50, which looked very similar to a Volkswagen. Approximately 13,000 of

these cars – which were built between 1936 and 1940 - were sold. Another successful model was the Steyr 220 which had a 2260 cc, six-cylinder, overhead valve engine. In total, Steyr manufactured 34,776 cars between 1920 and 1940.

Stoewer

The Stoewer company on the Falkenwalderchaussee in Stettin built its first motorcar in 1898. Prior to that time, they had already manufactured a lot of bicycles and motorcycles. Father Stoewer owned the company, but his sons Bernhard and Emil were responsible for the motorcars. The first Stoewers were powered by two-cylinder engines, but as early as 1902,

Between 1910 and 1911, 600 Stoewer LT4's were built. The 1556 cc, four-cylinder engine delivered 16 bhp at 1400 rpm.

thoroughly destroyed by Allied bombers. So thoroughly in fact that it could not be rebuilt. Once again another famous make had disappeared from the market.

The Stoewer R140 (1932-1934) was very popular.

the company launched one of the first German four-cylinder engines. It also proved to be a reliable engine. Bernhard Stoewer drove one of his cars from Stettin, on the Polish border, to Paris and back and that down roads which hardly deserved that name and without maps or petrol stations. In 1906, Stoewer was the first German car make with an 8821 c, six-cylinder engine.

In 1911, the engine was built into the Stoewer P6. Up until the twenties, the company specialised in cars with four-cylinder engines. Most engines were side-valve engines, only the F4 (1912-1916) and the R 180 (1935) were equipped with overhead valves. The same applied to the Greif Junior, Sedina and Arkona all manufactured immediately before the war. Up to 1940, Stoewer sold a total of 25,130 passenger cars. During the war the factory was

In spite of its price of 13,300 Reichsmark, which was high for that era, some 650 Gigants were sold. The car was 505 cm long and provided ample room for the entire family.

The G15 Gigant (1928-1931) was a very luxurious model powered by an eight-cylinder engine.

In 1920, the customer could choose from three different models with a six-cylinder engine. The cheapest was the Light Six, then came the Special Six. The most expensive model was called the Big Six.

Studebaker

Studebaker disappeared for good in March 1966. At that point in time, it was the oldest car factory in the world, but that fact was of more interest to historians than it was to the shareholders. In 1852, the brothers Henry and Clem Studebaker left California. They had made their money building covered wagons for the many gold diggers. They then settled in South Bend, where they started a coach factory. In 1902, they built their first electric car. 1,841 of these cars were sold.

It took till 1912 for the first Studebaker with a petrol engine to be built. In the meantime, the brothers gained plenty of experience with petrol engines as they had already assembled the Garford-Studebaker in 1904 and cars with petrol engines were built in their own factories Flanders and EMF. So it was only in 1912 that the first car with a petrol engine was launched under their own name. In 1913, the range consisted of three different models, two with a four- cylinder and one with a

In 1928, the Club Coupé was a popular model. The 'boot' doubled as seating for two passengers.

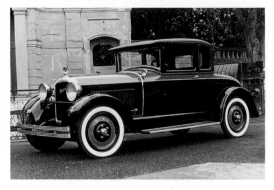

six-cylinder engine. In 1920, Studebaker stopped building carriages. The company started focusing entirely on cars. This activity proved to be very lucrative and in 1922 the company already had a turnover of $100 million.

Back then, the company primarily built large cars. The last small model with a four-cylinder engine was finished in 1919, from then on the company only manufactured six-cylinder engines. In 1926, Studebaker presented the Erskine, a cheap model with a six-

In 1929, there were three basic models in the range, the Dictator, the Commander and the President. The first was only available with a six-cylinderengine.

cylinder engine specifically intended for export. In the meantime, Studebaker had grown into a large company: in 1925 the company manufactured over

Studebaker also built successful racing cars. The car in the picture took part in the Indianapolis 500 in 1932.

In 1935, all the models were equipped with newbodywork. The high, narrow grill was an eye-catching detail.

The two-seater car seated four if you strapped the luggage to the luggage rack.

A 1939 Studebaker President in the five-seater convertible version. The eight-cylinder engine delivered 110 bhp.

A 1939 Studebaker President in the five-seater convertible version. The eight-cylinder engine delivered 110 bhp.

The dashboard of a 1935 Studebaker.

the President. The cars were powered by a six or eight-cylinder engine. In 1939, the range was expanded with the cheap 'Champion', which had a 2.7 litre, six-cylinder engine. In 1942, the company had to switch to manufacturing army equipment.

Stutz

Henry C. Syutz was born on 12 September 1876. In 1903, he moved to Indianapolis where he built racing cars in a small garage on Capital Avenue. The company was first called the Stutz Autoparts Company, but was rename the Stutz Car Company of America in 1913. Besides racing cars, which – incidentally – performed very well, Stutz built small sports and large passenger cars. The company became famous for the Bearcat, an open, two-seater sports car. The model offered no

100,000 cars for the first time. In 1928, there were approximately 21,000 on the payroll and the make was in fifth place on the list of American car manufacturers. Business was good, but the new director Albert Erskine made a few crucial mistakes. His Erskine sold very badly and buying the endangered car make Pierce-Arrow for $9.5 million in 1928 only made matters worse. In 1933, this company was sold again at a loss of over a million dollars.

The financial reserves were exhausted and the impending depression put Studebaker in even deeper trouble. In 1932, the company went in the red for the first time and only in 1936 could this loss once again be made up. In that year, the customer could only choose between two models, the Dictator and

The Bearcat was not much more than a chassis with a bonnet, two bucket seats and a large round petrol tank. The picture depicts a car from 1912.

A 1927 Black Hawk as a two-seater coupe. The dickey seat seated two additional passengers.

luxury whatsoever, but sold well in spite of its high price. The Bearcat was powered by a six-cylinder, overhead valve engine, initially in a 5.4 and later in a 6.5 litre version. Technically speaking Stutz's cars were ahead of their time. The 1915 racing cars featured a four-cylinder engine with a single overhead camshaft and four valves per cylinder.

In that same year, a new sports car, the Stutz Bulldog, was launched and this model also became a resounding success. Meanwhile, the factory had become too small so the company had to find more spacious premises. To be able to finance these, Stutz issued shares on the New York stock market.

The majority of these were bought by Alan A. Ryan who thereby gained a great deal of influence on the company. Stutz was so unhappy with this development that he left the company in 1919 and relocated to Florida. In spite of its owner's departure the company continued.

New models were regularly launched. In 1923, the customer could chose from an open two-seater or a closed five-seater limousine. The models were powered by a four or a six-cylinder engine. In 1926, the first model with an eight-cylinder engine was unveiled, the Stutz AA. The 4.7 litre engine was designed by the Belgian Paul Bastien, who had previously worked for the

The Black Hawk was the sporty version of the Stutz AA. The car depicted here left the assembly line in 1927.

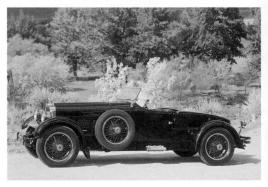

The 1929 Stutz Black Hawk was comfortable passenger car and you could even race it at the weekend.

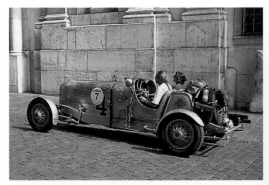

Belgian company Métallurgique. A sports version of the AA was launched in. 1927, which was sold as the Black Hawk. In 1928, a Black Hawk finished second in the 24-hour Le Mans race behind a Bentley. In 1929, the old familiar Bearcat name was reinstaed. This car was equipped with a compressor engine.

Stutz was always an expensive car. Due to the imminent depression production faltered as most customers could no longer afford an expensive car. After the depression the company launched a model with a 4.0 litre, six-cylinder engine with an overhead camshaft. Back then, the customer could also opt for an eight-cylinder, Continental engine.

When Cadillac, Lincoln and Packard presented their 12 or even 16 cylinder engines, Stutz had to lag behind: funds were not sufficient. Instead, the existing eight-in-line engine was equipped with a new cylinder head with two overhead camshafts and four valves per cylinder. This engine was built into the Stutz DV32 (Dual Valve = double the

A racing car engine: eight cylinders, two overhead camshafts, 32 valves and four carburettors.

number of valves (32)). This model saved the company's reputation. Almost everyone who could afford a Stutz DV32 bought one. The rolling chassis was provided with bodywork by various bodywork builders.

This meant the range featured 30 different body versions. The Speedster was once again christened the Bearcat. In spite of the enormous success, the company was forced to close in 1935.

This Stutz DV32 left the factory in 1933. The rear passengers sat behind their own windshield.

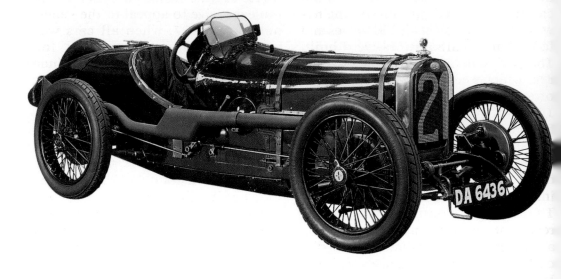

Sunbeam manufactured large numbers of racing cars. This two-seater appeared at the race tracks for the first time in 1922. It had a 1975 cc, four-cylinder engine with two overhead camshafts which delivered 88 bhp.

Sunbeam

At the end of the nineteenth century, John Marston was one of the many bicycle manufacturers, but in 1899 he built his first motorcar. In 1901 it was followed by a second prototype. Both models had single-cylinder engines and two-speed gearboxes. A third model was introduced in the Autumn of 1901. The power was provided by a 2.75 De Dion-Bouton engine. A small series of these cars was built, and, up to 1904, sold as the Sunbeam Mabley In 1903, it was followed by the 12 HP which had a 2.4 litre, four-cylinder engine. This car's special feature was its drive train. The chains ran through a continuous oil bath thereby protecting them from road dirt. In 1909, the Frenchman Louis Coatalen joined the company and beautiful models were created on his drawing board such as the 14/18 and the 12/16 HP which could be supplied with either chain or differential axle drive. The cars were powered by four-cylinder engines;

either 3402 or 2412 cc. The 12/16 remained in production until 1921 and could also be ordered as a sports car, people even raced them. So these Sunbeams finished in positions one, two and three at the French Grand Prix of 1912 which was held in Dieppe. During the First World War, the company primarily built aircraft engines. In spite of that, they did succeed in building a racing car which finished third at the 1916 Indianapolis 500. In 1920, Sunbeam merged with

Sir Henry Segrave paid £9,000 for this car with which he broke the land speed record in 1927.

Talbot and Darracq. In the new S.T.D. group, the Sunbeam make was primarily responsible for racing, but beautiful cars with 3.0 litre, eight-in-line engines with overhead camshafts, 32 valves and four Zenith carburettors were built. The engine delivered 108 bhp at 4000 rpm which was enough for a top speed of a good 109 mph (175 kph). From 1922 onwards, Sunbeam also manufactured ordinary sports and passenger cars. The models, which were once again named the 14 and 16 HP, were driven by a new engine with overhead instead of side valves.

The design and construction of cars for record breaking attempts soon became a Sunbeam specialisation. One of the company's best customers was Sir Henry Segrave. In 1926, he reached a speed of 152 mph (243.2 kph) in a Sunbeam Tiger.

A year later, Louis Coatalen designed a car especially for Segrave that was the first car to break the 200 mile and hour barrier. This car had two aircraft engines one in the front and one in the back. Together the V12 engines had a cylinder capacity of 22 litres and delivered an awesome 1,000 bhp. In 1926, the company unveiled two models with eight-cylinder engines with cylinder capacities of 4.8 and 5.4 litres, but the beautiful cars were far too expensive to appeal to the general public. In 1927, when all cars were equipped with brakes on all four wheels, the production of four-cylinder engines was discontinued. The customer could still choose between three different six-cylinder engines, the 16 HP with a 2-litre engine, the 20 HP with a 2.9 litre engine and the 25 HP with a 3.6 litre engine. The models were manufactured until 1933. They were followed by the Speed Model which had a 2.9 litre, six-cylinder engine. This model had to compete in particular with the Talbot 105 manufactured by the same company. In 1934, the Sunbeam Dawn was launched. This model had a 1627 cc, four-cylinder engine, largely made from aluminium. The car could also be supplied with a pre-selector gear box. When the STD group got into financial trouble in 1935 it was taken over by the Rootes brothers. A few more Sunbeams were built under their leadership, but the 1939 Sunbeam-Talbot looked more like a Talbot than a Sunbeam. Only in 1953 was a real Sunbeam once more introduced.

This 1922 racing car was powered by a V12 aircraft engine which delivered 350 bhp.

Talbot

As early as 1896, Alexandre Darracq drove round the streets of Paris in an electric car and three years later he did the same in a three-wheeler after a design by Bollée. Neither of the motor-cars agreed with him and so in 1900 he decided to build his own car. The car featured a 785 cc, water-cooled, single-cylinder engine. The rear wheels were driven by a cardan shaft. In that time, car racing was very popular in France. Darracq also decided to take part in them. Especially for this purpose he built cars with enormous engines. In 1905, he unveiled a racing car with a V8 engine with a cylinder capacity of some 22.5 litres. The car was so fast that Darracq managed to break a speed record with it. On the road between Arles and Salon he achieved a top speed of 111 mph (177.2 kph). Partly due to this success, his passenger cars such as the 1904 15, also sold well. This model was powered by a 3.0 litre, four-cylinder engine. Until 1909, Darracq also built smaller cars with single or

This AG 14/45 Talbot was built in England in 1930 and had a 1606 cc, four-cylinder engine.

The Talbot 75 was particularly popular in England.

The 14/65 was manufactured in the English factory on Barlby Road in North Kensington, London.

The Talbot Ten was unveiled in 1935. Shortly before, the company had been taken over by the Rootes brothers. No wonder that the car was the spitting image of the Hillman Minx.

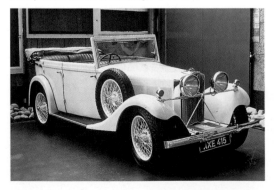

The English models had a very conservative look. The French cars, on the other hand, were very sporty. The picture shows the 1938 Talbot Lago LT 150 C.

The interior of the Talbot Lago: a lot of dials and meters in a beautifully finished wooden dashboard.

two-cylinder engines. In 1911, Darracq decided to experiment with the new rotary engine, invented by his country-man Henriod, but the engine was so unreliable that the company almost went into bankruptcy due to the count-less claims. Darracq stepped down as managing director and was succeeded by Owen Clegg. This Englishman designed two new models, one with a 2.1 and one with a 2.9 litre, four-cylinder engine. In 1913, the company was already manufacturing fourteen a day. During the war, the company switched to the production of aero-planes, but as early as 1919, the first post-war passenger car was presented, the 16 CV. In that same year Clegg

introduced the Model A which had a 4594 cc, V8, side-valve engine which delivered 80 bhp. In 1919, Darracq merged with the English makes Sunbeam and Talbot. In England the cars were sold as Talbot or Darracq and on the continent they were sold as Darracq. Besides joint models, the factories in France and England also built their own motorcars. For example, in England the 14/45 HP came out. A car with a six-cylinder engine designed by the famous designer Georges Roesch. The successful 45 was followed by the 75 and the 90, the 105 (1931) and the 110 (1935). In 1935, the S.T.D. company (Sunbeam-Talbot-Darracq) was sold to the Rootes brothers. The Talbot Ten, which looked a lot like the

This Talbot Lago SST was provided with bodywork by Figoni & Falaschi in 1937. The car became famous as the Goutte d'Eau.

The Talbot Lago 23 had a 4.0 litre, six-cylinder, overhead-valve engine which delivered around 110 bhp.

Hillman Minx – was launched under their leadership. In the meantime, the French side of the operation had not been idle either. In 1922, the 10 CV DC and 12/14 CV DC models were launched, which had 1.5 and 2.1 litre, four-cylinder, overhead-valve engines. In 1926, the DU was launched. This model featured a 2539 cc, six-cylinder engine. The engine delivered 70 bhp and gave the car a top speed of 75 mph (120 kph) in spite of the car's weight (1450 kg/3190 lb).

This engine constituted the basis for the subsequent series such as the DUS and the LT. The LT was powered by a 3.0 litre, six-cylinder engine and had a top speed of 94 mph (150 kph). Besides these expensive, deluxe cars, Talbot also manufactured smaller models such as the M67 and K74. In 1930, the Pacific and the Atlantic were launched with a 3.9 litre and a 3.4 litre, eight-in-line engine respectively.

Unfortunately both models sold really poorly. In 1935, a new director was appointed, Major Antione Lago. New models were developed under his leadership, such as the 4.0 litre 23 VC. This fast sports car had a top speed of 100 mph (160 kph). During the 1937 French Grand Prix the Lago Specials finished in first, second and third place.

Tamplin

Immediately following the First World War there was also a great demand for cheap motorcars n England. Factories which manufactured small, cheap cyclecars shot up everywhere and all too often disappeared again after only a few years. Carden, a former captain,

In 1919 this Tamplin took part in the Wycombe hill climb and won a race against a train on the route between Banbury and Carlisle.

also wanted to capitalise on the desire for car ownership. He designed the Tamplin. In the first models the passenger still sat behind the driver, but this changed in 1922. The new model had four wheels and was powered by an 8 bhp, JAP motorcycle engine.

The front wheels had independent suspension and the bodywork was made of plywood. In 1927, the Tamplin Motors company of Cheam, Surrey was forced to close down. The demand for small cars had collapsed entirely. In total, the company manufactured slightly less than 2,000 cars.

This Tamplin sports car left the factory in 1919. The JAP motorcycle engine can clearly be seen under the large headlight.

Tatra

Ignac Sustala's Nesseldorfer Wagenbau-Fabriks-Gesellschaft started building coaches and railway equipment in 1853. The company's first motorcar – the Nesseldorf President - was presented in 1897. The car was powered by a two-cylinder Benz engine. It was the first car in central Europe. In 1900, the company built its first engines and as early as 1906, cars with a 3.3 litre, four-cylinder engine with an overhead camshaft left the factory in Koprivnice. The model, designed by Hans Ledwinka, was called the Nesseldorfer S. In 1910, a model was launched with a 50 bhp, six-cylinder engine and by 1914 cars could be supplied with brakes on all four wheels. In 1916, Ledwinka left the company. When he returned to his former employer some six years later in 1922, the company had since been re-named Tatra-Werke AG. The first model the famous designer drew for Tatra was the Tatra 11. Instead of a chassis this car had a steel tube, 11 cm

Between 1930 and 1938, a total of 1,687 Tatra 52's were sold. The air-cooled engine had a 1910 cc cylinder capacity.

The Tatra 70 was a very luxurious car which could easily compete with a Mercedes or Horch. The 3406 cc, six-cylinder engine with an overhead camshaft delivered 65 bhp. 50 were sold in 1931 and 1932.

In 1938, the 57 A was entirely revamped. The new model was christened the 57 B.

in diameter, which ran from the front to the rear of the car. At the front of the car, the tube was directly attached to the aluminium oil sump of the air-cooled, two-cylinder boxer engine. The rear wheels were connected to the tube by means of axle half shafts. The type 12 was developed by boring out the engine. All-in-all, over 25,000 type 11 and type 12's were sold. After 1926, Tatra also sold models with a 2.0 litre and 2.3 litre, six-cylinder engine. And, in 1930, the range even included a V12 engine. The Tatra 57 was unveiled in 1932. Along with its successors, the 57 A and 57 B, it was to be one of the best

Small, but valiant: the 1155 cc Tatra 57 A had a top speed of 56 mph (90 kph). The 57 A was manufactured between 1936 and 1938.

The 1934 Tatra 77, had no rear windscreen. Note the large fin on the bonnet, which lent the car more stability at high speeds.

The magnificent Tatra 77 made Ledwinka world-famous. The car had a rear-mounted, air-cooled, V8 engine.

The Tatra 77's V8 engine had 2973 cc. In its successor, the 1935 77 A, the cylinder capacity was increased to 3380 cc. This increased the output from 60 to 70 bhp.

selling models. The cars were powered by an air-cooled, 1155 – or in the case of the 57 B 1256 cc – four-cylinder, boxer engine. Ledwinka became world-famous for the Tatra 77. This beautiful, streamlined car harboured an air-cooled, 3.4 litre, V8 engine. The model formed the basis for all the models the company was to build until long after the Second World War. Incidentally, Ledwinka spent six years behind bars in Czechoslovakia after the war. When he was released in 1951, he moved to Munich where he died in 1967.

The final pre-war model was the Tatra 87, which was manufactured between 1937 and 1950.
The 2968 cc engine delivered 75 bhp and a top speed of 100 mph (160 kph).

Tempo

The first Tempo was built in Hamburg in 1927. The car looked like a motorised trade bike, with a single rear and two front wheels. The rear wheel was powered by a 200 cc motorcycle engine. In 1933, a new model was unveiled which had two rear wheels and a single front wheel. The driver no longer had to sit out in the cold.

The car had front-wheel drive, but a motorcycle engine was once again used. The Tempo, originally designed as a delivery van, could be supplied with various bodies. The company did well.

As early as 1934, the 10,000th Tempo rolled off the assembly line. By then, the company had also started manufacturing four-wheeled cars. Off-road vehicles with two engines and four-

The Tempo's engine was mounted over the front wheel.

The back-seat passengers had to get in and out through the rear door.

The car was not particularly fast, but a top speed between 37 and 40 mph (60 and 65 kph) was possible.

wheel drive were built especially for the Wehrmacht. However, the three-wheelers made the most profit. They were even used to break records. In 1934, a Tempo broke the speed record for 1,000 km with an average speed of 34 mph (54.1 kph).

Terraplane

On 21 July 1932, the Hudson factory in Detroit unveiled a new make of car and this festive occasion was given a great deal of publicity. Amilia Earhart, the first woman to fly across the Atlantic on her own christened the Essex-

In 1933, the customer could choose from no less than 40 different models, of which 14 had an eight-cylinder engine.

Terraplane by smashing a bottle of aircraft fuel on its radiator grille. All the American Hudson dealers had come to the factory to personally receive their demonstration model. On that day a cavalcade of over 2,000 new cars drove through Detroit. Ford had hit the headlines a few months before with its new, cheap V8 and Hudson could therefore do with a little publicity.

The Terraplane was the successor to the Essex and was therefore first sold as the Essex-Terraplane The model was slightly cheaper than the new Ford and the six-cylinder engine delivered 5 bhp more than the competitor's V8.In 1933,

The Terraplane was first modernised in 1934. In that same year 56,804 cars were sold.

This 1934 Terraplane four-door convertible is probably equipped with European bodywork.

The dashboard of a 1934 Terraplane is conspicuously sober.

the car could also be supplied with an eight-in-line Hudson engine. It was the last model to be sold as an Essex-Terraplane. The name Essex disappeared for good. The eight-cylinder engine was only built into the 1933 Terraplane.

After all, there had to be a difference between the expensive Hudson and the cheaper Terraplane. In the latter's case the customer would have to make do with a six-cylinder engine. By this time, the make was so popular that this was even detrimental to Hudson. In 1938, the Hudson board of directors decided to change the make's name to Hudson-Terraplane and in 1939 the word Terraplane disappeared. Whether this improved Hudson's sales? Definitely not. In 1936, the company still sold 123,266 Hudsons and Terraplanes. In 1937 and 1938 that number had decreased to 111,342 and 51,078 Hudson-Terraplanes respectively. In 1939, only 82,161 Hudsons could be sold.

Thury-Nussberger

The Swiss M. Thury and M.R. Nussberger built their first three-wheeler in 1878. At that point in time, both of them were still studying at the Société Genevoise d'Instruments de Physique in Geneva. The three-wheeler was powered by a steam engine and seated four, who sat two-by-two back-to-back. The two-cylinder ran on coal.

At full throttle, the engine delivered 12 bhp at 350 rpm. The three-wheeler did not have a gearbox and the rear wheels were driven by chains. With a full 80 litre water tank the vehicle had a top speed of 31 mph (50 kph).

This Thury-Nussberger was almost entirely destroyed by fire in 1914. The car was recently fully restored and can now be seen at the Verkehrshaus in Luzern.

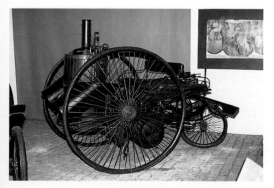

Toyota

Most car manufacturers started as bicycle and motorcycle manufacturers, but the Japanese Sakichi Toyoda (with a d) manufactured looms. A year before his death, Toyoda sold his patent for £100,000. His son Kiichiro used the money to build his first motorcar, among other things. In September 1934, Toyoda developed his own engine which looked suspiciously similar to Chevrolet's six-cylinder.

In May 1935, the first type A-1 left the workshop. The bodywork was a copy of the 1934 Chrysler Airflow. If Toyoda had known that this American car would fail miserably he would have imitated a different model. The 1500 kg (3300 lb) car seated five, but was not a success. In the first year, only three were sold. In 1936, Chrysler presented a new body for the Airflow, which caused the Japanese to copy its example. The new model was called the AA. The chassis and the

When Chrysler unveiled the new Airflow in 1936, Toyota followed with the AA model.

The 1939 Toyota AB in the four-door convertible version looked suspiciously like an army vehicle.

In 1908, the Tribelhorn still did not have a steering wheel. The front wheels were moved using a sort of rudder.

mechanical parts were 'borrowed' from the Chevrolet. An open version was presented in 1937 called the AB. The Toyoda family, then founded the Toyota (with a T) Motor Company. In 1938, the Toyota AC was unveiled, followed in 1939 by the smaller Toyota AE.

The dashboard of a Tribelhorn: a volt and amp meter.

The latter model was powered by a 2258 instead of 3389 cc engine. The impending war dramatically increased the demand for trucks.

Toyota also benefited from this development and built some 20,000 trucks and only 2,000 passenger cars up till 1942.

Tribelhorn

Around the turn of the century, there was no consensus as to how to power a car, whether it be with petrol, steam or electricity. Even decades later proponents of a particular system would could continue to defend their ideas fanatically. Each drive method had its own specific pros and cons. In 1899, the Belgian Camille Jenatzy

reached a speed of 66 mph (106 kph) with an electrically driven car. This reinforced the confidence of many car manufacturers in batteries instead of coal or petrol. And so, in 1902, the Swiss Tribelhorn company presented its first electrically driven car.

The passenger car could cover a distance of 62 miles (100 km) at a speed of approximately 15 mph (25 kph). The car housed so many batteries that there was almost no room for the passengers. The operating range was and still is the main problem facing electrically driven cars. Tribelhorn tried to solve the problem by building special charging stations along the main roads of Switzerland. However, this was of no advantage to the passenger cars as the charging stations were too spread out across the country. They did offer great advantages to the trucks of the Swiss postal service which always followed the same route.

Triumph

On 9 June 1984, British Leyland closed the Triumph factories. Up till that point in time, the company had manufactured beautiful sports and passenger cars. In 1883, the then twenty -year old German, Siegfried Bettmann emigrated to England. He started a bicycle factory in Coventry. Technical support was provided by Bettmann's countryman Schulte. The necessary capital, some £10,000 was provided by the White Sewing Machine Company. At the close of the nineteenth century, the company also manufactured motorcycles besides cars. Until the Japanese

The Triumph Gloria from 1936 was powered by a 1991 cc, six-cylinder engine.

motorcycles appeared on the market in the sixties, this represented the principal source of income. Immediately after the First World War, there was a large demand for small, cheap cars in England.

In 1920, some 59 manufacturers started manufacturing cars. One of these was Triumph, which built a new factory

The Triumph 10/20 Sports was a very successful model. The picture shows a 2+2 from 1923.

The dashboard of the 10/20 was very comprehensive.

A 1936 Gloria Southern Cross.

especially for this purpose in 1923. The first cars, the 10/20 type, were powered by a 1.4 litre, four-cylinder engine. The side-valve engine delivered 23.4 bhp. The two-seater bodywork had two auxiliary seats in the boot, which were called dickey seats in England. When Cecil Kimber unveiled his first MG, Triumph responded in 1924 with the 10/20.

This two-seater sports car had a beautiful aluminium body, but was considerably more expensive than the competition's cars. In 1925, the Triumph was provided with a 1.9 litre engine and four hydraulic brakes. Sales only started going well aft6er the introduction of the Super Seven in 1927, a counterpart to the Austin seven. This small car could be supplied in some

five different versions. The 832 cc engine could be equipped with a compressor at the customer's request. In 1929 and 1930, Donald Healey took part in the Monte Carlo Rally in a Triumph. In 1930 he even finished seventh. During the depression, bought the engines from Coventry Climax to save money. In 1930, it was such an engine which was installed in the sporty Southern Cross.

In 1932, Triumph recorded a loss of some £145,856. The following year, the then seventy-year old Bettmann left his company, Donald Healey had since been appointed technical director. The Triumph Gloria, a sports car with a four or six-cylinder Climax engine, was developed under his leadership. Healey even won his class in the Monte Carlo Rally in this car. Another model the 1937 Triumph Dolomite was a copy of the famous Alfa Romeo 8C2300. Most of the parts could even be exchanged trouble free. The Dolomite was an ordinary passenger car. In 1939, Triumph got into debt so deep that the company had to be sold to Thomas

The first single-seater Turicums were steered using the feet.

During the first years of its existence, Turicum only built small cars. The picture depicts a two-seater from this early period.

The type D Turicum was powered by a 1943 cc, four-cylinder engine. The car in the picture left the factory near Zurich in 1909.

During the first years of its existence, Turicum only built small cars. The picture depicts a two-seater from this early period.

definitely not bad. In 1913, the company had approximately 150 employees, who built over 200 cars. However, the factory closed for good when the First World War broke out.

Ward. He immediately switched to the production of army equipment and sold Triumph to the Standard Motor Company during the war.

Turicum

In 1904, Martin Fischer built his first motorcar on the outskirts of Zurich in the Swiss village of Niederuster. The single-seater car had an unusual form of steering. The wheels were steered using two foot pedals.

The single-cylinder engine delivered 7 bhp. In 1904, the company presented its first model with a four-cylinder engine. In 1908, Turicum was one of the first Swiss manufacturers with a branch in Paris. Fischer left his company in 1908. He started over again and built a few more cars under his own name. Most Turicums were powered by a 1943 or 2613 cc, four-cylinder engine, but the customer could also opt for a two-cylinder engine. Business was

Top to bottom: the beautiful horn, the massive headlight and the heavy leaf springs.

considerable demand for cheaper cars and particularly taxi-fleet owners liked the Unic. In 1907, Richard had only sold 690 Unics, but in 1911 the number sold already amounted to 1,219. In those days, those were considerable sales figures. In France alone, there were at least twelve car manufacturers that period, each of which manufactured over 1,000 cars per year. At the

Unic

Georges Richard and Henri Brassier built cars under the name of Richard at the turn of the century, but in 1905 Richard left the company. He rented a factory building on the Quai Nationale in Puteaux and started over again. He could no longer use the name Richard and therefore christened his new car the Unic. The car was powered by a two-cylinder, 10 bhp engine. A short while later, the customer could also opt for a four-cylinder. In 1909, a Unic with a 4.1 litre, six-cylinder engine was unveiled, but this model was not a success. There was a

The 1935 U4 B had a 2.2 litre, four-cylinder, side-valve engine. Ignition was brought about using a magnet.

Thanks to its grill, this 1937 Unic looked a lot like an American car.

The car in the picture had a factory body, an electric Cotal gearbox and independent suspension for the front wheels.

end of the twenties, Unic manufactured a large, luxury, eight-cylinder car. The results were poor, which led the company to concentrate on cheaper models once again. In 1937, the range consisted of the U4 and U6. The U4 was powered by a 2.0 litre, four-cylinder and the U6 housed a 3.0 litre, six-cylinder engine. The U6's wheel base was 9.5 cm longer than that of the U4. The cars had a top speed of respectively 75 and 87 mph (120 and 140kph). They were equipped with independent suspension and power-assisted, but mechanical brakes. After the U4 and U6, the company only built trucks.

The Unic was a reliable, but relatively unimaginative car. The make was particularly sought after by taxi drivers because the cars were very reliable and spacious. The picture depicts a five-seater convertible from the twenties.

Vale

Sports cars never sell well in times of crisis, but Messrs Downhall Dellow, R.O. Wilcoxon and Allan Gaspa nevertheless had the guts to launch a new sports car in 1932. They christened it the Vale, after the district in London in which their workshop was located. The Vale Engineering Co. Ltd. built cars with a great deal of love and craftsmanship. The two-seaters had a very low chassis and a tuned 832 cc, four-cylinder Triumph engine. The company did not have a network of dealers or a sales department. All the cars were sold straight from the workshop on Potsdown Road. In 1933, the company employed 17 people who built no less than 15 car per month. When Triumph

The 1932 Vale's low chassis was particularly striking.

stopped manufacturing engines, Vale also switched to Coventry Climax engines. Most cars had an 1100 cc, Coventry overhead valve engine, but the customer could also opt for a 1250 cc Meadows engine.

In 1934 the factory built a prototype with a 1500 cc, compressor engine. This car was raced very successfully. A Vale was always a relatively expensive car and therefore no great numbers were sold of any model. When the company got in debt in 1936, the board of directors decided to discontinue the make. All-in-all, only 103 Vales were ever built. The make can still be seen during classic car rallies.

In 1933, a Vale cost £192. A Morgan sports car could already be yours for £110.

In accordance with English tradition the spare wheel was mounted on the petrol tank.

A Vauxhall from just after the First World War. After General Motors took over the company, the cars were given American looks.

The 30/98 HP was the last racing car Vauxhall built. 586 were sold between 1913 and 1927.

Vauxhall

In 1857, Alexander Wilson founded a factory for ship's engines. He called the factory the Vauxhall Iron Works. In 1892, he left the company. The new owners decided that besides ship's engines they would also start manufacturing cars. In 1903, the first Vauxhall left the factory in London. It was an

In 1937, all the Vauxhalls were given new bodywork. The picture shows a Twelve from that year. All the models had a six-cylinder engine. The twelve had the least powerful engine with only 1531 cc.

open four-seater. The driver sat on the rear seat, which was very common in those days. The single-cylinder engine was mounted under the rear seat and powered the rear wheels by means of chains. The gearbox had two forward speeds, but no reverse. In 1905, the 12/14 HP was launched. It had a three-cylinder engine and a round steering wheel. The later renowned car builder Lawrence H. Pommeroy designed two new models, the 12/14 and the 18 HP, for the 1906 range.

Both cars were powered by a four-cylinder, side-valve engine. In those days, racing provided a lot of positive (or negative) publicity. In 1908, Vauxhall built the 20 HP. The car won a reliability trial over an awesome 2,000 miles (3,200 km). Moreover, it was the first English car to break the 100 mile an hour barrier at the Brooklands racetrack. On 28 October 1910, the 20 HP reached a top speed of 100mph (160 Kph). One of the most beautiful models was the 30/98 HP of 1913. The super fast car was powered by a 4.5 litre, side-valve engine. From then on the bodywork and the engine were regularly upgraded. In 1923, the 30/98 HP had an 4224 cc, overhead-valve engine. The last car in the series rolled off the assembly line in 1927. At that point in time, a total of 586 had

This 30/98 from 1924, was sold as a rolling chassis and was equipped with bodywork by the Wensum company.

In 1913, the Velie was powered by a 32 or 40 bhp, four-cylinder engine.

been built. In 1923, the company stopped racing. From then on Vauxhall concentrated on manufacturing passenger cars. In 1922, only 600 were sold, but in 1924 that number had already risen to 1,400. In spite of these satisfactory results, the board of directors accepted a take over bid from the American company General Motors. The Americans ran the business their way. They soon switched to mass production. 1928, saw the launch of the 20/60, a spacious, four-door with a six-cylinder, overhead-valve engine which only cost £475. Though the company also manufactured cheaper cars. For example, the 1931 Cadet which had a 2.0 litre, six-cylinder engine. This model only cost £280. In 1935, Vauxhall sold 25,000 cars and in 1938 this number had risen to over 60,000. In 1936, the cheaper Ten was launched. This model featured a 1.2 litre, four-cylinder engine.

Velie

Just like the Studebaker brothers, Willard Velie also started out building carriages and in 1909 he also attempted

The 1913 Velie was not aerodynamic. But that was not really necessary with a top speed of 25 mph (40 kph).

to build his first motorcar. The first motorcar that left the factory in Moline, Illinois was powered by a four-cylinder, Lycoming engine. The car was available as a five or two-seater. The models were called the Velie A and B. In 1911, Velie built his own four-cylinder engine. Howard Hall finished seventeenth in the first Indianapolis 500 in 1911 with one of these engines. In 1914, six-cylinder engines appeared which delivered 34 bhp to the large rear wheels. During the First World War, Velie was awarded countless government contracts which made him a wealthy man. In 1919, the Velie Motor Corporation built its first six-cylinder, overhead-valve engine. This engine was such a success that in 1920 production could be increased to 9,000 cars.

In order to save time, engines were also purchased, primarily from Continental. The 1920, Velie 34 was powered by such a six-cylinder engine. The model was only available with five-seater bodywork.

Velie manufactured a large number of different models, which were always of exceptional quality. The 1928 range also featured a Velie with an eight-cylinder Lycoming engine. In that same year, the 66 and 77 (with six-cylinder engines) and the 88 (with an eight-in-line engine) were launched. In total, there were some thirteen different

bodies available that year. Willard Velie died on 24 October 1928. He was succeeded by his son Willard Lamb Velie Junior. When he died shortly afterwards on 20 March 1929 of a heart attack the factory closed down for good.

Velox

The Prager Automobilfabrik Velox GmbH, primarily manufactured small passenger cars between 1906 and 1910. The company only manufactured one model, which was mainly used as a taxi in Moscow. The car was powered by a 1020 cc, single-cylinder engine, mounted under the rear seat. The gearbox had three speeds and reverse.

This Velox dates from 1906.

The foot brake used the gearbox and the hand brake one of the rear wheels. According to company specifications, the top speed was 28 mph (45 kph). Whether that speed was ever achieved remains doubtful.

Vermorel

As early as round the turn of the century, the Vermorel company started experimenting with cars in the French town of Villefranche, but in 1908 the company started tackling matters in a more professional manner. Vermorel hired the well-known car builder Francois Pilain. A Vermorel with a 1.8 litre, four-cylinder, side-valve engine and a four-speed gearbox was developed on his drawing board. Quite soon the engines' cylinder capacity increased to 2.2 and 3.3 litres. From 1922 onwards, all the cars were equipped with brakes on all four wheels. In 1923, the Vermorel could also be ordered as a sports car with an overhead-valve engine. The 16/60 was

In France the steering wheel remained on the right-hand side of the car for sometime, as demonstrated by this 1913 Vermorel.

unveiled in 1924 and had a 2.6 litre four-cylinder engine with an overhead camshaft. In 1928, the first model with a six-cylinder engine followed, the Vermorel AH. The engine had a cylinder capacity of 1869 cc and delivered 45 bhp. The Vermorel cars never caused a stir. When demand decreased in 1930, it was decided to discontinue the production of passenger cars.

Voisin

The car industry has always had its remarkable figures and one of these was Gabriel Voisin. Voisin started his career building aircraft. Until his death in 1973, he maintained that he built an aircraft before the Wright brothers did. In any case, he was definitely a pioneer in this field. During the First World War, Voisin had earned a fortune building over 10,000 aircraft for the French airforce. Once the peace agreement had been signed, a new phase in his career started. In 1919, he built his first

A 1911 Vermorel 2+2. The last two passengers had to sit in the boot.
The four-cylinder engine had 2074 cc.

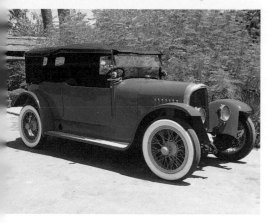

The C1 was actually a Citroën design. Voisin equipped the car with a four-cylinder, sleeve-valve engine.

cylinder cars. The hideously expensive Voisins were particularly popular with rich people. In 1923, the company had no less than 68 kings, maharajahs, lords and sultans as its customers and films stars such as Rudolph Valentino also owned one or more Voisins.

The company mainly sold the cars as rolling chassis. The customer could then select a bodywork builder, although a factory body was also an option. It was particularly the latter bodies which attracted the most attention. They were almost entirely made of

Voisin was not interested in a car's looks. It was more important to him that the car was light and yet still strong.

The roof of this four-seater 1927 Voisin was made of leather stretched over the wooden frame.

It is obvious that the C25 Aérodyne was designed by an aircraft manufacturer.

car. The aerodynamic bodies and almost silent sleeve-valve engines made his models striking. The first type C1 Voisin from 1919, was actually designed by Citroën. However, Citroën never took the model into production. The car was powered by a 4.0 litre, four-cylinder, sleeve-valve engine and had a top speed of 75 mph (120 kph). After 70 of these cars had been sold, the C2 was developed in 1920. This enormous car had a 7.2 litre, V12, sleeve-valve engine. Very few were sold and that is why, in 1922, Voisin once again switched to smaller, four-

The C25 was powered by a 2994 cc, 90 bhp, six-cylinder engine.

The roof of this Voisin could be completely opened-up. One of the round windows then served as the rear windscreen.

The 4882 cc, V12, sleeve-valve engine delivered 125 bhp at 4000 rpm, which was enough for a top speed of 87 mph (140 kph).

average speed of 113 mph (181.60 kph). During the depression, the company rapidly nose-dived. However, this did not mean that Voisin had given up hope.

On the contrary, he designed feats of technological prowess such as a five-cylinder, sleeve-valve engine with petrol injection, designed seven and nine-cylinder engines and various

The interior of the V12: why hide beautiful technology behind sheeting?

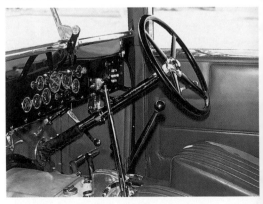

aluminium. The material was strong and lightweight and Voisin had already used it to build fighter planes during the First World War. Voisin also built various racing cars. On 13 April 1927, a Voisin with an 8.0 litre, eight-cylinder, sleeve-valve engine broke the speed record over 160 km. The car had a top speed of 128 mph (205.66 kph). In a 24-hour race it clocked an

There were very few people who thought the Voisin was a beautiful car. This car with a V12 engine left the factory in 1931.

Ferdinand Porsche drove 485,000 km in this Kraft durch Freude. This, the oldest Beetle can now be found in the museum in Wolfsburg.

models with front-wheel drive. In spite of his efforts, the board of directors switched to six-cylinder, American Graham engines in 1938. During the war Voisin worked for the Germans, but still had enough spare time to design a small passenger car. This open two-seater had a single-cylinder engine and front-wheel drive. After the war this midget was sold in Spain as the Bi-Scuter.

Volkswagen

Professor Ferdinand Porsche (1875-1951) had already presented his plans for a cheap car for the general public in 1922, but no one showed the least bit of interest, not even his boss at the time Austro-Daimler. When the Austrian started discussing his cheap dream car again at Mercedes, this meant the end of their cooperation. Porsche started his own company and was over the moon when his friend Adolf Hitler commissioned him to manufacture a car for the general public – the Kraft durch Freude car - in 1934. Hitler did not make it easy for him. The car's fuel

consumption had to be lower than 6 or 7 litres per 100 km and was not allowed to cost more than RM 900. Moreover, it was to have a top speed of at least 62 mph (100 kph). A savings scheme was developed, whereby each German saved at least RM 5 per week for the new car. Actually, the design was already finished.

In 1931, Porsche had already made the drawings for a model of this type. Zündapp had even already built three prototypes back then. NSU was also interested in the design, but when this company was taken over by Fiat this meant the end for the NSU-Volkswagen. Hitler's offer came right on time.

The post-war model differed little from this 1938 pre-war model.

The simple dashboard of the KDF car.

On October 12 1936, Porsche presented three running prototypes. Each car drove 50,000 km in seventy days,. When this distance was achieved without any substantial repairs, Hitler was satisfied. Hitler then personally sought out a suitable location for the factory.

Because the only two available factories, owned by Ford and Opel, were not purely German, Hitler

Before the indicator light was invented, these 'arrow' indicators were used.

ordered his Arbeitsfront to construct a new factory in Wolfsburg. Some 800,000 cars per year were to be built at the gigantic factory. On 26 May 1938, Hitler laid the first stone for the new factory and in 1940 the first car rolled off the assembly line.

But it was not a Kraft durch Freude car (the official name) but an army vehicle designed by Porsche. Only a few passenger cars were manufactured at the plant for the party's leaders. In any case, the German had lost their savings.

Volvo

Volvo, currently the largest industrial corporation in Scandinavia was founded in 1924 by Assar Gabrielson and Gustaf Larson. The two friends decided to manufacture cars. The designs for a first prototype were finished in 1925.

The bodywork was designed by the artist Helmer Mas-Olle. When the well-known ball-bearing company SKF expressed its interest in financially supporting the project, the Volvo ('I roll') company was founded. The first car left the factory on 14 April 1927.

This model the OV 4 or Jakob was to be manufactured until 1929. Initially 205 convertibles were sold, but because in this version the car was not really suitable for the harsh Swedish climate, it was decided to manufacture a closed version the PV 4. 791 were produced. To be able to realise this number, 200 convertible bodies were destroyed and replaced by a closed body. The first cars of this type were powered by a

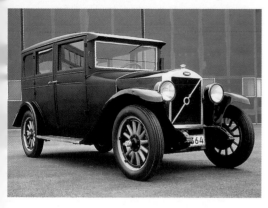

four-cylinder engine, but as early as 1929 a six-cylinder engine was presented, which was particularly favoured by taxi drivers. The PV 653 weighed approximately 1500 kg (3300 lb). Because the 3.0 litre engine delivered well over 55 bhp, the car still had a top speed and cruising speed of 69 mph (110 kph). The model, and its successor the PV 658, looked like sized-down American cars. The cylinders were then bored out further to 3266 and 3670 cc, which delivered between 65 and 85 bhp. When Chrysler presented the Airflow, Volvo launched a similar model in 1935, the Carioca. In total 501 were sold.

Incidentally, the Carioca was the first Volvo with an entirely steel body. 3,005 were sold of its successor the PV51 between 1936 and 1938. In 1938, the PV 801 was launched. This model was to be manufactured until 1947, primarily as a taxi. The car seated eight.

The 3670 cc, six-cylinder engine delivered enough bhp to give the car a top speed of 81 mph (130 kph). The last pre-war model with a six-cylinder engine was the PV 60. The car was manufactured between 1942 and 1950. The PV 60 was also the spitting image of a pre-war American car. In 1950, the model was very outdated.

The first Volvo was known as OV 4 or Jakob.

Ww

Wanderer

Johann Winkelhofer and Richard Jaenicke had a small workshop in Schoenau near Chemnitz (Germany) where they repaired bicycles. Several years later they built their own bicycles, motorcycles and typewriters (as the make Continental). In 1905, they built their first car. However, the car had so many technical problems that it took until 1907 before a second prototype could be built. This car was also far from reliable. Only in 1912, were most of the problems solved and could production start. The two Germans were

The passenger sat diagonally behind the driver in the 1918 Wanderer W1.

offered a design by Ettore Bugatti, but they thought their own car was far more beautiful. The small Wanderer W1, also known as the Puppchen was a success. The W1 seated two grownups, one behind the other. The car was powered by a 1140 cc, four-cylinder engine and because the car only weighed 500 kg (1100 lb) it had a top speed ofalmost 44 mph (70 kph). The model remained in production for almost fifteen years. The most important modification was moving the seats.

From 1913 onwards, the passenger seat was staggered behind the driver's. In 1921, the company launched a second model, the W 6. The W 6 housed a 1.5 litre, four-cylinder, overhead-valve engine. Many car makes started with small cars, but presented increasingly large models over the years. And Wanderer was no exception. In 1928, the W 10 was launched which had a 2.0 litre engine and in 1929, followed the large and more expensive W 11. The car was powered by a 2.5 litre, six-cylinder engine and cost the then astronomical sum of RM 8,000. When the Auto Union was founded, Wanderer

W 23 (1937-1940) was powered by a 2632 cc, six-cylinder, side-valve engine which delivered 62 bhp.

The W24 looked like a downsized version of the W 23. The car had a 1767 cc, four-cylinder engine and a top speed of 65 mph (105 kph).

was put in charge of the medium-priced cars. The new board of directors had the relatively conservative bodywork modernised. The W 15, of which 400 were sold in 1932, was re-christened the W 21. Production of the model increased in 1933 and 1934 to 5,000.

Dr. Ferdinand Porsche developed a compressor engine for a sports car the W 25 for Wanderer, but unfortunately the engine proved unreliable and that is why only 250 were sold. In 1937, the W 23 was launched, which had a 2640 cc, six-cylinder engine.

An advertising shot of the W 25 K. It looked good like this, but in practice it was a letdown.

Ferdinand Porsche designed the compressor engine for the sports car. The 1963 cc, six-cylinder engine delivered 85 bhp, enough for a top speed of 90 mph (145kph).

Waverly

This model was to be built for the Wehrmacht until 1941. After the war, the Wanderer factory lay behind the Iron Curtain and the production of cars was discontinued.

The Waverly Electric Company was founded in 1898 as the result of a merger between American Electric Vehicle Company and the Indiana Bicycle Company. The company, which specialised in vehicles with electro-motors, was located in Indianapolis.

The first 'cars', were basically carriages with electro-motors. They were not equipped with a steering wheel, instead of a steering rod, until 1911. In 1913, a two-seater roadster, the Waverly 90 was launched. Only a few of these cars were sold. In 1915, the company stopped developing and manufacturing motorcars.

This Waverly Electric, 75 Brougham was unveiled in 1910. The electro-motor was mounted over the rear axle. The front of the 'car' is on the left in this picture.

In 1928, the customer could choose from a Whippet with a four or a six-cylinder engine.

Whippet

The Whippet was a Willys-Overland product. The car was manufactured between 1927 and 1931 in the Overland factory in Toledo, Ohio. The early models were equipped with a four-cylinder engine. It was the smallest car ever built in America. The model had a mere 254 cm wheel base. Later on, the Whippet could also be supplied with a six-cylinder engine.

One of these cars drove non-stop for 24 hours at an average speed of 56.52 mph (90.432 kph) round the oval Indianapolis circuit. The Whippet was not only small, but also cheap. The four-cylinder version cost less than a comparable Ford. It was even the cheapest, six-cylinder car in the world.

In the first year of production, the factory sold 110,000 cars, but the impending great depression also caused problems for Willys-Overland. As a result the Whippet make was discontinued in 1931.

Wikov

Passenger and sports cars were built in the Czechoslovakian town of Prostejov, not far from Brno, between 1926 and 1937. The cars were sold as Wikov, a contraction of the names of the factory owners, Wichterle and Kovarik. The company was well-known for its agricultural machines, but just like so many companies in that era Wikov also tried its hand at cars. The first cars were

The Wikov 40 was the most popular model (330 sold). The car was manufactured between 1933 and 1937.

The 1934 Wikov had a beautifully streamlined body. The two spare wheels were not a luxury in those days.

very similar to the Italian Ansaldo. The engine in particular was conspicuously similar. The model 28 was powered by a 1480 cc, four-cylinder engine with an aluminium engine block and a cylinder head with an overhead camshaft. The engine delivered 28 bhp at 2800 rpm. In 1931, the cylinder was bored out to 1740 and in 1933 to 1940 cc. This led to the 35 and the 40 models. As early as 1930, all the models were equipped with

hydraulic brakes. Like most car makes, Wikov had its own racing team. In 1929, during the first race the cars took part in they failed to impress. Only in 1931 did a Wikov come third in the 1.5 litre class. In 1933, a Wikov won a road race from Prague to Pressburg with an average speed of 57 mph (92 kph). In 1931, the famous aerodynamics expert, Paul Jaray designed a number of beautifully streamlined bodies. When

The 1935 Wikov sports car can be seen in the Czech Museum in Prague. According to the factory, the car had a top speed of 90 mph (145 kph).

Central Europe was also hit by the depression, Wikov tried to survive by manufacturing some cheap models. This Wikov baby was much less successful than it deserved to be. The Baby's engine was mounted in the rear of the car and the wheels had independent suspension.

The chassis consisted of a central tube after Hans Ledwinka's design. Only eight were sold. In 1933, a larger car with an eight-in-line engine was also launched, but this model was also a failure. In 1937, the company decided to limit itself to the manufacture of trucks.

Windsor

The Moon Motor Car Company was founded in 1905 in St. Louis. Most of the cars it built were powered by a Continental engine. In 1929, the company unveiled a luxury car called the Windsor. This Windsor was also equipped with a Continental engine, but in contrast to the Moon, the new car was provided with an eight-cylinder engine under the long bonnet.

The two passengers of this 1930 Windsor two-seater convertible could sit in the dickey seat if they strapped the luggage to the luggage rack.

The brake system was hydraulic. The Windsor was large and had a 318 or 358 cm wheel base. There were six different body versions available for the car. The smallest, a two-seater roadster cost $1,845, and the largest, a seven-seater limousine, cost $2,195. The company was closed in 1930, the umpteenth car make to disappear.

Wolseley

Frederick York Wolseley had a factory which manufactured sheep-shearing equipment, when he too decided to try his hand at manufacturing cars in 1896. The first car he built was designed by Herbert Austin. It was an obvious copy of the Frenchman Léon Bollée's three-wheeler. The car was powered by a two-cylinder, boxer engine with an overhead camshaft. The second model, which had a single-cylinder engine, never made it out of the prototype stage.

In 1899, the company unveiled the 3.5 HP. Once again, Austin had mounted a single-cylinder engine in the car, but the model had four instead of three wheels. In 1901, some 327 cars were sold. This made Wolseley one of England's premier car manufacturers.

An astonishing 800 cars were built in 1903. The company earned enough to be able to invest in racing. This was tackled on a grand scale. In that same year, a car with a 11.283 cc engine was unveiled which delivered 70 bhp. In 1905, this engine was tuned to 96 bhp. Charles Rolls finished eighth in the French Clermont Ferrand Grand Prix. In 1905, Austin left the company. His successor was John Davenport

Siddeley, who was later to become famous for the Armstrong Siddeley. In 1914, Wolseley was England's largest car manufacturer with a total production of 4,000 cars. Ford built 7,000 T-Fords in England in that year, but after all Ford was an American company. In 1914, all Wolseley's were equipped with electric lights. In that same year, a new model was introduced, the Stellite which had a four-cylinder engine and a two-speed gearbox. The Wolseley Ten of 1918 had an engine with an overhead camshaft. The model sold badly which led to a decrease in the company's income.

The board of directors decided to manufacture a small, cheap car with a two-cylinder, boxer engine. With a sales price of £255, the model could not compete with the Austin Seven which cost a mere £165. In 1926, the company had another go with an expensive model with a 2.0 litre, six-cylinder engine. By then, it was already too late. Wolseley went bankrupt and was sold to its former rival Morris for £730,000. The new six-cylinder engine

was further developed by Morris. In 1928, Wolseley presented a very luxury car with a 2.7 litre, eight-cylinder engine, but this model was also a failure. The company did not make the headlines again until 1930 when it introduced the Hornet 6. The car was powered by a 1271 cc, six-cylinder engine, mounted in a Morris Minor chassis. The engine initially delivered 32 bhp, this was later increased to 35 bhp. Beautiful sports cars were built on the basis of the Hornet. One of the most famous versions was that of bodywork builders Jensen and William Lyons.

In 1934, the Hornet could also be ordered with a four-cylinder engine. A year later, the Wasp was launched, the last Wolseley with an engine with an overhead camshaft. This system proved to be far too expensive and therefore had to make way for ordinary overhead-valve engines. In the meantime, Wolseleys looked more and more like Morrises and the engines were also interchangeable. In 1939, the Wasp was provided with a new engine which was also mounted in the MG TC after the war.

Zédel

Around the time of the First World War, Zédel was a reasonably well-known make of car. The company was owned by Ernest Zürcher and Hermann Lüthi. In the early years of the twentieth century, the company in the Swiss village of St. Aubin near Neuchatel, primarily manufactured engines for motorcycles and three-wheelers, but the company also manufactured auxiliary engines for bicycles including for the Belgian make Minerva. In 1902, the company moved to Pontarlier, just over the French border beside the river Doub. In this way, the board of directors wished to limit import duties, because most of the engines were sold to French companies. In 1906, the Fabrique de Moteurs et Machines Zédel built its first motorcar and as early as 1914, it manufactured some 400 per year. The first Zédels were powered by an 1128 cc, four-cylinder engine. The bodywork seated two people. In 1908, the first four-seater was introduced and in 1912, Zédel presented a medium-price range car with a 3563 cc, four-cylinder engine. After the war, Zédel launched two models with 2120 and 3168 cc, four-cylinder engines respectively. It was around that time that the company was sold to the Swiss company Donnet. From then on, the cars were sold under the name Donnet-Zédel. In 1927, the company moved to Nanterre. Once again the name was changed, this time to Donnet. In 1933, the Donnet make was sold to Simca.

Zédel primarily became well-known for its small cars, but large deluxe models such as this Landaulet were also produced.

Register

Word of thanks

The publishers and author would like to thank the following people for their assistance in producing this book. They either supplied photographic material or allowed us to photograph their cars.

in alphabetical order:

Slot Aalholm, Nysted, Denmark
Tom Barrett III, USA
Blackhawk Collection, USA
Fred Brechtbühl, Switzerland
Ivo Celechovsky, Tatra, The Czech Republic
Frank Gardner, USA
Fred Hediger, Switzerland
Lukas Hüni, Switzerland
Rick Lenz, USA
Reinhard Lintelmann, Germany
Ton Lohmann, the Netherlands
Nationaal Automobiel Museum [National Motorcar Museum], Raamsdonksveer, the Netherlands
Petra Nemeth, BMW Munich, Germany
Oldtimer Garage, Switzerland
Renault, France
Ernst Ritzmann, Switzerland
Reinhard Schmidlin, Switzerland
Matt Stone, USA
Max Stoop, Switzerland
Volvo, Sweden